PENGUIN BOOKS

THE NATIONAL TRUST BOOK
OF THE ENGLISH HOUSE INTERIOR

Dr Geoffrey Beard is Chairman of the Furniture History Society, of which he was a founder in 1964. He also edited its first ten annual journals. He has written a number of books on interior decoration in the seventeenth and eighteenth centuries, including standard texts on decorative plasterwork and craftsmen at work in England. His *Craftsmen and Interior Decoration in England, 1660–1820* (1981) was awarded the Sir Banister Fletcher Prize. His study of English furniture in National Trust houses in this series was published in 1985, and his study of the celebrated wood-carver Grinling Gibbons appeared in 1989. He now lives in Bath, having left university teaching to concentrate on writing and lecturing. He is currently writing a book entitled *The Compleat Gentleman*.

GEOFFREY BEARD

THE NATIONAL TRUST
BOOK OF THE
ENGLISH HOUSE INTERIOR

*For my friends
Woods and Clarissy
williamson
As ever
Geoffrey Beard*

PENGUIN BOOKS
IN ASSOCIATION WITH THE NATIONAL TRUST

PENGUIN BOOKS

Published by the Penguin Group
Penguin Books Ltd, 27 Wrights Lane, London W8 5TZ, England
Penguin Books USA Inc., 375 Hudson Street, New York, New York 10014, USA
Penguin Books Australia Ltd, Ringwood, Victoria, Australia
Penguin Books Canada Ltd, 10 Alcorn Avenue, Toronto, Ontario, Canada M4V 3B2
Penguin Books (NZ) Ltd, 182–190 Wairau Road, Auckland 10, New Zealand

Penguin Books Ltd, Registered Offices: Harmondsworth, Middlesex, England

First published by Viking 1990
Published in Penguin Books 1991
1 3 5 7 9 10 8 6 4 2

Filmset in 11/13 Monophoto Palatino

Printed and bound in Great Britain by
Butler & Tanner Ltd, Frome and London

For
John Summerson

CONTENTS

PREFACE

ix

ACKNOWLEDGEMENTS

xi

1. MEDIEVAL PATTERNS
*The House Plan; The Roof; Floors; Walls; Ceilings;
Windows; Doors; Fireplaces; Staircases; Services: The
Kitchen; Services: Garderobes.*

1

2. TUDOR SYMMETRY
*The House Plan; Halls, Galleries and Chambers;
Chapels; Floors, Walls and Ceilings; Panelled Walls;
Painted Walls and Ceilings; Plastered Walls and
Ceilings; Windows; Doors and Interior Porches;
Chimneypieces; Staircases; Services: The Kitchen;
Services: Privy Chambers.*

24

3. 'SOLIDITY, CONVENIENCY AND
ORNAMENT': THE SEVENTEENTH CENTURY
*The House Plan; Halls, Chambers, Galleries and
Saloons; Floors; Screens and Panelled Walls; Painted
Walls and Ceilings; Plastered Walls and Ceilings;
Windows; Doors; Chimneypieces; Staircases.*

69

4. THE SPIRIT OF BUILDING,
1700–1760
*The House Plan; Floors; Wainscoted Walls; Painted
Walls and Ceilings; Plastered and Stuccoed Surfaces;
Windows; Doors; Chimneypieces; Staircases; Services.*

139

5. VISIONS AND REVIVALS,
1760–1830

*The House Plan; Rooms and their Uses; Plastered Walls
and Ceilings; Painted Walls and Ceilings; Windows;
Doors; Chimneypieces; Staircases; Services.*

187

6. CONVENIENT, SPACIOUS OR SNUG,
1830–1914

*The House Plan; Rooms and their Uses; Decorated
Walls and Ceilings; Windows; Doors; Chimneypieces;
Staircases.*

238

NOTES ON THE TEXT
275

GLOSSARY
287

BIBLIOGRAPHY
294

PERSONAL NAMES INDEX
298

GENERAL INDEX
303

PREFACE

For over forty years I have been fortunate in being able to pursue research into country houses in Britain, and, in particular, the craftsmen who created much of enduring quality. My researches in the history of interior decoration began in 1946 at the behest of the late Margaret Jourdain. She urged me, during one of a number of meetings at which she imparted information with typical generosity, to give some substance to an aspect she had been unable to deal with in her *English Decorative Plasterwork of the Renaissance* (1926). This was to identify and list work by plasterers and stuccoists. Two books by me on these subjects appeared, rather belatedly, in 1975 and 1983, the second one dealing with stucco in Europe.

I have long realized that those elements of an interior less likely to disappear than the furniture and fabrics are the structural parts. It seemed sensible, therefore, to divide this book into periods and to describe the structural parts in sequence in each chapter, showing how these parts developed in response to changing influences and emphases, from the Middle Ages to the early twentieth century. Naturally enough, different parts had unequal importance at different periods, and I have taken this into account. For example, the types of material used in the construction of floors were well established by the late eighteenth century and I have therefore allocated the space from that chapter onwards to 'Rooms and their uses'. My arrangement is, of course, not a new idea: it is the one used by Edith Wharton and Ogden Codman in their book, *The Decoration of Houses*, first published in 1897, and attention was also given to the parts of the whole by John Fowler and John Cornforth in their invaluable *English Decoration in the 18th Century* (1974). In my own *Craftsmen and Interior Decoration, 1660–1820* (1981) I was able to underpin consideration of interior decoration with facts about men and techniques.

In recent years study of the daily life in, and the services of, great English country houses has been given new impetus by the researches and writings of a number of scholars. I have the pleasure of numbering most of them as friends, and like others, have profited in particular by conversations and by the writings of Professor Mark Girouard, John Cornforth and Peter Thornton. I also had the advantage of a number of conversations on the nineteenth-century house-plan with the late Dr Jill Franklin, to whose published study of the subject we are all indebted.

I have included some words on smaller houses, but in their internal arrangements they are less constant than greater ones and consequently few illustrations of them at various periods are available. Distinguished studies of the architecture of vernacular and terrace houses are, of course, noted in the Bibliography. It should not be assumed that all the houses mentioned are necessarily open to the public, but this information is available in the annual lists of country houses. Properties administered by the National Trust are denoted in the Index.

I decided at an early stage of writing this short text to conclude it at the opening of the First World War as most of the houses administered by the National Trust are of earlier date. It also leaves a distinct gap between the historical past and the present day. I was, in any case, short of space, and in terms of the country house, the period from the Edwardian years to the present day has been impressively dealt with by three more friends. Clive Aslet's *The Last Country Houses* (1982), John Martin Robinson's *The Latest Country Houses: the Continuation of a British Tradition 1945–1983* (1984) and Merlin Waterson's editing of *The Country House Remembered: Recollections of Life Between the Wars* (1985) provide fascinating reading for those interested in the twentieth century.

Finally, I am very happy to record my indebtedness to Margaret Willes, Gervase Jackson-Stops and Alison Rendle at the National Trust, to Eleo Gordon at Viking Books, to Maureen Barton for typing the manuscript efficiently and to my wife, Margaret, for her selfless encouragement and help.

GEOFFREY BEARD
Bath, January 1989

ACKNOWLEDGEMENTS

The ornaments used on the dedication page and at the end of each chapter have been taken from the three volumes of *The History of the Rebellion* by Edward, Earl of Clarendon, Oxford, 1704.

All the photographs are by courtesy of The National Trust, with the following exceptions:
Olive Smith for an Edwin Smith photograph, no. 27.
The British Library for nos. 1, 105.
Country Life for nos. 24, 29, 32, 43, 45, 77, 78, 80, 88.
The Courtauld Institute for no. 121.
Mrs E. Croft-Murray for no. 56.
Department of the Environment for nos. 68, 75.
English Heritage for no. 25.
A. F. Kersting for nos. 3, 34, 53, 54, 58, 59, 64, 65, 66, 74, 81, 84, 93, 94, 96, 99, 108, 111, 120, 133, 135.
The Metropolitan Museum of Art, New York for no. 35.
Royal Commission on Historical Monuments: National Buildings Record for nos. 40, 41, 42, 47, 113.
Philadelphia Museum of Art for no. 91.
Canon M. H. Ridgway for no. 20
Trustees of the Victoria and Albert Museum for nos. 51, 103, 104.
The author for nos. 44, 61, 67, 83, 87, 89, 90, 92, 97, 138.

Coment noe feigr comenda a noel faur vne arche et y mettar vne paur de coufs beftes pour le deluge

1. *The construction of a timber-framed building, fifteenth century, with carpenters using plane, auger, axe and saw. Illustration from an illuminated manuscript.*
(British Library Add. MS 18850, f. 15)

One

MEDIEVAL PATTERNS

The course of art has left a great series of buildings as documents for the history of civilization. Their structural forms were lavishly decorated by a large number of craftsmen, working to the orders of patrons in a period when the architectural profession had not emerged. Master mason and master joiner were pre-eminent in their craft and led their teams with assurance.

Whilst much decoration was destroyed and dispersed during the Commonwealth, there is still a rich and astounding Medieval 'survival' (that is, the remains of an earlier style enclosed in a later structure), particularly in English churches. It shows the achievements of the medieval carver and his sources of inspiration as well as delighting with a robust display of pattern, or, as in church misericords, with a striking portrayal of events in daily life. The processes were only hampered if there was too slavish an imitation in wood of what was carved in stone as the different weights and textures of each material hindered effective transfer of motifs.

Some chroniclers of the past, perhaps swayed by the rich diet of Sir Walter Scott's historical novels – splendid and robust as his descriptions are – have assumed that medieval life was always hard and that people lived in houses lacking comfort and privacy. In *Ivanhoe*, Scott writes of a twelfth-century castle: 'magnificence there was, with some rude attempt at taste; but of comfort there was little, and being unknown, it was unmissed . . .'

However, there is abundant documentary evidence of the sophistication of many monastic and secular dwellings. For example, Geoffrey Chaucer's 'Miller's Tale' (in *The Canterbury Tales*, written c. 1387) shows the private room of the poor Oxford scholar, Nicholas, as being spacious enough for his books and instruments and as being sweetly perfumed, and in *Pierce the Ploughman's Crede* (c. 1390–1400) there is a description of the chambers of the Dominican Friary in London 'with chymneys and chapells gaie'.

2. The thirteenth- and fourteenth-century tithe barn at Bredon, Hereford and Worcester, under restoration after a fire in 1980. The main frames were reared into position as one unit.

In fairness to Scott, it is always possible to argue that the poor were badly housed when comparing their dwellings with the buildings that their labour created – not only the great castles, churches and houses but the smaller manor houses, farmhouses and barns, which were under constant repair. The Black Death of 1348 had swept away about a third of the English population and labour was scarce. Parliament tried to parry the inevitable rise in wages and prices by passing various Statutes of Labourers (1349–51) and the City of London issued ordinances regulating prices and wages in many crafts. Carpenters could, however, usually find plenty of work within and near to their home towns, and this led to their setting up guilds to control activity and promote standards at a far earlier date than the masons.

Workers in wood may not have needed to band together in teams or 'schools' in the early medieval period, but there is reason to think that they followed, whenever possible, the experienced guidance of a master-carpenter. Before the late fourteenth century most work in wood was the carpenter's undisputed province. He did all tasks from felling and sawing the timber to its final placing in the structure. Later, the joiner shared in these tasks, although there were often arguments over the demarcation of jobs between those working in wood. Whilst knowledge of how the building would react to the weight of its component parts and to the weather was imperfect, enough survives to show a reasonable competence in erection. This is particularly true of the complex timber construction of barns and of the great halls in many houses.

The fourteenth century saw the beginnings of English dominance in the trades of wool and cloth. This led to a wealth which was partly expressed in the architecture and decoration of many fine parish churches and manor houses, with their adjacent great barns. Many of these were tithe-barns, built to hold the 'tithe', or tenth of agricultural produce conceived as due to God and hence payable for support of churches and the priesthood.

The fourteenth-century tithe-barn at Bredon, Hereford and Worcester, is 132 ft long and, whilst restored with traditional materials after a fire in 1980, is still a wondrous run-away space. It is the only aisled barn in the county, with the main frames of its construction being formed on the ground and then reared into position. There are perhaps half a dozen comparable surviving barns – at Glastonbury, Wells and Pilton in Somerset; Abbotsbury, Dorset; Harmondsworth (a property of Winchester College as early as 1391); and Great Coxwell, Frocester and Ashleworth in Gloucestershire. The Frocester barn is the best preserved. Internally it is 186 ft long and 30 ft wide, with thirteen bays supporting a roof that is carved in one span. The Ashleworth barn was built at the end of the fifteenth century and is a mere 125 ft long and 25 ft wide with ten bays, surmounted by timber roof trusses, with queen-posts helping in their support. Whether barn or house, the principal material used was timber, of varying proportions. This led to serious depletion of resources and alarmed the Tudor economists, for timber was vital too for the great ships of the Navy. A progressive reduction in the scantling of timbers (that is, the size to which they are cut) and an increase in the space between them became inevitable.

THE HOUSE PLAN

In the medieval town house there were two main types of plan, related to the placing of the hall. It could either be parallel to the street or at right

3. *Westminster Hall, London, with hammer-beam roof by Hugh Herland,*
windows dating 1394–1402 and Norman walls.

angles to it.[1] In either case, the typical medieval house had a very simple
plan; indeed, until the end of the thirteenth century most timber-framed
houses consisted of a single room, which served as living-room, bedroom
and kitchen. Simple sub-division allowed this to become a hall with aisles
and spaces at each end – one for preparing food and the other for sleeping
apartments. These annexes were built at right angles to the hall with that
for the bedrooms usually being of two storeys. The upper was known as
the 'solar', a name sometimes applied to the whole of that wing. A building
of more than one storey required a timber construction of girders (or
'summers') mortised to the principal posts in order that a timber floor could
be supported. The wall space between the principal posts was framed with

narrower upright posts and on the frame thus formed a filling of wattle-and-daub, plaster, or later, bricks, was used. Light was provided through unglazed openings protected at night by wooden shutters.

By the fourteenth century the hall was usually at ground level and aisleless, and in the larger houses it had separately framed and glazed windows. Much of the constructional work, or 'framing', would be done on the ground, as with the Bredon tithe-barn. This involved cutting the mortise and tenon joints and pegging the timbers together before delivering them to the site ready for rearing into position. The process was helped by

4. *Detail of the barn roof timbers at East Riddlesden Hall, Yorkshire, which are joined with wooden pegs.*

marking the timbers and in some medieval roofs the cut marks are still visible on the trusses. The tie-beam and its principals would bear the same mark, with an increasing number for the successive trusses. The 'rearing' involved several men who, ideally, would have set the ground-sills on a low wall of brick or stone. Sills laid directly on the ground were more prone to decay and involved much levelling and beating down of the soil. The principal posts were inserted into the prepared mortises in the ground-sills, and were held together temporarily by tapering wood pins. This allowed for some movement in the insertion of other subordinate timbers before the more permanent process of pegging the posts together. The tenons on the upper ends of the principal posts were mortised into horizontal beams known as 'wall-plates', a term applied whether they were supported by timber posts or by brick or stone walls. From the wall-plate sprang the timbers for the roof.

In developing the plan it was necessary to consider apartments not only for the family but for guests and retainers. Those for the family were often arranged, as in monastic or collegiate buildings, around a small quadrangle, with a gatehouse in the side opposite to the hall doorway. This pattern can be seen clearly at Compton Castle, Devon; unfortunately, the great hall has gone, but the withdrawing-room, with its large, polygonal bay window, and the chapel, both of c. 1420, survive.

The most important of the private rooms in the early Middle Ages was the 'solar' or great chamber, which acted as a private bed-sitting-room.[2] Servants often slept in the same room as their master, on a low truckle bed that was pushed under the principal one during the day. It was convenient for this great chamber to be near to the hall, and it would usually have a fireplace on the same wall as that in the hall. It must be borne in mind, however, that in earlier times the normal position for the fire in a medieval hall was the centre of the room, requiring a smoke-vent or louvre in the roof above. This often developed into a decorated lantern which served both to ventilate and light the space beneath, even when the central hearth was superseded by the fireplace in the wall, with a chimney, as in many college halls. The Hampton Court great hall louvre, hexagonal in shape, was allowed for in the accounts as late as 1535. The louvre opened like a modern Venetian blind with horizontal movable slats controlled by cords. However, the opening for smoke can still be seen in the soffit of the east-end window of the hall at Clevedon Court, Avon, c. 1320.

At one end of the hall there was a raised dais where the high table was placed. Important guests took their places, according to rank, 'above the salt', to the right hand of the host.[3] A great window was sometimes set above, behind the table. The early fourteenth-century hall at The Treasurer's House, Martock, Somerset, has a window lighting the high table, which has been re-opened from earlier blocking: not many such windows remain for they were in a position where cross-wings could be inserted to give more accommodation for a growing family. This led to lighting the high table from a bay window in a lateral wall.

The hall at Haddon Hall in Derbyshire exemplifies the typical medieval arrangement: erected originally in about 1370 by Sir Richard de Vernon IV, Haddon still retains the screen (c. 1450), the screens passage separating the hall from the kitchens, and a raised dais lit from side windows. However, at Cotehele, Cornwall, there is no screens passage. At one end three doors

5. *The hall at Cotehele, Cornwall, with its fifteenth-century roof,*
which has added principals steadied by purlins and braces.
Watercolour by J. C. Buckler, 1821.

lead into offices, while at the other end, behind the high table, lies the great chamber, with the chapel beyond. During a time – the early fifteenth century – when hammer-beam roofs were already popular, the Cotehele roof is conventional, with arched members steadied by purlins and tautened by braces: it is a technique to be observed at Penshurst Place, Kent, perhaps the finest of the fourteenth-century manor houses. Here, the entire screens passage arrangement survives and the hall itself, some 62 ft long and 39 ft wide, is complete in its medieval state including its central hearth, although the smoke louvre has disappeared. The timber roof has crown-posts on collar-beams resting on richly modelled purlins, with arched braces coming down on to the wall-plates, against which hang large wooden figures. Wall-paintings are traceable in outline between the windows. The original dais is in the west bay one step up, and the tiled floor is also fourteenth-century work.

The ground floor of the medieval house was usually vaulted in stone, which provided resistance to fire. The living-rooms, raised on the first floor, had access by a staircase to this additional and valuable stone-built living space. This in turn could be used to make the house more defensible, as a pele-tower, particularly in northern England where Scottish border raids were frequent. These vaults were often used for storage as well as defence, and had their own stylistic development – barrel-groined and ribbed. The barrel vault was shaped like a tunnel, at first semicircular and then, in the thirteenth century, in pointed form. The groined vault was formed by the intersection of two barrel vaults, and stone arches strengthened the groin

6. *The Canon's Parlour, thirteenth century, at Anglesey Abbey, Cambridgeshire.*
The quadripartite vault is of soft limestone; the columns have Purbeck shafts.

intersections in the ribbed vault. The introduction of the Gothic arch in the second half of the twelfth century allowed the vault to be higher and to be more complex in arrangement with the various ribs meeting at a ridge rib. The late twelfth-century subvault survives at Burton Agnes House in East Yorkshire with 5 ft thick walls and three cylindrical piers supporting the radiating ribs and vaulting.

Each medieval household needed to be self-sufficient and I have noted that storage space was essential. Additionally, there was a continuing search for comfort and privacy. The rooms beneath the great chamber and adjacent to the hall could be turned into small living areas where the family could dine or retire to from the high table. Here, with a wall fireplace, a less draughty room could be devised and the great hall could be kept for festive occasions and for the entertainment of visiting lords and their entourages. This change began to take place in the fourteenth century: in fact, Langland in *The Vision of Piers Plowman* dated *c.* 1362 noted that the lord and his lady no longer like to sit in the hall but 'eat by themselves.../In a privy parlour' and 'leave the chief hall/That was made for meals, for men to eat in'. These extensive residential rooms can be seen at Broughton Castle, Oxfordshire, *c.* 1300, at the upper east end of the hall.

THE ROOF

One of the main differences in the construction of English medieval timber roofs is that between single and double framing.[4] Single framing came first: in this case, the roof frame was constructed so that all the identical transverse rafters carried a share of the total weight. The rafters were strengthened by inserting a collar-beam and this was braced in its position by diagonal timbers. In addition, verticals were sprung from a wall-plate to support the rafters at a lower level.

In a double-framed roof extra strength was given by the additional use of longitudinal timbers, such as a ridge beam at the apex of the roof and purlins at regular intervals along each slope. The 'triangular' section of the roof was supported at its foot by a tie-beam and at a higher point by the collar-beam. These beams could be connected to the ridge at a central position by a king-post, whereas the symmetrically placed vertical queen-posts fulfilled the function of connecting the tie- and collar-beams.

The layman with any knowledge of timber construction always remembers the 'hammer-beam roof' as a term. Such a roof consists of three major triangles. That supporting the ridge consists of two upper principal rafters,

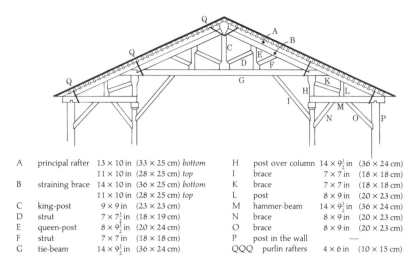

A	principal rafter	13 × 10 in	(33 × 25 cm) *bottom*	H	post over column	14 × 9½ in (36 × 24 cm)
		11 × 10 in	(28 × 25 cm) *top*	I	brace	7 × 7 in (18 × 18 cm)
B	straining brace	14 × 10 in	(36 × 25 cm) *bottom*	K	brace	7 × 7 in (18 × 18 cm)
		11 × 10 in	(28 × 25 cm) *top*	L	post	8 × 9 in (20 × 23 cm)
C	king-post	9 × 9 in	(23 × 23 cm)	M	hammer-beam	14 × 9½ in (36 × 24 cm)
D	strut	7 × 7½ in	(18 × 19 cm)	N	brace	8 × 9 in (20 × 23 cm)
E	queen-post	8 × 9½ in	(20 × 24 cm)	O	brace	8 × 9 in (20 × 23 cm)
F	strut	7 × 7 in	(18 × 18 cm)	P	post in the wall	—
G	tie-beam	14 × 9½ in	(36 × 24 cm)	QQQ	purlin rafters	4 × 6 in (10 × 15 cm)

Fig. 1. Roof construction, with typical dimensions.

with a collar-beam and a king-post at the centre. Below this on either side are the two other triangles, each having a broad base – the hammer-beam – overhanging the wall on either side. A hammer-post, often richly carved and ornamented, rises vertically to the base of the upper triangle creating a stable structure. Arched braces could give additional strength.

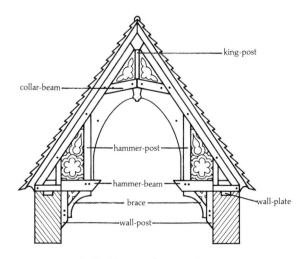

Fig. 2. Hammer-beam roof.

FLOORS

The excavation of many deserted medieval villages in recent years has been a useful source of information on the flooring materials used in the small house. At Wharram Percy Manor House, East Yorkshire, the late-twelfth-century undercroft was in hard-beaten chalk, probably sealed with sour milk, and at Beere, North Tawton, Devon, a thirteenth-century house had one floor composed of small gravel and another of rammed earth.[5] The latter was often used, with rushes and aromatic herbs overlaid to keep down the dust, but in grander buildings, such as castles, stone floors were usual and other substances, for example clay mixed with fine ash, brick and cobbles were also common. Plaster floors, although rare, were also fashioned, as a hard finish can be obtained by mixing lime with brick dust. Vitruvius outlined the preparation of various building-mortars in his *Ten Books of Architecture* in the first century AD. Sand or *pozzolana* was added to the well-slaked lime. *Pozzolana* was a variant form of sand, volcanic in origin, which was used for certain mortars, especially in Roman building construction.[6]

The use of tiles (thin bricks) in the floors of monastic buildings is well known. As early as 900 AD the Abbot of St Albans, Ealdred, had destroyed the ruins of Roman Verulamium but had put aside the tiles and stones for building his church.[7] There is no evidence that the Saxons made either tiles or bricks but production was well re-established by the fourteenth century. Henry III, who married Eleanor of Provence in 1236, had learnt of tiles in France and they were used in the three chapels at Westminster Palace – 'decently paved with painted tile' (L. F. Salzman) – and in 1241 in the whole of the hall at Winchester Castle.

Henry III's favourite residence was Clarendon Palace, Wiltshire.[8] The surviving Liberate Rolls, which have been published, show that it had many elaborate tiled pavements of *c.* 1250. Part of one was found in 1935 and is now in the British Museum; six long panels are decorated with lions and griffins, lattice-work, interlacing circles forming quatrefoils, and foliated crosses, all in bright colours – red, yellow, olive green and a rich brown.[9] Important tile-manufacturing centres in the fourteenth century were at Great Malvern, Hereford and Worcester, London, Coventry in Warwickshire and Penn in Buckinghamshire. The decoration of inlaid tiles was produced by impressing a wooden stamp on to the damp clay and then spreading pipe clay into the indented shape. In painted tiles only the relief part of the pattern formed by the stamp was covered in colour, usually yellow against brown or red.

7. *The great hall, fourteenth century, at Alfriston Clergy House, Sussex,*
with its floor of rammed earth.
This was the first building bought by the National Trust, in 1896.

In the early medieval period, timber floors were confined to upper rooms, although there was also some use of lime and wood-ash mixed together to form durable surfaces. Oak was the first choice but because of its weight elm was sometimes substituted. This surface often formed the ceiling of the room below, thus allowing painted patterns to be applied, a practice that was popular in Scotland, in particular, during the sixteenth century.

WALLS

In the thirteenth century, plaster – a mix of lime, sand, water and chopped animal hair – was not used in a decorative sense but as a thin protective coating for walls. This could be whitewashed by mixing powdered chalk and water with a little size. Alternatively, the whitewash could be applied direct to the stone surface, which was done, for example, at the Keep of the Tower of London in 1248, hence its name, 'The White Tower'. A popular idea for interior work was to mark the creamy-white surface with brown or red lines to represent blocks of masonry. In 1251 Henry II ordered the sheriff of Nottingham to have the Queen's Chamber at Nottingham Castle whitewashed, together with the wardrobe and chapel and 'to point' the walls 'lineally', that is, to mark them out in squares.[10] Simple ornament might then be added in the form of painted devices – flowers were popular, in particular the early forms of rose.

Whilst lime for plaster was plentiful, the important deposits of the finer white gypsum (calcium sulphate) came from Paris at Montmartre – hence 'plaster of Paris', which was formed by burning the gypsum. It was better known and of a better quality than the lesser English deposits at Nore Down, Purbeck, and Matthew Paris, in describing Henry III's visit to Paris in 1254, noted how the King was impressed by 'the elegance of the houses, which are made of gypsum, that is to say plaster'.[11] It was imported into England from the thirteenth century onwards and was used for fine work particularly over fireplaces and chimneys as it withstood the heat better than a crude mortar plaster.

Sometimes the simple whitewash formula was varied by adding colour – red lead or red and yellow ochre were the most common and the yellow ochre was sometimes varnished, with the ochre and varnish even being applied to the oak timbers of the great hall. The medieval painter was skilled enough to attempt the marbling of surfaces, and those working for Henry III were often asked to decorate surfaces with his favourite design, a green background with gold stars. At Clarendon Palace in 1245 one chamber was

8. The east front of the movable screen in the great hall,
c. 1470, at Rufford Old Hall, Lancashire.

to be so painted, with a border depicting the heads of kings and queens and the walls showing the four Evangelists and the story of St Margaret, all 'with good and exquisite colours'.[12] What the king favoured, his court wanted, too, and there is a splendid early-fourteenth-century example of wall-painting, hidden under layers of limewash until 1945, in the Painted Chamber at Longthorpe Tower, Northamptonshire. The 'Nativity', the 'Seven Ages of Man', the 'Labours of the Months' and much else is set out in bright yellow and red ochres, with traces of gold, vermilion and black. It would, perhaps, be unwise to regard this splendid survival as typical of the decoration in all fourteenth-century houses of any pretension. It has been called 'by far the most impressive piece of medieval secular mural decoration in the country'.[13] However, it was certainly common for the walls of parish churches to be painted with stories from the Scriptures.[14]

From early times, it was as customary to panel rooms in wood as to paint them, at first simply and then in more elaborate forms of wainscot. Even something resembling a picture rail could be set above the panels in order that tapestries could be hung. The simplest wainscot consists of vertical planks of soft Norway fir that were usually painted. The most attractive type of wainscot has linenfold panelling, in which the ribbed panels are carved in the form of folded cloth.

One of the important features of the medieval hall was the screen at the lower end, which, in spanning the width, was virtually a wall, albeit a lavishly carved one. Its original purpose was probably that of separating a part of the room from the preparation of food. Later it shut away from sight the 'screens passage' leading to the service areas, and protected those dining in the hall from draughts. This arrangement is still intact in several houses. At Compton Wynyates, Warwickshire, c. 1500, the screens passage is preserved behind the screen, which has richly carved doors set off by the surrounding delicate linenfold panelling. The buttery also survives, with its original doorway and wooden partitions.

Perhaps the most impressive medieval survival, however, is the screens passage and lavish movable screen at Rufford Old Hall, Lancashire, dating from the 1470s. Beneath the five hammer-beam trusses of the hall roof bearing carved angel figures is 'the only originally preserved movable screen, a monster of a screen, and movable only if you accept a very optimistic meaning of the term' – the phrase is Sir Nikolaus Pevsner's. Eight traceried panels are set within a massive frame topped by three fantastic pinnacles, which are carved with ropes, shells, and barbaric gargoyle-like shapes. The 'spere' type of screen, originating from skins suspended between spears, was, at first, movable between the 'speres' but evolved into more solid forms. The late-fifteenth-century example at Chetham's Hospital, Long Millgate, Manchester, projects from the side of a doorway, is original except for its cresting, and now has two entrances. I shall return to this subject when considering interiors of the Tudor period.

CEILINGS

It was usual in the medieval house to leave the beams and crossing joists supporting the upper floors exposed to view from beneath. The great hall, of course, had its own elaborate roof structure and the adjoining upper solar or great parlour could also have exposed beams, with a chamfer or moulding on each edge. The space between was often decorated with painted designs; much of this survives in Scotland (as at Pinkie House, Musselburgh and Delgatie Castle, Aberdeenshire) but little remains in England and examples show only a simple pattern rather than one containing beasts, figures or heraldic devices. An alternative to painting was merely to whitewash the boards. Plastering as a form of decoration became popular from the sixteenth century.

—————— WINDOWS ——————

A house built for fortification had little need of windows, but improvements in glazing, the need to use the hours of daylight for many indoor tasks and the desire for overall comfort and convenience led to an increasing use of great windows, particularly those projecting as an 'oriel' from an upper storey. The Latin word *oriole* (*oriolum*) denotes any projection or built-out gallery,[15] and in medieval times such a gallery was often reached by an external staircase. Later it became a projection usually containing a window and the term now denotes a window not starting from the ground but resting on a corbel, or shaped projection from a wall, to support its weight. Handsome oriels can be seen at many houses,[16] including several National Trust properties. Three of these, chosen at random, are Great Chalfield Manor, Wiltshire; Bradley Manor, Newton Abbot, Devon; and Lytes Cary, Somerset. Those oriels at Great Chalfield, *c.* 1480, are semicircular and have lierne vaults (in which the short intermediate ribs do not rise up from a springing point). Externally one of the oriels has attractive stone fleur-de-lis cresting and blind panelling to the dado, whilst the other has no supporting buttress and a blank dado. The two Lytes Cary oriels, *c.* 1530, are lighting the upper floor of a two-storeyed porch and the adjacent chapel. The parapet of the porch oriel surmounts the eaves of the main roof. The array at Bradley Manor is impressive with a further three-sided oriel being inserted when a central third gable was added to the frontage, *c.* 1495.

The early-sixteenth-century bay windows at Thornbury Castle, Gloucestershire, are multi-angular, following a polygonal plan that was used with great distinction in the Henry VII Tower at Windsor Castle and in Henry VII's great chapel in Westminster Abbey (1503–19).[17]

Whilst the oriel allowed light to enter through an elegant architectural feature, there were other smaller windows for light and ventilation in the medieval house. The Norman loops of the twelfth century were small narrow windows with rounded heads, seen to perfection in the great tower of Castle Hedingham, Essex, c. 1135. Norman windows of the two-light, round-head form can also be seen at Hemingford Grey Manor House, Cambridgeshire, and at Boothby Pagnell Manor House, Lincolnshire, c. 1200. Internally the opening was splayed to make the most of the light that entered. Glass itself, even by the thirteenth century, was scarce: whilst in use in Roman and Saxon times it only slowly supplanted the use of translucent animal horn.

Windows gradually became more elaborate in shape and larger. Trefoil lights in the apex became common. The early wing (c. 1250–60) in the Treasurer's House at Martock, Somerset, has trefoil-headed lights with a quatrefoil above. However, most of the surviving medieval houses date from c. 1350 onwards and their windows have pointed Gothic trefoil heads to the lights and slender 'Perpendicular' mullions. Those at Stokesay, Shropshire, a house with a great hall, c. 1285, are typical of the late thirteenth century, with twin trefoil-headed lights, a large circle at the head and a protecting pointed arch. Within the room the window embrasures could be used for seats, and shutters were added, barred with iron, for night-time security. The holes for the shutter-bars can still be seen at Longthorpe Hall, Northamptonshire, built from 1260 onwards but with a fourteenth-century square tower containing amazing murals of the Nativity and the Seven Ages of Man.[18]

By the fifteenth century, glass was a little less expensive, owing to the greater availability of materials and the increased number of craftsmen skilled at fashioning them. However, glazed windows were still regarded as a luxury and one which, in coloured form, was used to denote rank by proud heraldic display. At Ockwells Manor House, Berkshire, the hall windows contain eighteen shields of armorial stained glass in which, c. 1455–60, Sir John Norreys recorded his allegiance to the kings he had served: Henry VI and Edward IV. Henry's arms and those of his wife, Margaret of Anjou, are surrounded by those of Norreys's court colleagues, and Norreys's own arms are supplemented by the badge of the Wardrobe – Norreys served Henry VI as Master of the Wardrobe – and by his motto, 'Feythfully Serve'.

DOORS

One of the important elements in the design of a room was the placing of doors. In a Saxon hall it has been noted[19] that the entrance might be on an end wall or centrally in a side wall, often facing another doorway. By the twelfth century the door was placed at the lower end of the hall, giving easy access to the screens passage while remaining at a distance from the high table. Horton Court, Avon, has a north wing of Norman date, c. 1140. This is the remains of a prebendal house and its north doorway is therefore in line with the priest's door in the adjacent church of St James, built in the fourteenth century on the site of the Norman church. It has a single-storey hall with a second entrance opposite the north doorway. Both doorways are decorated with chevron-moulded arches and the jamb shafts are adorned with early foliated capitals of the stiff-leaf variety.

The siting of a staircase, considerations of light, and access to private and service areas were three factors dictating door positions. At the fine house of Ightham Mote, Kent, with its moat providing a perfect setting, the hall doorway, c. 1330, is faced by a window of c. 1500. The door leads straight into the hall, not into a screens passage, but in the north-east corner of the hall, a fourteenth-century doorway leads to what is now a seventeenth-century staircase.

The great chamber usually adjoined the upper hall and access to it was made by a doorway in the partition in the corner behind the high table. However, if the hall and chamber were on separate levels it necessitated a 'hidden' staircase and there is little evidence that staircases ever rose against the internal side wall of the hall itself. At Stokesay Castle, Shropshire,[20] the arrangement was complicated; after dining the family left the high table by the end door, passed down to the great chamber basement, through an outer door and came up an external covered staircase to the great chamber. When the great chamber extended beyond the hall as a cross-wing its entrance could be put in the extension of the end wall, leading to a covered external staircase in the re-entrant angle made by the two buildings. Such a staircase would be lit by loops, although at Penshurst Place, Kent, there is an elaborate hall oriel and evidence of another, which was entered from a side wall of the hall, has also been found at Compton Castle, Devon. Oriels were used to light the stairs (which allowed diners to leave the hall unobtrusively) and to shield the great-chamber door from draughts.

At this early period in English domestic architecture it is the doorway that has more chance of being in its original form than the door it frames. Most are familiar with the Norman round-headed and dog-toothed arch of the eleventh and twelfth centuries, often enriched with shafts in the angles. However, this type of doorway is mainly confined to churches or to special settings such as the Jew's House in Lincoln (c. 1170–80).[21] There is a magnificent shafted entrance (c. 1170) incorporating three greater and two lesser orders, to Bishop Pudsey's Building at Durham Castle. On a small scale it echoes the great transept arches of Durham Cathedral itself, finished sixty years previously and soaring to a little over 68 ft high.

In thirteenth-century doorways the outer arch is often pointed or four-centred. This means that its curves were each drawn from centres on or below the springing line (the level at which an arch rises from its supports) to meet in a point at the top. It persisted as a form through the fourteenth century but in the last quarter was often incorporated within a square frame. In the late years of the fifteenth century the four-centred form was replaced by a two-centred or Tudor arch. Here, also, the curves were struck from centres, but on the springing line. Variations were the ogee, popular in the fourteenth century, and the depressed or basket arch in which the head was straight with only the angles rounded. Few early ogee-headed doorways exist although the form is common enough in mid-eighteenth-century Gothick Revival work in a house such as Lacock Abbey, Wiltshire.

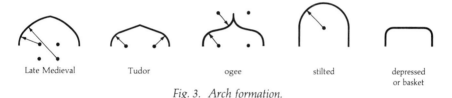

Late Medieval Tudor ogee stilted depressed or basket

Fig. 3. Arch formation.

The earliest form of door, properly called a 'leaf', consisted of vertical boards fastened at the back by horizontal battens or ledges, and occasionally with additional diagonal braces. The Saxon north-door leaf at St Botolph, Hadstock in Essex, consists of four wide planks with D-section oak ledges for the frame and the horizontal members, whilst the Saxon door leaf at Westminster Abbey in the east range of the cloister is formed of five oak planks strengthened by three horizontal ledges.[22] Those in domestic use must have been similar, with iron spikes hammered through the outer planks and ledges and with the points being bent back and driven into the ledges.

The refinement of this form of construction consisted in rebating the vertical planks so that stronger joints were formed and the ledges were, dovetailed into the outer frame. By the mid-fifteenth-century, the main surface of the door could be lavishly carved – the two pairs of entrance doors at St Martin's Palace in Norwich,[23] dated between 1446 and 1472, exemplify the skill of contemporary carpenters at precise, linear, Per-pendicular-style decoration. Internal doors, whilst lighter in construction, followed the development of those for external use and were eventually panelled to match the wall-panelling. Most doors were hung on iron strap and hook hinges, often of elaborate shape. The carpenter also provided the window shutters which may be regarded as window doors. They were braced like doors, that is, with ledges holding the battens or planks together.

FIREPLACES

I have noted that the hall in its early plan was heated by a central hearth and this design continued in some houses until the early sixteenth century. However, the development of the great chamber and other rooms above the hall rendered this practice inconvenient and even dangerous. The solution was to place the fireplace against the wall and eventually to sink it into the stone and connect it to a chimney or funnel, through which the smoke could escape to the outer air. The earliest Norman fireplaces were round-headed with chevron ornament.[24]

A practical amendment to the wall fireplace was the introduction of a hood which projected into the room. It was the predominant form in the thirteenth century and was refined in appearance throughout that time. Triple-clustered shafts, corbel supports, pyramidal stone or plaster hoods, and even angle brackets to support lamps were common features, partly decorative and always functional. At Conway Castle in North Wales the hall has two fireplaces, basically of the late thirteenth century, the west one having a hood of pyramidal form, whilst that to the south has been made vertical in the fourteenth century. The most elaborate late-thirteenth-century fireplaces are found at Aydon Castle, which stands high above the Cor Burn and near to Corbridge and Hadrian's Wall in Northumberland. It is, in fact, a fortified house (having no keep), but it was licensed to crenellate — that is, to have battlements — in 1305. The slightly earlier hall range is on the first floor, reached by an outer staircase, and in a room below the hall there is a fireplace with a massive stone lintel, which has an elaborate scroll-moulded string-course and convex-shaped corbels. In the great chamber and the basement beneath are two further fireplaces, ogee corbels and dog-tooth foliage; and a stone plinth with a rich cornice carved with heads. At the west end of the south range there are two more fireplaces in two upper storeys, one above the other, proving that this part was once three-storeyed.

By the second half of the fourteenth century, the pyramidal hood had passed out of fashion in English houses, although it persisted in France. Other shapes were used, particularly the arched fireplace, or those with a segmental or a square head. Many have stone traceried panels, as miniature expressions of the Gothic style, and are especially resplendent when they display coloured heraldic shields.

STAIRCASES

It is understandable that no internal wooden stairs of early date survive especially as stone was the dominant material, although there are a few oak treads at Stokesay Castle, Shropshire, serving doorways in the hall. A spiral staircase took up little space and could be built in the thickness of a Norman wall or in a corner turret. They could therefore be put into the defensive position, in the angles of great towers, and were usually built clockwise so that the defender had space for his sword arm.[25] There are two excellent fifteenth-century domestic staircases rising in a clockwise direction at Clevedon Court, Avon, although the early-sixteenth-century Sandford Orcas Manor, near Sherborne, Dorset, has both clockwise and anti-clockwise examples. At both Lytes Cary, Somerset, and Sandford Orcas, the newel, or central pillar round which the steps wind, has a wooden top with stone below.

When the hall of the house was divided laterally to give upper rooms it became necessary to put the staircase in some form of stairs tower. Doe's Farmhouse, Toothill, Essex, has a handsome stairs tower containing its original newel stair and mullioned windows.[26] By the early sixteenth century, the circular staircase, now with newels and steps of wood, was being replaced by a straight or double-backed form, in an open well, with a handrail and balustrade rather than a second enclosing wall.

SERVICES: THE KITCHEN

The arrangement in the great hall of a raised dais at one end and a screen and screens passage at the other meant that diners only saw the arched openings to the service areas. These included the kitchen, pantry and buttery and, perhaps, the stairs to wine and beer cellars. There could also be areas for bakery and butchery and for the servants themselves to eat. Cooking was done on open fires although the baking was in brick-lined ovens.

A number of these fine, high, medieval secular kitchens survive, for example at Raby Castle, Durham, from the mid fourteenth century, at Haddon Hall, Derbyshire, from the end of the fifteenth century and at Stanton Harcourt, Oxfordshire, from *c.* 1485, where there is a splendid octagonal timber lantern allowing ventilation. The ecclesiastical kitchens

*9. Detail of the great kitchen, early sixteenth century, at Compton Castle, Devon,
showing part of the hearth, which extends the whole width of the kitchen,
with bread ovens to each side.*

are always impressive and there is an excellent late-fourteenth-century
abbot's kitchen at Glastonbury, Somerset.

It has been shown that the three arches in the screen had a ceremonial
as well as a practical function. They acted, of course, as entrances when
food was carried into the hall, but the ceremonial could be lavish, with
musicians in a gallery above. The dressed swan or boar's head was carried
through the central arch to great acclaim, with the accompanying retinue
of servants and servers filtering through the other two. 'The lord was then
facing a fanciful portal crowned with trumpeters', and as the kitchen staff
sent forth the platters they 'could burst into sound at the exact moment
that the food and its escort emerged from underneath it'.[27]

This arrangement can be seen clearly at Penshurst Place in Kent, an
impressive survival of the 1340s, and in a setting of about 150 years later
at Haddon Hall, Derbyshire. At Penshurst, the service areas are hidden by
a later screen but access to them originally was directly through the three
arches in the kitchen wall. At Haddon Hall, entry from the lower courtyard
is through a west door directly into the screens passage. On the left, lie the
buttery and pantry with a passage leading to the old kitchen, which retains
its medieval fittings. There is an enormous stone-arched fireplace and
originally a second hearth stood against the northern wall. During the

restorations in the 1920s, this was taken out to give access to the tunnel from the new kitchens (which had its own small 'railway' to transport food). Passing from the kitchen there was a bakehouse, with its own ovens, and a butcher's shop with bench, salting-trough, hanging-rack and chopping-block.

SERVICES: GARDEROBES

It is easy in a modern society, with elaborate and efficient systems of plumbing and sewage disposal, to forget that English house interiors in the past had to include privies, or as they were politely called 'garderobes'. As a term, it seems to derive from the French *garde-robe* or medieval storage chamber for dress materials and for dressmaking. The king and queen's storage room, or wardrobe, will be encountered many times in later pages. To these rooms, which also served for dressing, a privy chamber was a sensible addition, with rain-water diverted for flushing the privy shaft.[28] It could be incorporated in a thick wall, or be corbelled out to resemble an external buttress, and there are examples of this on the north tower at Stokesay Castle, Shropshire, at Broughton Castle, Oxfordshire, and at Longthorpe Tower, Northamptonshire. Such privies discharged by a shaft into a stream, river or cess-pit, and precautions were taken in medieval castles to build covers in order that an intrepid invading party could not enter up this shaft in time of siege. The eventual tendency was to separate the privy from the dwelling-house, and life was intended to be a little easier when Sir John Harington, godson of Queen Elizabeth I, invented the water-closet.[29] Unfortunately, no one took much notice of his efforts and the old and noisome practices continued.

Two

TUDOR SYMMETRY

England in the Tudor period was spanned by the reigns of five monarchs, commencing with that of Henry VII in 1485 and concluding, in 1603, with the death of Elizabeth I, after her forty-five-year rule. In architectural terms, the Elizabethan Age is regarded as something different and apart from the one immediately preceding it, and the exuberant and richly decorated 'prodigy houses' of the late sixteenth century are often referred to, rather confusingly, as manifestations of an Elizabethan Baroque. What many of the houses had in common was a ground-plan based on buildings arranged around a courtyard, or in the formation of a letter 'E' or 'H'. The debt owed to the similar plans used in the building of monastic houses and collegiate buildings is evident.

THE HOUSE PLAN

One of the main concerns of the medieval builder had been the defence of his home, and comfort did not coincide readily with this aim. Across the deep moats of fortified houses such as Oxburgh Hall, Norfolk, or Baddesley Clinton, Warwickshire, owners could feel secure, dining in their great halls on the side of the inner courtyard[1] furthest from their castellated gatehouses. These important buildings at the entrance demonstrate that the owner was part of a court circle well versed in up-to-date architecture. They sometimes stood proud and detached, but as often were connected to the front of the building, announced by a wing or retaining wall, as at Cotehele, in Cornwall. The concerns of the Tudor builder in the 1520s, however, related more to the overall symmetry of his expensively contrived façades and less to defensive towers. The hall window bays could be spaced out equally on the main high front, with side-wings balancing each other as they swept forward to enfold the amazed onlooker.

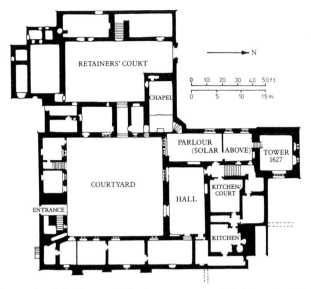

Fig. 4. Cotehele, Cornwall; the house was remodelled in 1485–1539,
the entrance being placed on the south side and the early courtyards increased in size.
(Plan by courtesy of the National Trust)

The early Tudor preoccupation with buildings grouped round a courtyard surrounded by many towers had been given encouragement by Henry VII in his palace at Sheen (called Richmond Palace) finished in 1501. Of its exact plan we know little,[2] and only part of the outer range, including the main gatehouse on Richmond Green, now remains. However, the palace had many timber galleries, made by the master carpenter Thomas Binks, overlooking a courtyard 'which renders all the roomes ... that lie inwards to bee very light and pleasant'. At Thornbury Castle, Gloucestershire, all but completed by Edward Stafford, 3rd Duke of Buckingham, before he was executed in 1521, we can still see a building derived from Richmond Palace. The main buildings are again around a courtyard, with the south side containing the rooms of state, overlooking the enclosed Privy Garden. These plans give an idea of what was being built for Cardinal Wolsey at Hampton Court. Begun in 1515, Hampton Court was presented by Wolsey to Henry VIII in 1525. It was an astute move calculated to try to regain the king's favour and stem the decline of power. This was not achieved, even after the gift of such a mighty bauble, because the devious, hard-working cleric-diplomat was already in disgrace.

Wolsey's Great Gatehouse at Hampton Court, with its oriel windows and slender towers, allows entry from the Outer Court into Base Court and thus in turn leads to what is now called 'Clock Court'. However, of the surviving Tudor buildings only the great hall, 1532–4, is well documented, with its many carved embellishments 'of Italianate character, set slightly incongruously in the traditional framework of the Gothic roof'.[3] The courtyard arrangement at Hampton Court may have given ideas to the king to have an inner and outer court at his Palace of Nonsuch, which he began to build in 1538 near the old village of Cuddington in Surrey.

Only fragments survive of the sixty or so houses owned by Tudor monarchs. For example, some parts of a gatehouse with octagonal turrets, and the Chapel Royal (1532–40), are all that remain of St James's Palace. What suited a monarch was often of little use to his courtiers — they had less need for indulging in regular and lavish entertainments, however ambitious they might seek to become. Nevertheless, the separate suites of apartments appropriate for a king and his queen were deemed as necessary for a powerful courtier and his wife, but they needed to be on guard, when enlarging their houses, against charges of exceeding their positions. Ben Jonson describes the modesty of the country house in his poem *To Penshurst* (1616):

> Thou art not, PENSHURST built to envious show
> of touch, or marble; nor canst boast a row
> of polish'd pillars, or a roofe of gold ...

and contrasts this with other edifices:

> Those proud, ambitious heaps, and nothing else ...

It has a continuing echo from the early Tudor years, when the king's mood was fickle and the axe sharp for those who stood out too soon as serious rivals to self-aggrandisement.[4]

After Wolsey's downfall in 1529–30, royal management of the land-market and other devices, such as the rendering of feudal dues, discouraged the construction of houses for a short time.[5] However, at the Dissolution (1537–8), many residences were built on monastic lands, which were given as rewards, sold to the highest bidder, or offered to courtiers during the occupancy of an important office in the Crown's service.

When the defensive functions of the medieval gatehouse and the inner courtyard it 'guarded' were less necessary it was an easy step to fashion a plan with extended wings and a central gatehouse or raised frontispiece. Sir John Strode, in building Chantmarle in Dorset as late as 1612 (this date and the word 'EMMANUEL' appear on the keystone of the porch doorway), wrote in his diary: 'Constructa est in forma de littera E, scilicet Emanuel, id est, Deus nobiscum in aeternum.'[6]

There was now a pedantic stress on symmetry, and no better place than to state an owner's concern with the classical orders than on the frontispiece (of which, inside the house, the chimneypiece was often a minor copy). This frontispiece could be a towering array of misunderstood and unrelated decoration, cribbed from such influential foreign sources as Philibert de l'Orme's frontispiece of the late 1540s at the Château of Anet.[7] The medieval plan persisted, however, and even in the seventeenth century the old arrangement of hall with upper and lower end chambers was not obsolete, although outmoded.

As the sixteenth century progressed, there was a concern for more comfort and a new house could afford better heating, lighting and arrangements for sanitation. This involved careful consideration of the plan. The rich collections of sixteenth-century drawings by John Thorpe and by the Smythsons[8] show designs based on a wide range of geometrical shapes, using ideas borrowed from foreign pattern-books and engravings by such designers as Wendel Dietterlin, Vriedeman de Vries, Jacques Androuet Du Cerceau and Sebastiano Serlio. The five *Books of Architecture* by Serlio were of great importance in spreading knowledge of Classical forms in England. They were published in France between 1537 and 1547 in an odd sequence, with Book Four appearing first. The ideas propounded therein were used at an early date, *c.* 1549–52, by Lord Protector Somerset's unknown architect when building at Old Somerset House, with fronts facing the Strand and the River Thames, in London. The Strand front had a symmetry and rhythm that made it appear more in the Renaissance style than it actually was. Whilst Serlio remains the chief source used, knowledge of recent French building was also probable.

Being an architectural theorist, Serlio ensured his position as an important disseminator of interior designs by issuing a book of doorways – the *Extraordinary Book* – in 1551. The popularity of his books continued throughout the sixteenth century and many motifs taken from his wood engravings were used to decorate doors, chimneypieces, coffered ceilings and pieces of furniture.[9]

There are many examples of house plans formed around buildings acquired after the Dissolution of the Monasteries.[10] A large number of the abandoned abbeys and priories became quarries for expensive, well-fashioned building-stones. In 1536 Sir William Sandys acquired the Augustinian house of Mottisfont Abbey (or more correctly, Priory), Hampshire, by exchanging the Manor of Chelsea with the king. He made his adaptation of the priory into a residence the chief activity of his declining years – he died at Calais in 1540. Whilst little of his double-court mansion is now

*10. The thirteenth-century monks' cellarium at Mottisfont Abbey, Hampshire,
constructed from Caen stone, with a groined vault.*

visible, much is incorporated into the priory itself. In fact, the nave and
crossing of the church formed the principal part of his new house. The
cellarium with its mighty vault and the chapter house had wings raised over
them to give him a 'U'- or even an 'E'- shaped house, assuming there was
a central porch.

In amending their houses, few were as meticulous as Sir William Petre,
Secretary of State to Henry VIII, Edward VI, Mary Tudor and Elizabeth I,
who had sought absolution from the Pope for the monastic sites he had
acquired. He rebuilt Ingatestone Hall in Essex, which had been a manor of
the nunnery of Barking, but still ranged his buildings in an old-fashioned
way, round a large inner courtyard. Ideas were given to many owners about
what to build from the disposition of existing buildings. For example, the
medieval hall often had an upper parlour inserted in the sixteenth century
and this then became a pattern for the more confined and symmetrical space
of Elizabethan halls. There was also little need, as a more peaceful period
rendered the security of a property less urgent, for windows only to look
inwards to a courtyard. Houses could rise high and become 'outward-
looking' and the organization of interior space could be considered in terms
of comfort rather than defence and the storage of supplies for long isolation.

The mid-seventeenth-century chronicler, John Aubrey, writing when Elizabethan architecture was not admired, and was even despised by some, noted that it 'made no progress but went backwards'.[11] 'Outward-looking' as some lavishly glazed houses were, with a similarly perceptive attitude in their owners, the native Perpendicular Gothic traditions were still very strong and hard to shake off, except in rare cases. Even the 'glass walls' of Hardwick Hall, Derbyshire, seem to have had their origin in the huge square-headed windows provided by the Gothic church builders – the domestic counterpart of the Henry VII Chapel at Westminster Abbey or of King's College Chapel, Cambridge, albeit given a special character by its architect, Robert Smythson. He was, of course, drawing on English Gothic traditions but combining them with Renaissance details for a different and subtle emphasis.

HALLS, GALLERIES AND CHAMBERS

Elizabethan architecture has been seen, by one writer, as 'a magnificent last flowering of the Gothic age',[12] yet with richly carved surface trappings based on foreign influences. This is apparent in certain of the halls, chambers and galleries of sixteenth-century houses. Montacute in Somerset has an

11. *The timber screen (c. 1530–40) in the hall passage at Bradley Manor, Devon.*

impressive stone screen, *c.* 1600, incorporating pillars, two rusticated arches and strapwork decoration topped by an elaborate cresting with carved rams' heads, a motif often found in Romanesque sculpture. The sources of the decoration are, however, grounded mainly in Netherlandish patterns. By contrast, the hall screen at Hardwick Hall, erected by William Griffin in 1597, is a pure piece of Italian Classical design, amid much that emanates from the pattern-books published at Antwerp and the Mannerist architecture of the Low Countries. Many spaces therefore broke with Gothic building traditions in a variety of ways: for example, the important Elizabethan interiors done for Sir William Sharington at Lacock Abbey, Wiltshire, or, as noted, for Lord Protector Somerset at Old Somerset House, London.

A final indication of diversity in the Elizabethan period can be seen in the use of different building materials; in halls, for example, timber-framing occurs at Ightham Mote, Kent, and Speke Hall, South Lancashire. At Ightham, there are traces of earlier structures, such as the doorway, and at Speke, the two-storey hall had the arrangement of a prefatory screens-

12. *The screen, c. 1600, in the great hall at Montacute, Somerset,*
from a watercolour by C. J. Richardson, c. 1830.

13. *The great hall (c. 1340, but with some nineteenth-century restoration)*
at Ightham Mote, Kent, showing a medieval fireplace with later surround;
a roof of open-timbered trussed rafters and a fourteenth-century doorway.

passage. Whilst dated *c.* 1500 it may equally be of any date before 1598,
when the north front was finished. Amendments in structure were common:
the hall in the east range at Baddesley Clinton, Warwickshire, has both
fifteenth-century beams and a large stone chimneypiece of *c.* 1580 that was
originally in a room over the gateway.

If the great hall of the sixteenth-century house declined in importance
because of the need for more privacy, with people increasingly dining and

taking leisure in smaller rooms, the long gallery and the great chamber developed in importance. The gallery, owing to its dominant position in the plan and its impressive length, frequently occupying the whole of one side of the house, often remains intact. In 1531 a visitor to Whitehall Palace recorded that he had seen 'three so-called galleries, which are long porticos or halls without chambers, with windows on each side looking on rivers and gardens'. They became spaces primarily intended for recreation and exercise from the early sixteenth century onwards.

When Sir William Sandys, whom I have noted altering Mottisfont Priory, started to amend The Vyne, also in Hampshire, in the late 1520s, he created a remarkable plan. This broke with current fashion and anticipated planning of later years. Lord Sandys was trying hard to finish his work before Henry VIII's intended third visit of 1531 and one of his innovative touches was to build a long gallery, in the manner of those provided for Henry VII at Richmond Palace and Cardinal Wolsey at Hampton Court. Lord Sandys had spent a great deal of time in France, where the gallery had been developing as a space from the fourteenth century, and whilst it has been much altered, his gallery at The Vyne is one of the earliest surviving examples in a private house in England.[13] It occupies the whole of the first floor in the west wing and could therefore be lit from both sides. Despite its great broken-pedimented chimneypiece designed by John Webb in the 1650s, and its eighteenth-century ceiling, it is a Tudor room in structure, although there is reason to believe that the oak panelling, much of it sixteenth-century, was not made for the gallery. Indeed, some in the end-bay is *c.* 1820 – despite many Tudor emblems and devices, including those of Catherine of Aragon and Cardinal Wolsey.[14]

When a gallery could not be set within the ground- or first-floor plan, to look either out, or into, a courtyard, it was frequently skied even higher, particularly in the late sixteenth century. The most notable of these skied or attic galleries are those at Hardwick Hall, Derbyshire, Burton Agnes, Yorkshire, and Montacute in Somerset; there are others of seventeenth-century date noted in Chapter 3. Sir Sacheverell Sitwell has written evocatively of the great gallery at Hardwick Hall: 'all but two hundred feet in length, hung with tapestry from end to end ... we can look out, from the windows in the long bays, upon the park and the stag-antlered trees.'[15]

Equally, Mark Girouard has described in considerable detail[16] the interchange of ideas between Elizabeth, Countess of Shrewsbury, 'Bess of Hardwick', and her architect, Robert Smythson (*c.* 1535–1614), who utilized height as a feature in the 'Old' and the 'New' Hardwick Halls in the 1580s and 1590s. Old Hardwick is now a picturesque ruin but the new house

14 (above). The Oak
Gallery, c, 1525, at The
Vyne, Hampshire, with
linenfold panelling; the
Classical marble chimney-
piece was designed by John
Webb, c. 1655.

15 (right). Detail of the oak
linenfold panelling at The
Vyne, Hampshire, showing
a pomegranate (the device
of Queen Catherine of
Aragon), c. 1525.

(1590–99), rearing astride the hill-top, with its six towers each bearing the stone initials 'ES', and with its façade pierced by the great area of glass windows, is a magnificent statement of Elizabethan opulence. Its gallery, 160 ft long, was a useful space in which Bess of Hardwick could receive important visitors and take exercise on inclement days. In fact, in 1603, Sir Henry Brounker, a Commissioner sent by Queen Elizabeth to sort out the intrigues of Bess's granddaughter, Lady Arabella Stuart, noted: 'My Lady of Shrewsbury ... sent for me in her gallery where she was walking with the La: Arabella and her son, William Cavendish.'[17]

A gallery was also a place to hang paintings, particularly portraits (that of Queen Elizabeth herself is among many at Hardwick) and to have 'entertainments'. Roger North's description of galleries, which appeared in his *Treatise on Building* in 1695–6[18], is equally relevant to galleries of the late sixteenth century: they should enable people to move around freely and take exercise; they should be easily accessible, preferably on the first floor; they should have bow windows fronting on to the gardens and they should be decorated with carving, paint or pictures.

The skied galleries were at variance with North's concern for ease of access but there is no denying the splendour of those at Hardwick and Montacute, set so high and long across the plan of the house. The second-floor gallery at Montacute House in Somerset is the longest surviving one, of some 172 ft; only two other galleries exceeded this one in length: the gallery designed by Smythson, at Worksop Manor, Nottinghamshire (now demolished) and the remodelled one at Longleat in Wiltshire. An account of Montacute in 1667 gives this description: 'a faire Gallary of 200 feete long Wainscoted, with divers good lodging Chambers adjoyning, and 3 very faire and large Stairecases all built with the same Freestone ...'

During the nineteenth century, this wainscoting was replaced by pine panelling to dado height which was, in turn, stripped out except around the fireplaces and in the oriels at each end. As the setting now for about ninety Tudor and Jacobean portraits from the collections of the National Portrait Gallery, the Montacute gallery fulfils Roger North's edict that it be 'set off with pictures'.

The great Elizabethan gallery at Haddon Hall, Derbyshire, was created in about 1598. This date is on an heraldic glass panel in the first of the south window bays beyond the stone stairs, commemorating the liaison of the Manners and Vernon families. The gallery is 110 ft long and 17 ft wide and its panelling and plaster ceiling are worthy of description in the relevant sections which follow. Again, as the wing protrudes to look over the terraced gardens of the south front and the upper courtyard to the north,

16. *The long gallery, c. 1597–9, at Hardwick Hall, Derbyshire,*
showing the simple ribbed ceiling and one of the two chimneypieces by Thomas Accres.

windows are placed on both sides and at the east end; these are square, with stone mullions and transoms and undulating diapers of greenish-white glass.

The last of the smaller Elizabethan galleries, that at Little Moreton Hall, Cheshire, is perhaps the most charming, as it is within a courtyard house which itself delights, by its disordered, half-timbered black-and-white array. In 1559 the carpenters William Moreton and Richard Dale, whose names are carved above the upper and lower polygonal bay windows, remodelled the living-rooms and started building the south range, which is the one first encountered when crossing the moat. They reared up a long gallery across the ship-like, wooden length of the gate house, with a roof formed, internally, of a collar-beam, two tiers of concave wind-braces and a plastered tympanum at each end. It is an early precursor, in a light and fanciful moment only, of all those late-Elizabethan houses which let in air and sunshine through great expanses of glass – the side-walls are almost entirely composed of leaded lights. But Little Moreton is, of course, built without Classical thought or precedent, a carpenter's proud achievement. It owes nothing to great patronage, or to the precise lined instructions set out on the 'platt' or to a drawn elevation submitted by a knowledgeable surveyor. It strains and tips like a wooden man-of-war rearing on its anchor, incongruous in the green Cheshire fields.

The siting of long galleries over great halls or loggias gave further variety to the plan, but many have been remodelled, or disappeared at an early date. As a space, the gallery was often near, or gave access to, other important rooms and even, in a few cases, to the chapel. This happened at Copthall in Essex, c. 1570–80,[19] which, alas, only survives in plans and views, having been supplanted by a new house in 1753. The principal room to be served was the great chamber, which was usually sited over the parlour and was sometimes formed with a two-storey solar. From medieval times the great chamber had been a room of state for special occasions but in the Tudor period its use gradually became more defined. It served for entertaining and formal dining, marriage celebrations and even the lying in state of a body before burial. The room could also be used as a state bedchamber at the visit of an important personage.

At Lytes Cary, Somerset, the great chamber is reached by a stone staircase at the great hall archway. It has excellent plaster decoration (described below) dating from about 1533, and this gives an approximate date to the room itself. Next to the great chamber is a little chamber, as well as a small ante-room, which corresponds to the oriel, off the hall. Almost all the original wainscot in the great chamber has disappeared, but a common use for the room is suggested now by a canopied oak bed. The great chamber would often be lighted by an oriel built over another oriel below, which in turn may have been formed out of the space occupied by the oriel window of the medieval-hall plan. In the Lytes Cary great chamber the stone arch of the oriel has, moreover, the same Perpendicular Gothic panels as that in the great parlour beneath.

I have already mentioned the hall in the half-timbered house, Speke Hall, near Liverpool. Its great chamber has a lovely vine-pattern plasterwork ceiling and an elaborate wooden overmantel to the chimneypiece, representing three generations of the Norris family.

It is, however, in the great 'prodigy houses' (the apt phrase is Sir John Summerson's) of Queen Elizabeth's reign that the finest great chambers are found, the most supreme example being at Hardwick Hall, Derbyshire. This great house for Bess of Hardwick was built a few years after Wollaton Hall at Nottingham, which Robert Smythson designed for Sir Francis Willoughby from 1580–88. Externally Wollaton survives almost untouched. However, the magnificent hall within has an elaborate hammer-beam roof (modelled on the one at Longleat) which Mark Girouard has shown to be a fake: 'It does no useful work but is in fact slung from the ceiling which it appears to support'.[20] Short timbers were scarfed together in order to span the 32 ft width of the hall. Around this and built high were two great chambers, to north and south. They survive (but with their original decoration long since gone) and are approached up matching staircases. The east side of the plan was given over to a long gallery, all of it symmetrical and based on plans in books by Du Cerceau and Palladio. Mark Girouard captures the spirit of the house in this description:

Wollaton has something of the quality of nightmare. For many it must have been an experience unforgettable but awful to climb the long avenue up the hill, to round the corner, and to stagger back – amazed and excited, yes, but also appalled, by the basilisk glare, the crash and glitter, of that fantastic façade.[21]

Of the Smythson houses, Hardwick Hall is the best known, not least because of the architect's determination to construct a building worthy of its creator, Bess of Hardwick. There are, of course, differences in the Wollaton and Hardwick plans and Hardwick Hall contains less of the mature, brilliant carving than the Willoughby house.

The High Great Chamber at Hardwick Hall is arguably one of the most beautiful rooms in Europe. It is approached, winding up through the light and dark of the house, by a stone staircase that never reveals where it is going until the last sharp turn to a bright, tapestry-hung landing. Bess's

17. *The High Great Chamber, c. 1597–9, at Hardwick Hall, Derbyshire,*
with its deep, coloured plaster frieze by Abraham Smith and others
and a chimneypiece by Thomas Accres, surmounted by the royal arms.

arms are set in plaster over the elaborately panelled door to the High Great Chamber and a fine medieval German lock on the door helped to introduce or bar supplicants to her presence.

Within, the High Great Chamber draws its interest from the deep, robust plaster frieze, the chimneypiece, the decorated panelling and the sheer scale of the space, completed in 1599. As a rectangle it measures 50 by 30 ft with the protruding bay of the south-west tower, lighted on three sides, adding a further 27 by 15 ft. But mere measurements cannot convey the splendour of this room, with its colourful plaster representations of the court of Diana, a flattering allusion to the court of Elizabeth I. The 1601 Inventory shows[22] that Bess was able to sit there beneath a canopy on 'a Chare of nedlework with golde and silk frenge' with her feet on a footstool, surrounded by a company on six forms and sixteen stools. They would eat at 'a long table of white wood', covered with carpet and a damask tablecloth, served by a rigid hierarchy of servants, and at the end of the meal they could listen to music or watch the sun setting over the forbidding façades of Old Hardwick Hall, before attending family prayers in the chapel below.

Both the Old and New Hardwick Halls had two great chambers. In New Hardwick the Low Great Chamber was far from Bess's bedchamber and those of her son and granddaughter beyond. It was part of a domestic suite and was used for family dining, for playing table-games and even as a common room by the upper servants.

CHAPELS

In addition to rooms for parade and estate, Elizabethan houses followed their medieval predecessors in having a chapel. At the south-east corner of The Vyne, Hampshire, the Tudor chapel (with its adjoining tomb chamber built in the late 1760s) is prefaced by a chapel parlour and an ante-chapel. The parlour is lined with crisp linenfold panels from the time of Sir William Sandys's work but the ante-chapel is a typical product of the deliberations of the Strawberry Hill Committee. This was composed of Horace Walpole's friends, John Chute (1701–76) being one of the closest. The chapel retains its Tudor windows and woodwork but at Horace Walpole's suggestion trompe-l'œil paintings of groins and vaults were put on the ceiling. The Tudor stalls are in two tiers of enriched panels with cusped heads, each end having poppy-head style finials, one representing a woman and three acrobats. The stained glass is of Flemish origin and of the early 1520s:[23] it is bright and colourful and only equalled in importance by that in the windows of King's College Chapel, Cambridge.

At Ightham Mote, Kent, the Tudor chapel is placed on the north side of the ground floor of the house. It was built between 1521 and 1529 by Richard Clement, who had been in royal service to Henry VII and Henry VIII. However, despite looking entirely Tudor, the chapel was rebuilt in 1890–91, using original materials as far as possible. The stalls, screen, pulpit and linenfold panelling have very little restoration and the stained-glass windows are filled with glass thought to originate in Cologne, c. 1525. There is a fine painted ceiling (described a little later in this chapter) which adorns a wooden barrel vault. The oak door at the west end is of c. 1460 with the usual cross-banding held by clenched nails, an example of a feature older than the surrounding structure being re-used during the expensive stages of building.

As well as having two great chambers, Hardwick Hall also had two chapels. The lower chapel, on the ground floor of the south-east tower, was

18. *The chapel, c. 1525, at The Vyne, Hampshire, with three late-Gothic windows
filled with Flemish glass, and encaustic tiles before the altar.
The windows depict the Passion of Christ.*

used by servants whilst the upper one, in the same tower on the first floor,
was used by the countess, her family and guests. It was richly upholstered
and prefaced by a landing frowned on by heads in splendid plasterwork
cartouches. An open-work screen now separates the chapel from the landing
as, perhaps originally glazed, it then separated the kneeling pious from the
bold stares of the curious lower servants.

19. *The chapel, c. 1521–9, rebuilt 1890–91, at Ightham Mote, Kent.*
The stalls, screen and pulpit are original with little restoration.
The barrel-vault ceiling is painted with chevrons and royal badges.

FLOORS,
WALLS AND CEILINGS

Since the Middle Ages floor surfaces have undergone as many changes as other structural features in houses. The most common flooring materials were stone, bricks, marble or wood, but occasionally hard plaster or tiles were used.

The weight of stone usually confined its use to paving for the basement and ground floor. It came frequently from quarries on or near the site, although the use of some highly prized stone meant seeking it at a distance. Most Tudor houses seem to have been built with stone[24] from within a radius of about twenty-five miles of their location. The thin flat paving stones needed for floors were dressed on site from the larger rough blocks sent by water and cart from the many quarries.[25] York sandstone is formed of thin 'laminations' that can be split apart easily and it was in considerable demand for all areas where a hard durable surface was needed. Portland limestone, whilst achieving its greatest use after the Fire of London (1666), had been used for building and flooring since the fourteenth century. It is close-grained with an even texture and whilst not easy to work, because of its hardness, has always been thought one of the finest building-stones in England.

The first bricks were introduced into Britain by the Romans and, although manufacture died away after they left, it was re-established in medieval times. Cardinal Wolsey and Henry VIII used bricks in structural and decorative ways at their palaces of Hampton Court and St James's but the use of brick alone for floors was rare. It was tiles, which have much in common with bricks (often being made in brick-kilns), that were chosen for flooring. The early years of the sixteenth century had seen a decline in the English monastic production of tiles at houses such as that of the Benedictines at Great Malvern. Tiles were therefore sometimes obtained from abroad: the maiolica portrait tiles on the chapel floor at The Vyne, Hampshire, for example, have been attributed to the workshop set up in Antwerp in 1512 by an Italian from Urbino, Guido de Savino. Among the portrait tiles at The Vyne is one with the profile head of Federigo da Montefeltro, Duke of Urbino. They are a colourful foil in their glazes of lemon-yellow, orange, green and cobalt blue to the already radiant stained-glass windows of the chapel. Flemish paving tiles were supplied in green and yellow for use at Hampton Court in 1535[26] at a charge of 5d a hundred.

One of the richest effects for flooring was achieved with coloured marbles. Marble is a fine-grained limestone containing a high proportion of calcium carbonate. Under great natural heat and pressure it is recrystallized and the fissures formed become filled and stained with calcite and mineral colourings. One of the attractions of using marble for interiors is its ability to take a high polish, even if this is gradually lost in a damp atmosphere. Pure forms of white English marble are rare, but impurities such as iron oxide give it an attractive range of warm colours. Some English marbles also contain many fossil-shells of the freshwater snail and this gives an elaborate figuring when cut and polished.

The best of the English marbles were quarried in Kent, Derbyshire, Sussex, Surrey and in Dorset, near St Aldhelm's Head, where the famous Purbeck marble was found.[27] In its dark-grey polished state, Purbeck marble was used extensively in English churches (as far away from its source as Durham Cathedral). However, I know of no Tudor Purbeck-marble floor in a domestic interior.

The material most used for floors in the Tudor period was undoubtedly wood, in particular, oak. When a room had a small span the wooden planks were supported by wooden joists that ran across from one wall-plate to the opposite one. Where the span was over about 15 ft, one or more 'summers' (horizontal beams) were inserted with the joists laid on them longitudinally. The joists were then usually mortised into the summers, with endplates laid on top of them. William Horman in his *Vulgaria* recorded this method in 1519 when he wrote:[28] 'The carpenter or wryght hath layde the summer bemys from wall to wall and the ioystis a crosse.'

Throughout the Tudor period there was an appreciation that dry, seasoned oak was best but it was not in plentiful supply. It was also very heavy – a cubic foot weighing some 55 lbs – and expensive. Other timber of varying sorts and sizes was provided from the Baltic through the trading efforts of the Hanseatic League of North Germany. By the beginning of the fifteenth century the League had control of the Baltic and much else, thus excluding English merchants from its lucrative trading in timber, pitch, tar and fish.

Evidence suggests that early Tudor houses were not always models of tidiness and hygiene. Erasmus, in a letter to Cardinal Wolsey's physician in the late 1520s, wrote that in English houses: 'The floors are commonly of clay, strewed with rushes under which lies unmolested an ancient collection of beer, grease, fragments, bones, spittle, excrements of dogs and cats and everything that is nasty.'

Strewing of rushes on the floor was a common occurrence and in the household of the 2nd Viscount Montagu at Cowdray, as late as 1595, the regulations stipulated that: ' ... the galleyes and all lodginges reserved for strangers [be] cleanly and sweetly kepte, with herbes, flowers and bowes in their seasons.'[29]

Some part of this entry may refer to the bags containing sweet-smelling herbs that were placed in rooms to scent the air or between linen; 'perfuming pans' in which scented pastilles were burned were also in use.

Finally, we should note that in a number of houses, both large and small, floors were composed of hard plaster (*glacis*). This type of flooring can be seen in the late 1570s at Burghley House, Lincolnshire and in the 1590s at Hardwick Hall, Derbyshire, where some remnants survive in the 'banqueting houses' (that is, the small vantage towers) on the roof, almost indistinguishable from hard cement.

PANELLED WALLS

The *Oxford English Dictionary* gives the date for the first use of the word 'wainscot' as 1352, and the introduction of such panelling undoubtedly made rooms more comfortable for daily life. William Harrison in his oft-quoted *The Description of England*, written in 1577, noted that rooms which were lined or 'sealed' with oak wainscot were 'made warme and more close than otherwise they would be'.[30]

Early wainscoting was firmly established in the early thirteenth century and although none survives from that date, examples have come down to us from the late Middle Ages, and by the early sixteenth century the carver's skill had developed to a high degree. The best-known pattern, as I have noted in Chapter 1, was the linenfold, the earliest form of which comprised a single rib dividing the ornament into two folds. Alternative forms of panelling were those in which a narrow board was grooved into thick upright posts and this was often used in screens to form tall narrow panels. It was necessary to use seasoned oak, mortised and tenoned into a frame and pinned with oak pins. Shakespeare referred to the importance of avoiding unseasoned wood, which would warp, in *As You Like It* (III, 75–7): 'This fellow will but join you together as they join wainscot; Then one of you will prove a shrunk panel and like green timber, warp, warp.'

The panels at Paycockes, Great Coggeshall, Essex, have close-set ribs in which the linenfold ribbing is 'stopped' at top and bottom by a semicircle across all the hollows or in a variant, across each separate hollow. 'Wavy woodwork' (*lignum undulatum*) was the term used to describe this form of ribbed boards, 'linenfold' being a nineteenth-century word, with 'parchemin' – applied to panelling in which the rib branches to the four corners –

being of even more recent usage. The 'sealing of drapery panell' was quoted at 21d a yard for the work at Westminster Palace in 1532, along with 'pleyne sealing' and 'creste panell' at 12d and 19d a yard respectively.[31]

The many Fleming craftsmen in England in the fifteenth and sixteenth centuries hastened on the normally slow processes of decorative change and growing interest in classical ornament. Henry VII also encouraged Florentine artists to come to London to work on the chapel that bears his name in Westminster Abbey. The apartments at Hampton Court, started by Cardinal Wolsey and completed for the king in the 1530s, continued to show this trend. Both Wolsey and his imperious master, Henry VIII, were responsible for bringing Italian artists to England to work for them, but none was of the calibre of Leonardo da Vinci, Cellini or Primaticcio, all of whom were invited to France by François 1er. Craftsmen such as the king's master carpenter, John Nedeham, and his successor from 1532, William Clement, were trained in a late-Gothic style and needed to work hard to update and blend their skills with those of German, French and Italian origin.

The walls of the 'Wolsey apartments' at Hampton Court were framed and panelled by joiners using oak supplied by Hanseatic merchants in London. This was overlaid with a profusion of mouldings, cornices and carved embellishments. Taken along with the new great hall (1532–4), the remodelling of the chapel interior (1535–6) and the new lodgings for the king and queen (1534–7), they presented large areas for the work of skilled craftsmen.[32] These men were keen, if their masters were, to absorb the new ideas of the Italian Renaissance artists and to build in the 'antique' as well as they could.

A splendid example of this duality of early interest in the Renaissance is found in the panelling of the Abbot's Parlour at Thame Park, Oxfordshire. Built on the site of a Cistercian Abbey, the present house incorporates work of many dates including that done for Abbot Robert King between 1530 and 1539. The parlour is lined with linenfold panelling and has an internal porch. A deep frieze is carved with a lavish filigree pattern of scrolls set in small panels, each one being separated by heads in medallions, or alternately of mermaids and urns framing shields. The frieze was originally coloured and gilded and was obviously done by a competent carver. The name of Richard Rydge, who worked on the great hall of Hampton Court, has been suggested but there is no precise evidence of his involvement.

Medallion heads and carved cartouches supported by *amorini*, grotesques, candelabra and various scrollings appear in many panels of the Tudor period. This was described by contemporaries as 'Romayne work' and is found, for example, in the hall of Magdalen College, Oxford, on the screens at King's College Chapel, Cambridge, at Carlisle Cathedral, Langleys, Essex, at Thame, Oxfordshire and in the dining-room alcove at Haddon Hall, Derbyshire.

20. Carved oak panel in the style known as 'Romayne' work, c. 1545,
often seen in country houses, but here on the Salkeld screen at Carlisle Cathedral.

Oak panelling, c. 1530, from a house near Waltham Abbey, Hertfordshire, can be found in the collections of the Victoria and Albert Museum, London. The museum houses the Inlaid Room from Sizergh Castle in Cumbria, dated to 1575–85. The wainscoting rises up to the plaster frieze below the ceiling, having bays formed by Ionic pilasters in the lower and the upper section. The last bay has two round-headed arches enclosing lesser arches with a circle above them, an almost Venetian evocation of the windows of the Palazzo Vendramin-Calergi in Venice, begun by Codussi, c. 1502. There is no knowledge that Alice Boynton, who commissioned the panelling, ever went to Venice, but the foreign inspiration is strong, although the use of holly, bog oak and cherry for the inlays is essentially English. So, too, was the occasional deviation from the traditional use of oak: a parlour in Elizabethan Chatsworth, now long gone, was described in the inventory as 'fayre waynscotted with white wood', which may have been a type of deal. The panels in the great chamber of Gilling Castle, Yorkshire, have lozenge-shaped centres and angular knot-work. They were purchased and taken to America in 1929 by the late Randolph Hearst, but fortunately returned to Gilling in 1952. They stand again beneath the great painted frieze with its arms of Yorkshire families (described below).

<h2 style="text-align:center">PAINTED WALLS
AND CEILINGS</h2>

The use of wainscoting, sometimes overhung with tapestries, gave a warm, if dark, appearance to early Tudor rooms. This trend towards comfort was continued by adorning walls and ceilings with paintings on plaster and with plaster decoration itself. The paintings could be of the simplest form, made from cut-stencils[33] (there is an excellent collection of such wall paintings, gathered locally, in the Saffron Walden Museum, Essex), or they could be composed of more elaborate patterns or even of scenes from mythological and biblical stories. Whilst most of this latter work is, understandably, painted on church screens, there is an early and amazing series of secular panels, either by the Florentine, Toto del Nunziata (1499–1554), or the Modenese, Nicolò Bellin (fl. 1516–68), on the walls of the hall at Loseley Park, Surrey.[34] The panels, painted a little after 1543, are of grotesques, incorporating cartouches with the royal arms, cyphers and emblems of Henry VIII and Catherine Parr. They are attributed to the Italians who were working at the king's palace at Nonsuch, Surrey, in the 1530s.

Another example of work done by a foreign artist of considerable distinction is the chapel ceiling at St James's Palace, London, attributed to the German artist, Hans Holbein (1497–1543). The ceiling is coffered in octagonal, cruciform and hexagonal panels filled with heraldry, mottoes and the cyphers of Henry VIII and Anne of Cleves.

Equally, there is much lesser work[35] by unknown painters. When some panelling was moved in 1927 at the White Swan Hotel, Stratford-upon-Avon, wall decoration of c. 1570–80 showing scenes from Tobias and the Angel, divided by simulated pilasters, was found in distemper on the plaster.[36] The same painterly anonymity surrounds the depiction of the life-size figures of the 'Nine Heroes of Antiquity', c. 1576–8, uncovered from under later lime-washing in 1939 at Harvington Hall, Worcestershire.[37]

Formal sixteenth-century patterns were occasionally realized in crude form, as at Ightham Mote, Kent, Haddon Hall, Derbyshire, Canons Ashby, Northamptonshire, or Little Moreton Hall, Cheshire. The work at Ightham Mote is an early and important scheme of c. 1525, painted on the timber barrel vault of the chapel ceiling. The long narrow compartments have chevron and triangular patterns alternating with the Tudor portcullis and the pomegranate. It is believed that it was originally a tilting pavilion ceiling and as it is from the time of Catherine of Aragon it could have been used at the Field of the Cloth of Gold. A succession of royal badges and Spanish emblems, including the castle of Castile and the arrows of Aragon, enhance this faded decorative scheme of great rarity. In the low parlour at Haddon Hall the painted ceiling was carefully restored by the 9th Duke of Rutland in 1926. It was painted, c. 1510, with diamond and squared patterning, and this is enhanced by the prominent display of the Tudor rose and the Talbot dog. Sir Henry Vernon, Treasurer to Prince Arthur, had married Anne Talbot, daughter of the Earl of Shrewsbury. It is above later panelling inserted by Sir George Vernon about 1545. The date is incorporated in the combined shield shared with his wife, Margaret, which is to the left of the fireplace.

In the Winter Parlour at Canons Ashby painted decoration of the 1590s was found under many later layers on the panelling. Some small areas were revealed by the last tenant of the house and are of arabesques and early masonic symbols. Further investigation showed that the panels themselves contain brightly coloured crests and other devices, set off by strapwork cartouches and with a series of moral inscriptions in Latin, in long panels below the cornice. It all seems to date from the time of Sir Erasmus Dryden, who inherited the property in 1584 and died in 1632. The painted shields commemorate his ancestry and connections; many emblems and rebuses were also incorporated to provide amusement for the onlooker in unravelling their meaning. The regular repeat pattern of diamonds within squares, with an interlaced pattern of Celtic complexity on the divisions, was painted at Little Moreton Hall in a naïve but attractive way.

Much grand Elizabethan work at the royal palaces has long disappeared and is known only from archival references. Perhaps the most elaborate surviving schemes are those at the Hill Hall in Essex, in the great chamber at Gilling Castle, Yorkshire, and that in the High Great Chamber at Hardwick Hall, Derbyshire. Hill Hall is one of the most important of the early Elizabethan houses in England. This is partly due to its builder, Sir Thomas Smith, who travelled abroad extensively in the 1540s, took a doctorate in civil law at Padua and became Vice-Chancellor of Cambridge University.

21. *The winter parlour at Canons Ashby, Northamptonshire.*
The painted decoration of the 1590s with crests and other devices in strapwork cartouches
was done for Sir Erasmus Dryden (d. 1632).

The cycle of wall paintings, *c.* 1575, shows scenes from the story of Eros and Psyche. As one would expect from one of Smith's erudition, they are based on engravings after Raphael's designs and have a classical elegance all too rarely attained. The Gilling Castle great chamber has a deep frieze above the wainscot which is hung with the shields of arms of various Yorkshire families on stylized trees, and which has two wonderful panels of ladies and gentlemen playing musical instruments against a backing of rich foliage. No wonder late-nineteenth-century designers such as William Morris fell in love with these rich patterns: this frieze could be an illuminated page in the copy of Chaucer's *The Canterbury Tales* printed by Morris at his Kelmscott Press were it not firmly dated to 1585.

At Hardwick Hall, the building-accounts for 1591–8[38] show that John Balechouse (or 'John the Paynter') received frequent payments for colours and must therefore have carried out most of the painted decoration: however, his only certain work is the long gallery frieze of strapwork and foliations painted in a grey-green monochrome. In the High Great Chamber,

22. *Detail of a band of painted ornament in the parlour at Little Moreton Hall, Cheshire, showing the wolf's head and crest of the Moretons, c. 1585.*

23. Frieze in the great chamber, 1585, at Gilling Castle, Yorkshire.

which is dominated by the deep coloured plaster frieze (described below), he may have painted the feigned marquetry that is decorated with engravings of the heads of classical philosophers and the Caesars and stuck on a canvas backing. One print in the set of emperors is signed by 'Peter Balthazar', better known as Peter de Coster, an Antwerp artist active in the late sixteenth century. These paintings bring a Mannerist touch to this Derbyshire room at the top of Bess of Hardwick's fantastic house.

PLASTERED WALLS
AND CEILINGS

Before describing the late-1530s stucco-work executed by Italians for Henry VIII at Nonsuch Palace, Surrey, it is sensible to explain the differences between stucco and plaster. Both contain lime or gypsum, sand and water, but tensile strength was given to stucco by the addition of powdered marble dust and to plaster by chopped animal hair of ox, horse or (for finer work) of the goat and its young kid. These constituents were mixed together and then applied either direct to the wall (as is usual with stucco) or to a framework of thin wooden laths, about five ft in length, which were fastened by hand-made iron nails to wall studs or ceiling joists. Additionally, stucco is modelled around a wood or metal armature. The white mix was usually applied in three successive thin coats, each being allowed to dry before the next coat was trowelled on. Some of the mix passed through gaps left

*24. Detail of late-Elizabethan lath and plaster ornamentation
at Clenston Manor, Dorset.*

between the laths and formed a good key for the subsequent layers. Only at that point, when a flat white surface had been created, was ornament applied. To make the ornamentation, the mix was pressed into greased iron moulds, allowed to set and turned out into trays to await application. A light Tudor rose, say, could then be scratched on the back with a nail to assist adhesion after a liquid slip of plaster had been brushed on. It was fixed into position on the ceiling and held until set by a timber prop from the scaffolding-boards erected at a working height below the ceiling.[39]

Plaster as a decorative medium has a long existence, but in England it only developed from the reign of Henry VII. The king granted a charter in 1501 to the 'Worshipful Company of Plaisterers' of London, giving their 'art and mystery' its formal recognition. One important patron, anxious at an early point to use painters and stuccoists, was Cardinal Wolsey. His apartments at Hampton Court contain Classical ceilings and friezes, formed in the usual way of lath and plaster, but with the superimposed wooden ribs given a plaster coating. This accorded with Italian Renaissance methods where many ornate ceilings – for example, those in the Doge's Palace in Venice – were formed of wooden ribs, with a gesso or plaster layer,

25. *Detail of the plasterwork, featuring Tudor roses, on the Wolsey Closet ceiling, c. 1527, at Hampton Court, Middlesex.*

subsequently gilded. The ornamental work of the frieze in the cardinal's closet contains dolphins, vases, mermen and mermaids surrounded by roses, the Prince of Wales's feathers and Wolsey's motto, *Dominus michi adjutor*, although this is made of papier mâché. It has been suggested that all this work was done for Henry VIII at the Palace in the 1530s, perhaps as late as 1537, when Prince Edward was born there. This seems most unlikely in view of the dominant position of Wolsey's motto.

The presence at Nonsuch of Nicolò Bellin of Modena (who had been in the team of painters and stuccoists at Fontainebleau before coming to England) encouraged a few unknown workers to attempt copies of his work. The splendid drawing-room chimneypiece at Loseley, Surrey, was probably copied from one at Nonsuch, and is noted below. During the long reign of Queen Elizabeth, from 1558 to 1603, architecture and decoration entered a new and bolder phase. But though English plasterers still relied on the use of emblem-books and illustrated versions of the Bible, they turned increasingly to foreign architectural treatises and engravings by Wendel Dietterlein, Marten de Vos, Jan Vriedeman de Vries, Abraham de Bruyn and others to inform their own ideas. For example, the devices on the

THE·WHEELE
OF·FORTVNE

WHOSE·RVLE·IS
IGNORAVNCE·

26. Detail of plaster tympanum based on Reynold Wolfe's Castle of Knowledge *(1556)
in the long gallery, c. 1560, at Little Moreton Hall, Cheshire.*

tympana at the ends of the gallery at Little Moreton Hall, Cheshire, are
meant to represent the Wheel of Fortune and are based on the *Castle of
Knowledge* printed by Reynold Wolfe in 1556.

While English plasterers may have learned some of the techniques used
by Italians, they never acquired their skill in design, nor indeed was this
necessary. The requirements in an English house were those of covering a
flat wall or ceiling with suitable plaster decoration, finished in plain, cream-
white limewash. Villas such as the Villa Madama in Rome had white
stuccoes certainly, but these were set amid the rich reds and blues on
soaring vaults and pendentives, painted by Raphael and his followers in
the 1520s. And England, through the schism with Rome, was well insulated
from all Romish devices, perhaps for too long.

Elizabethan plasterwork is characterized in England by a complex arrangement of low-relief ribs. Most of these ribs were set up or 'run *in situ*' by
the use of a mould, which was pushed along a layer of ductile plaster to
form a simple profile, with its cutting edge. The compartments created
between the raised interlocking ribs were filled with moulded ornamentation

27. *Detail of the plaster frieze, c. 1599, in the High Great Chamber,*
Hardwick Hall, Derbyshire, depicting 'Diana and her Court'.

of flowers and heraldic devices. Finished with creamy-white limewash, the
settling dust 'raised' the pattern to give interesting visual effects.

One important exception to these geometric plaster ceilings was the
work done in the High Great Chamber at Hardwick Hall, where all the
attention was given to the large frieze. The ceiling itself has no decoration.
Abraham Smith led a team of over twelve plasterers, of whom the principals,
apart from himself, were John Marcer and Robert Orton. In August 1595
scaffolding was erected for them and the total cost of doing this implies
that it was probably to work on the frieze, which runs all round the room.
Using designs based on the engravings of the Flemish artists Martin de
Vos and Nicholas de Bruyn, the plasterers worked at it, on and off, for
several months.

The theme of the Hardwick frieze is Diana and her court. Diana is
depicted surrounded by a profusion of lions, elephants, boars, camels,
monkeys, deer and other animals cavorting amid real saplings. The latter
are fixed to the laths and covered in plaster. It is a lively scene and, intended
as a compliment to Queen Elizabeth I, was given a dominant position in

the best chamber. To either side of the window recess there are two allegorical figures, of Spring and Summer, based on designs by Marten de Vos. On the east wall, the frieze is interrupted by the royal arms supported by a lion and a dragon. Had the Hardwick frieze been left white, washed with a solution of Crich lime as all else in the house was, its spirited relief-work would still amaze us. But the effect is made more dramatic, and especially so after the long climb to the second floor, by the use of colour. Whilst now faded, the soft browns, greens and pinks of the applied earth colours make it the supreme achievement of Elizabethan plasterers: a unique statement of their abilities.

WINDOWS

The large bay windows that are such a feature of houses such as Sutton Place, Surrey (1521–33), and Hardwick Hall, Derbyshire (1590–7), had been increasing in size and importance from the fourteenth century onwards. By the early sixteenth century, it was one of the most commanding of the many features on a façade, allowing more light to enter, as well as providing an interesting rhythm of light and dark along the inner wall surfaces.

The majority of windows were built with vertical stone mullions and horizontal transoms to give space for glazing and or subsidiary tracery in the upper parts of pointed openings, in particular. A casual glance at any repository of illustrations of Tudor and Elizabethan houses[40] will show that the majority of the windows, ignoring oriels and shaped bays, were rectangular, with many lights in tiers, one above the other. The ruined great hall of Cowdray House in West Sussex has a bay with thirty-six lights in six tiers behind the dais on which the high table stood. At Melbury House, Dorset, there is a splendid prospect tower, c. 1540, which rises as a lantern above the stairs and is lighted on six sides by windows with twelve lights, filled with diamond latticing. But the fenestration, whilst adequately lighting the stairwell, bears no comparison with the many windows of Hardwick, Derbyshire, which are spread in three storeys over four façades.

The stone window frames were set by the masons John and Christopher Rodes between 1592 and 1594. There are forty-four windows in each of the second and third storeys. The windows in the north-west were height-ened from 64 to 89 ft in 1594 – presumably at Bess of Hardwick's insistence on a light house – and the roof was on by November 1594. The total cost of cutting and setting the glass over the great expanse due to the glaziers, Richard Snidall and 'Jury', was £290, excluding the cost of the glass itself.[41]

Bess had glassworks at Wingfield that probably supplied what was needed. Others were not so fortunate.

Glass for windows was always expensive and was restricted to churches and larger houses; horn or blinds made from cloth or canvas (called fenestrals) had long been used. They were inferior substitutes and, as the Tudor period progressed, there was an increasing use of the diamond lattice, in which small quarries of glass were held in place by strips of lead, turned down over their edges and soldered at the junctions. Tallow was often used to pack the leading and make the window weatherproof but by the 1530s a type of 'cement' had replaced the tallow. Yet as late as 1567 the windows of Alnwick Castle, Northumberland, were removed in the owner's absence to protect the glass of the windows from extreme winds.[42]

The best sources for white and coloured glass were the Rhine lands of Burgundy and Lorraine, Flanders and Normandy, as Harrison records in his *Description of England* in 1577: 'some brought out of Burgundie, some out of Normandie, much out of Flanders, besides that which is made in England, which would be as good as the best, if we were diligent and careful to bestow more cost upon it.'

Most of the quarries were filled with white glass to admit the maximum light, but the depiction of arms and patterns in coloured glass became as common in domestic settings as they had long been in churches. The first stage in the making of stained-glass was to draw out a full-size design in outline on a table with the colours for each part indicated. This done, glass of the required colour was placed upon the outline and its relevant shape traced with thick chalk water. The glass was then broken along the outline with a hot iron and its edges cleaned with a grozing-iron. Details of figures, faces and beasts, whatever the design needed, were painted on each surface with a paint of iron- or copper-oxide, mixed with gum arabic, water and vinegar or urine. The gum made the paint adhere to the glass and the vinegar or urine rendered it insoluble when it had dried: 'depth' could be obtained by repeated applications of the paint.

Many glass-painters came to England from Germany and the Netherlands and settled in Southwark, where English glass-painters had been gathered since the end of the thirteenth century.[43] This inevitably caused dissent and their presence was bitterly resisted. Most patrons went for the best solution, one of compromise. Sir Thomas Kytson, a London merchant building at Hengrave Hall, Suffolk, in the 1520s, turned to both the Englishman Richard Wright of Bury St Edmunds and the Dutchman Galyon Hone, the King's Glazier, for the shields and representations from Genesis and the Life of Christ in his chapel. They can still be seen behind the bay windows of the south front. Another Dutch artist, Bernard Dininckhof, worked on the windows in the great chamber of Gilling Castle, Yorkshire, in 1585 and later. This glass also had a stay, like the panelling, in the crates of the American collector, the late Randolph Hearst, but returned to Gilling in 1952. A great deal of the glass-painters' work was, however, done in the great churches and much was therefore destroyed in the unstable period of the Commonwealth in the 1640s.

DOORS
AND INTERIOR PORCHES

Doors in smaller Tudor houses were regarded as part of the wainscoting and their presence is often indicated solely by iron hinges. In a larger house, the door became an important feature of the interior, vying with the chimneypiece for visual attention and often given prominence by carving, flanking pilasters or free-standing columns supporting an elaborate entablature. These features were usually in stone with a wooden frame set in the reveal (that is, the part of the jamb lying between the door and the outer wall surface). The door itself was made of panels that matched those of the wainscoting in size. Within these larger panels smaller ones would be set so that the door might have six, eight or nine panels altogether. Extra prominence was given to an entrance by thrusting an interior porch enclosing the door into the room. This was useful where the door opened on to a draughty stair landing and could itself be a splendidly decorated feature.

A small group of interior porches survive in English houses[44] and that at Montacute, Somerset, is a typical form. The porch there, originally in the Parlour below, was set up for Lord Curzon in about 1916 at the entrance to the great chamber (now the Library). It has been shown[45] that the Montacute porch is closely related to Plate E in Vriedeman de Vries's *Das Erst Buch* (1565).

Two porches in Devon, at Bradfield House and Bradninch Manor, are richly carved with small sculptured figures and strapwork cresting in the upper stages, employing decorative motifs also found in a number of West Country churches and houses, and on an important oak bed at Montacute, made in about 1612. The porch from the Inlaid Room at Sizergh Castle, Cumbria, is semi-octagonal in plan, and has a fluted frieze and cornice supporting compartments in a frame, which is itself further supported by fluted columns. This porch originally allowed a small room in the Deincourt Tower at Sizergh to be reached without passing through the great hall. The

28. *Elizabethan interior porch at Montacute House, Somerset,*
in a watercolour by C. J. Richardson, c. 1830.

interior porch at Broughton Castle, Oxfordshire, is flamboyantly surmounted by obelisks and a strapwork cartouche, which is also allusive to
another Plate (F) in de Vries's *Das Erst Buch*.

CHIMNEYPIECES

A fireplace properly describes the grate or hearth for a fire in a room. Early
fireplaces were in the centre of medieval halls, with the smoke drifting
upwards to a slatted louvre in the roof. When a recessed fireplace and
chimney became more common in the late fifteenth century, the mantel of
wood, stone or marble around this was called the chimneypiece. By the
early sixteenth century, the chimneypiece had become an important feature
of a room, although it still had a medieval look because of its flat four-
centred stone arch and simple Gothic-style ornament in the slight corner
spandrels. These early survivals are rare, and the principal change as the
sixteenth century advanced was the abandonment of the Tudor arch for a
rectangular opening and the decking of the best examples with caryatids,
columns and lavish carving in alabaster, stone, wood or moulded plaster.

During the latter half of the sixteenth century, the chimneypiece became
an object for flamboyant display, with coats of arms carved prominently
alongside an array of Renaissance-inspired ornament. Two of the most
spectacular examples of this trend are the drawing-room chimneypiece at
Loseley Park, Surrey, *c.* 1565, but perhaps brought to the house *c.* 1680, and
one at Broughton Castle, Oxfordshire, in the Star Chamber, *c.* 1554. Both
derive from chimneypieces in Nonsuch Palace and may well have been
done by the group of artists working there under the decoration of Niccolò
Bellin.

The exact story of both fireplaces is obscure. That at Loseley has been
described as 'an Anglo-Flemish hybrid of the late 1540s', but the Loseley
archives also contain a petition of *c.* 1562 from the London plasterer Thomas
Browne, which may indicate that he at least set up this piece. Whatever
the truth, it is a two-storeyed wonder, with coupled columns, elaborate
rustication, strapwork ornament and four caryatids in various stages of rest
or action, all carved with great skill. That at Broughton[46] has a panel within
a cartouche based on an engraving by Boyvin of the dance of the dryads
taken from Ovid's *Metamorphoses*. Boyvin's depiction was based on a
fresco of this subject by Rosso Fiorentino in the Galerie François 1er at
Fontainebleau, which would have been known to the artists journeying
from France to serve the king at Nonsuch.

29. *The chimneypiece, c. 1565, in the drawing-room at Loseley Park, Surrey, showing a lavish use of Renaissance-inspired ornament in solid chalk.*

30. Detail of one of the two chimneypieces in the long gallery at Hardwick Hall,
Derbyshire, designed in alabaster and blackstone by Thomas Accres, c. 1597.

At Reigate Priory, Surrey, there is a so-called 'Holbein' chimneypiece dating to just after the 'Nonsuch period', *c.* 1550–60. The stone fireplace is simple enough but has a most elaborate frieze. All of this is dwarfed by the great wooden surround with niche seats, surmounted by high canopies and flanked by coupled Corinthian columns resting on corbels fashioned as giant paws. This use of coupled columns had been anticipated only by Holbein in a drawing of the 1540s after he had visited Lyons and perhaps even Fontainebleau.[47] The centre of the overmantel is a cartouche with a strapwork frame bearing the royal arms and abundant Tudor roses. Many sources are given as to its origin but the most likely suggestion is that it came from Bridewell Palace in London which was being built from 1515 for Cardinal Wolsey, and which belonged to the king for a few years in the 1520s. As a chimneypiece, it has nothing to do with Holbein and it was only given this appellation on 11 August 1655 when John Evelyn saw it *in situ* at Reigate Priory and said that it came from Bletchingley in Surrey. It is crazily imitative of many styles without revealing any particular one as dominant.

One of the most flamboyant of the Renaissance-style stone chimneypieces is that in the hall of Burghley House, Lincolnshire, *c.* 1570, which contains a fireback dated '1571' bearing Lord Burghley's arms. This had been taken at some point from the house but was returned to the 9th Earl of Exeter in the late eighteenth century. The rectangular opening of the lower stage is flanked by enormous volute consoles. The chimneybreast is of tall concave (and Classical) shape, terminating in a pediment. A circle round the coat of arms is connected by flat bars to the four sides and seems to derive from the extensive use of Serlian motifs at Old Somerset House, which was built for Protector Somerset in the years immediately following Henry VIII's death in 1547. It should be remembered that William Cecil, the future Lord Burghley, had been the Protector's private secretary during the building of Old Somerset House.

The finest chimneypieces of the 1590s, using Derbyshire alabaster and blackstone, are those fashioned by Thomas Accres at Hardwick Hall, Derbyshire. He had started work for Bess at Chatsworth in 1576, and went on to work in 1585 for her architect Robert Smythson at Wollaton Hall, Nottingham. Accres arrived at Hardwick Hall in 1594 when it was being roofed; he worked easily in both stone and marble and was principally responsible for the two chimneypieces in the long gallery, which are again allusive to woodcuts in Serlio's *Architettura*. Smythson expected his masons to be able to work from Continental engravings and Accres had already done this with the stone screen in the hall of Wollaton, adapted in part from the engravings in Vriedeman de Vries's *Das Erst Buch* (1565). In the upper stages of each chimneypiece there are two alabaster statues of 'Justice' and 'Mercy' respectively, backed by an oval frame set against a strapwork ground and with twin half-Doric columns at each side. Above it all, is the painted frieze which John Balechouse executed in 1598 and which runs the entire length of the gallery.

31. Detail of the carved oak panel above the hall fireplace,
c. 1585, at Benthall Hall, Shropshire,
showing heraldic details of the Catholic Benthall family.

The availability of motifs in the repertory of skilled masons may explain some of the simpler stone chimneypieces such as that in the great hall in Baddesley Clinton, Warwickshire. It bears shields commemorating Ferrers family marriages, placed around a central achievement that quarters Ferrers with three other families. Dating from the 1580s, it shares its overall design of curiously shaped pilasters either side of the opening with the lower stages of the chimneypiece in the gallery at Arbury Hall, also in Warwickshire. The Arbury chimneypiece is grained to resemble marble and has a late-Elizabethan painted wood overmantel which does not fit the chimneypiece exactly. Nevertheless it makes a dominant statement that here was an owner who wanted things Italianate, or at least 'foreign', around him.

The two chimneypieces in the long gallery at Cobham Hall, Kent, have Corinthian columns and caryatid figures, as at Loseley, but the large coat of arms on one is dated '1599'. The second chimneypiece, less robust in pale mottled marble, has an overmantel relief of three Fates.

The chimneypieces in smaller houses and farms usually had simple stone surrounds, but even in remote country districts they could be given some additional importance by carved panels or by crude plasterwork overmantels. There are many such examples, particularly in Devon and Cumbria, and it should be remembered that many of the masons who erected the smaller church monuments were capable of dressing stone for domestic use with the same skill.

STAIRCASES

The staircase always occupies a prominent position on any house-plan and as interest grew in Classical architecture, considerable attention was given to its appearance and position. I have shown in the first chapter how staircases, usually made of stone (and therefore the mason's job) were inserted in corner towers, often surrounding the great hall, and were lighted by oriels or by smaller windows. I am, however, not sure that masons took any notice of Andrea Palladio's injunction, in 1570, that staircases should be placed so that no part of the building 'should receive any prejudice by them'. He further noted that three openings were necessary to any staircase: the doorway leading to it, the windows by which it was lighted and the landings by which one entered upper rooms.[48]

Staircases are basically of two sorts, either straight or of the 'vyse' (winding) newel type. It was important to ensure that the person ascending had enough 'headway', the distance between any step or landing to the underside of the ceiling or other part immediately above it. It was also necessary to decide about the *newel*: in a winding staircase this is the upright cylinder or pillar round which the steps turn and are supported from the bottom to the top. When the steps ascend in geometrical flights, being pinned into the wall at left or right and there is no central pillar, the staircase is said to have an *open newel*.

In England there was no intermediate stage between the stone spiral and the straight flights of wood, and in any case construction became the joiner's, rather than the stone-mason's, task. One important early decision was to settle the proper relation between the height and width of steps; normally eleven to thirteen steps were considered sufficient for a flight before a landing became necessary. Rooms on the upper floors that were in great use, such as the great chamber or long gallery, led to the need to develop an adequate staircase approach. Perhaps the most elaborate of the sixteenth-century stone staircases is that at Burghley House, Lincolnshire, of *c.*1575. It ascends around a masonry core and has a stone wagon-vault ceiling, carved with coffering and rosettes. It probably owes something in inspiration to the staircase at the Louvre (begun 1546), those in the French *châteaux* of Blois and Chambord or even those in Italian *palazzi* by Codussi, Peruzzi or Sansovino. But Lord Burghley had no direct knowledge of these and, whilst he is reputed to be one of the group responsible for introducing Renaissance architecture to England, he leaned (relatively speaking) more towards the Gothic style in the later stages of his career.

Of the plain straight stone staircases, that at Hardwick Hall, Derbyshire, is the most significant. It rises through the alternating areas of light and shade of three floors until its last eight steps swing sharply to the right to end at the landing outside the High Great Chamber. John Adams hewed and set the 'battlement' on this great staircase but John and Christopher Rodes, the principal masons, were responsible for its main construction from top to bottom. Many entries relating to this staircase appear in the accounts for 1595, such as the following: 'Payd to John Roods the 14th December for setting 12 steappes for the great steare 11 foot 3 ynnches lonng at $\frac{1}{2}$d the foot.'

His eight turning steps at the end of the flights were likewise done at $\frac{1}{2}$d the foot for 100 ft.[49]

It will be appreciated that a stone staircase puts a considerable strain on the supporting walls around it and even when built around a central well it still needed a masonry core. In contrast, placing timber 'strings' of baulks of wood between landings and then covering them with wood treads and risers meant a much lighter load. Consequently, the side to the well could be open and newels, handrails and balusters could be inserted to protect those ascending. This need gave impetus to the long-established trade of turning, in which wood was 'turned' on a pole-lathe, and the cylindrical forms of baluster produced rapidly replaced the flat pierced balusters common by the 1580s.

Whether the house was large or small, it had a staircase, or more than one, which followed these rules and forms: in other words, it was in stone and of straight flights with landings, or with each flight turned on itself inside a stairwell. As the lighter material of wood was substituted for stone, the staircase could have an open newel, as described, and a greater feature made of the cut or turned balusters. They were developments which came to splendid fruition in the early seventeenth century.

SERVICES: THE KITCHEN

All houses need a kitchen, whether a small manor-house such as Snowshill, Gloucestershire, with its main structure, although much amended, dating from the mid sixteenth century, or a spectacular fortress such as Compton Castle, in south Devon. It was an essential space, but often much altered by the insertion of great cast-iron ranges in the nineteenth century. It was also often well removed from the main block of the house by being in a wing or separate building, because of the risk of fire, and this has led to its being superseded in the present day by something smaller, warmer and more convenient.

At Compton Castle, Devon, the great hall that the kitchen serviced no longer exists. It was separated by a small courtyard from the main gateway and was surrounded by the five towers that John Gilbert (d. 1539) built in the new curtain wall. He also built at the east end of the hall to give better service areas, including a great kitchen, with a solar attached. This had become necessary because Compton is basically a fourteenth-century house that was converted into a stronghold with a dry moat on three sides in about 1500.

At Hardwick Hall, Derbyshire, the baking was done in a separate room in the north turret beyond the buttery, cellars and kitchen. The 1601 inventory for the kitchen lists a great number of utensils, many of which were engraved with the Devonshire crest or coat of arms, including brass and copper pans, knives, hatchets, dripping pans and ten spits over the open fires. The kitchen was originally equipped with a hatch to the servery, which was adjacent to the screens passage of the hall.

SERVICES: PRIVY CHAMBERS

Medieval monasteries (and royal palaces) had controlled and comparatively efficient systems of bringing in water from a spring on higher ground through conduits to the kitchen and *lavatorium* and of sluicing it through the complex drainage systems. The majority of Tudor houses had some such arrangement but many had to rely on the gathering of rain water, on wells or even on water brought in from a distance and stored in lead cisterns. The privies were connected by vertical shafts to sewage pits and if water could run through the smelly shafts it was helpful. The privies were often grouped on a cool northern or western side of the house in a privy tower, with parallel vertical shafts connecting to each floor, and they required constant maintenance. The recent exposure of the great drainage system at Wollaton Hall, Nottingham, shows how elaborate this had become by the end of the sixteenth century. Built on its hilltop, Wollaton had immediate problems with its water supply, and a brick-vaulted tunnel brought water from an underground spring to the basement of the house. At Hardwick Hall, water was pumped to a high cistern near the Old Hall and fed by gravity to the north side of the New Hall.

Many Elizabethan houses relied on the use of close-stools, and there are many listed in the 1601 Hardwick inventory. Sir John Harington's new water-closet, which he pioneered in the 1590s, remained a mere curiosity: it may have satisfied its inventor but no imitators followed his lead. Servants still had to do much for their lords and masters without grumble and at some personal distress.

Three

'SOLIDITY, CONVENIENCY AND ORNAMENT'

THE SEVENTEENTH CENTURY

When Dutch-born Sir Balthazar Gerbier (1592–1663) wrote his book, *A Brief Discourse concerning the Three Chief Principles of Magnificent Building*, issued at London in 1663, he categorized them in the words of this third chapter title: 'Solidity, Conveniency and Ornament'. They accurately describe the nature of much interior decoration in the seventeenth century. By contrast, the dates of kings are of little moment to this discussion except to give some meaning to words such as 'Stuart', 'Jacobean', 'Caroline', 'The Commonwealth' and 'William and Mary'. On the death of Queen Elizabeth at Richmond in March 1603, her Scots cousin, James VI, the great-grandson of Henry VIII's sister, Margaret, ascended the English throne as James I. When he died in 1625, he was succeeded by his son, Charles I.

Following the Civil War (1642–9) and the king's execution in its last year, the Rump Parliament that was formed abolished the monarchy and, despite an attempt by Charles II to usurp the Parliamentary forces at the Battle of Worcester in 1651, he was forced to spend eleven years as a wanderer at the European courts. Oliver Cromwell was Lord Protector in the Commonwealth period (1649–1660). The deposed monarch finally entered London after Cromwell's death and was restored to his throne on his thirtieth birthday, 29 May 1660. The king's interest in artistic matters, first fostered by his father, the patron of Rubens and Van Dyck, soon encouraged foreign artists to come to England and enter his service, to embellish the empty royal palaces and to work for favoured members of his courtly circle.

The following short reign, that of the Catholic king, James II (1685–88), was soon ended by his nephew and son-in-law, William of Orange, who, as William III, returned England to the Protestant cause at his accession in 1689. With Queen Mary (the daughter of James II and an ardent patron of building) as joint monarch, every encouragement was given by the king to Sir Christopher Wren, Antonio Verrio, Grinling Gibbons and others to build and decorate the royal palaces. It was in the grounds of Hampton Court, to which William had increasingly retired, after the death of his beloved wife in 1694, that he fell from his horse and died a fortnight later, on 8 March 1702. He was succeeded by his sister-in-law, Queen Anne, the last of the Stuart monarchs, who reigned until 1714.

THE HOUSE PLAN

Firstly, let me summarize the position at the end of the sixteenth century. The typical Elizabethan plan had been, as in the medieval house, to allow entry to the area of the hall through a screens passage, and in smaller houses to have a simple 'spere' or partition instead of a screen. With the hall at the centre of the plan, the kitchen was placed at the screens end and the parlours at the other. The accompanying desire for façades of symmetrical form was, however, imposed on the traditional plan against the easy planning of a house. This led to variations in the siting of the porch and various service rooms, and to plans of 'E' and 'H' shapes.

The depletion of timber supplies without replacement meant that by the reign of King James I stone-masons had become very active in the construction of buildings, and carpenters turned more to adornment. Nevertheless, the house plan chosen tended to be a variation of the Elizabethan style, with wings and courtyards, until the King's Surveyor, Inigo Jones (1573–1652),[1] produced the first Classical Italian villa in England at the Queen's House at Greenwich. This was based on ideas put forward in the writings and villa plans of Andrea Palladio and gave rise to the 'double-pile' plan, described below.

Even so, few courtiers adopted the Classical purity of Jones's royal work; most expanded on the Elizabethan plan by building large projecting wings, as at Hatfield, Audley End and Temple Newsam House, Leeds. One of the most percipient patrons, who had obviously studied Jones's Newmarket Palace, was Sir Roger Townshend. After a false start (1619–22), he went on to build his house, Raynham Hall, Norfolk (1635–8) with a T-shaped saloon and hall reminiscent of Palladio's Villa Pogliana. Its temple-like elevation was also loosely based on Jones's Lodging for Prince Charles at Newmarket and there are other Jonesian features[2] about the house. It anticipated Sir Henry Wotton's statement in his *The Elements of Architecture* (1624) that:

Everymans proper *Mansion* House and *Home*, being the *Theatre* of His *hospitality*, the seate of *selfe-fruition*, the Comfortablest of his owne *Life*; the *noblest* of his sonnes *Inheritance*, [is] a kind of private *Princedome* . . .

There were, of course, many houses designed to more modest plan. Inigo Jones designed one, of five bays with a central doorway and a hipped roof, for Lord Maltravers in 1638. It was not built and, for the most part, his Classical designs existed in nearly complete isolation. The master masons, working in a way that Sir John Summerson has labelled 'Artisan Mannerism',[3] did much more that was in the 'manner of the best London craftsmen: joiners, carpenters, masons, bricklayers...'. Their 'oblong square houses' (which anticipated developments in the early 1660s) brought together parts taken from a wide range of useful sources. Many of these were English, but foreign architectural books by Serlio, Palladio and Sir Peter Paul Rubens (*Palazzi di Genova*, 1626) were combed for ideas. Some houses were given plans and elevations that rivalled in scale the grandest medieval abbeys.[4] One such was Bolsover Castle, which Sir Charles Cavendish, Bess of Hardwick's third and youngest son, set out on a Derbyshire hilltop from November 1612 onwards. His son, Sir William, added a great gallery, 200 ft long, with strange external buttresses across its façade that resemble cannon-barrels and seem to have 'no parallel or precedent in England or abroad'.

This interest in grand form, gathered and displayed with care or abandon, focused itself in the career of a gentleman-architect, Sir Roger Pratt (1620–84). He took the idea of the small compact plan, which had long been in existence, and designed a warm and convenient house which he described in his notebooks,[5] coining the name of 'double-pile' plan. He wrote that this plan was most useful because it gave 'much room in a little compass' and needed very little ground to build. Essentially, a rectangular block was divided across its length by a corridor, with rooms to either side of it, giving a house two rooms deep. On the short axis, the central staircase hall rose through two storeys and faced a great parlour, which had a saloon, or dining-room, on the first floor above it. Pratt used the double-pile plan at Coleshill House, Berkshire, when building for his cousin in about 1657 (destroyed by fire in 1952) and at Kingston Lacy, Dorset (1663–5, altered in the nineteenth century). At a slightly later date, in the 1690s, Roger North (1653–1734) listed[6] the 'inconveniences of a pile' plan (meaning the 'double-pile'), as he saw them, including the problems of all noise being heard everywhere, smells being a nuisance in all rooms and some of the

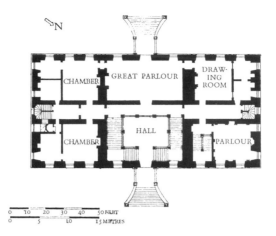

*Fig. 5. Coleshill House, Berkshire, 1650–62, a 'double-pile' plan
by Sir Roger Pratt, from* Vitruvius Britannicus, V, *1771.*

rooms being built too high or too low. He concluded that 'Designe ought
to be above such shifts', and one who did manage an effective twist on the
usual plan was North's friend, the architect Hugh May (1621–84) when
building at Eltham Lodge, near Greenwich (1663).

The Eltham plan is 'double-pile' but with two staircases rising from the
west and east in the central corridor. A more flexible arrangement of rooms
could thus be managed on both the ground and the first floors than was
possible at Coleshill House. Professor Andor Gomme has written that
Eltham's plan:

set the pattern for an endless progeny ... but its principal effect ... was on the
design, country wide, of innumerable small manor houses, rectories, farmhouses,
schools: shrunk to five or even to three bays, with the frontispiece removed,
it proved an astonishingly flexible envelope for endless varieties of internal
arrangement.[7]

These smaller buildings might be regarded in social and architectural
terms as 'vernacular houses'. In a masterly study[8] Eric Mercer regards
such buildings as of traditional form and materials, built in traditional ways
and using traditional ornament. They are common within, peculiar to one or
more limited parts of the country and are mean in comparison with some
of their neighbours. The vernacular examples of the double-pile plan did
not always rise to the same height at front and back and an 'outshut', or
extension under a lean-to roof, often housed the service areas. An important
consideration throughout the development of vernacular houses was the

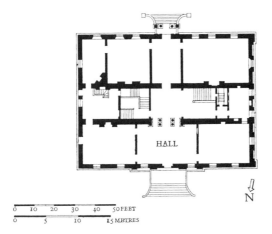

Fig. 6. Eltham Lodge, Greenwich, London, 1663, by Hugh May.
(Courtesy of the Royal Commission on Historical Monuments)

position of the chimney. When it was placed centrally it not only heated a room directly but, through its flue built in its rear wall, provided some radiated heat to an adjoining room. Its position could also be used to create a lobby between its flank and a side wall so that a 'lobby-entrance' could house the outer door. There were immediate advantages from a porch which shielded rooms from draughts and eliminated the need for a through-passage. The central chimney of the 'long-house' was replaced gradually by two or more, forming part of the end-elevations and making it a simple matter, with the use of the flexible double-pile plan, to give balance and symmetry to the façades of a house and the rooms behind them.

HALLS, CHAMBERS,
GALLERIES AND SALOONS

English noble society in the early seventeenth century found itself in a dilemma about building. Many possessed houses of considerable size dating from the medieval and Tudor periods.[9] The 'prodigy houses' of the late years of Queen Elizabeth's reign had been the exemplar to aspire to. Now, in 1615, there was Inigo Jones, fresh back from his second Italian journey and ready to put into practice the ideas he had absorbed from the buildings of Palladio and Scamozzi, and his modular systems for building.[10] In Rome, on 19 January 1615, Jones had noted that: 'in Architecture on[e] must studdy the Parts as loges, Entranses Haales, chambers staires' – in other words, the relationship of the parts of a building to the whole. What Palladio's work suggested to Jones and all of perception who had looked only at his plans of Italian country houses in the *Quattro Libri* (1570), was the way in which two large rooms could form the centre of a house, with other rooms in an ordered arrangement around them. Such a plan could be adapted to have a great chamber above a central hall, an immediate and convenient advantage over the great houses of Hatfield, Hertfordshire, and Audley End, Essex, which, intended in part for the entertainment of the king and queen, had been equipped with separate lodgings, spread out in a long and symmetrical array of wings.

The sort of porticoed great chamber of which Jones (and Palladio) would have approved was built by Sir Roger Townshend at Raynham Hall, Norfolk, in the 1630s, and I have already noted the Palladian and Jonesian cast of his great house. The great chamber at Raynham was set behind a row of Ionic columns with its central prominence marked by the pediment above them – in Roman buildings the pediment was a sign of rank. To either side of this great chamber were withdrawing chambers, bedchambers and closets.

Many early-seventeenth-century interiors were, for a variety of reasons, altered within a few years of their creation. Sir Thomas Vavasour's splendid mansion, Ham House, Surrey, was built from 1610 in three storeys on the 'H' plan. Its central entrance opens into one end of the great hall, a survival of the medieval practice of entering by a screens passage, yet the great hall was enlarged in the 1630s. Some of the fine 1630s work will be described when considering the great staircase and its landings. The former great dining-room still has plasterwork and decorative paintings of that date, as does the withdrawing-room, to which guests retired after dining. The Green Closet, with its deep painted cove, is one of the earliest 'cabinets' in England and a rare survival, but the long gallery, useful for exercise and for displaying paintings, was again remodelled in 1639.

In the early 1670s more alterations were made for the 1st Duke and Duchess of Lauderdale, including the creation of a chapel from a room previously used as a parlour, and the extending and repositioning of the duke and duchess's apartments. In about 1690 the duchess had the floor of the great dining-room (now the Round Gallery) pierced with an octagonal opening, surrounded by a balustrade, to give a good view of the great hall and entrance doorway below.

Certain aspects of the processes of renewal are true of most houses, large or small, with their varied owners; some knowledgeable, large of vision and well versed in the best authors of architecture; others content to amend and

32. *The Cartoon gallery looking east, c. 1607–8, at Knole, Kent.*
The room takes its name from the copies of Raphael's Cartoons hanging in the gallery,
presented by Charles I to the 1st Earl of Middlesex.

compromise casually and almost without thought. At Knole, Kent, Thomas Sackville, later Lord Buckhurst and the 1st Earl of Dorset, and also cousin to Queen Elizabeth (by whom he had been given the house and estate in 1566) was well acquainted with the leading Elizabethan surveyor, John Thorpe (c. 1563–1655), who may have helped him with designs. Yet the earl could not ignore the fact that he had inherited Archbishop Bourchier's great mid-fifteenth-century house and that it was cheaper to remodel it than build new, elsewhere on his estate.

In the great hall at Knole, built c. 1460, the earl put up the plasterwork ceiling, oak screen and panelling and the chimneypiece. He seems to have used part of Bourchier's medieval house to create the 88-ft length for the Brown Gallery and the apartments beyond, consisting of three galleries and four bedrooms. By the early seventeenth century, a hall was being used less for family dining and a list of seating arrangements for meals at Knole, made between 1613 and 1624, suggests that (as at Hardwick) the family took their meals in private. The steward presided over the household and estate servants who used the hall for their own meals. It was a considerable social move from the hall's former highly regarded status.

The Cartoon Gallery at Knole, Kent, *c.* 1607–8, takes its name from a set of six large copies of Raphael's Cartoons that were presented by Charles I to Lionel Cranfield, 1st Earl of Middlesex. The gallery runs along the south side of the house with six windows and a bay looking south, and another bay window looking into the Green Court, the largest of the seven courtyards at Knole. Early inventories call it the 'Matted Gallery', in respect of a type of rush matting that originally covered the floorboards. The solar or chief living-room (now called the ballroom) is, again, part of Archbishop Bourchier's work of about 1467. It is 70 ft long with a door in the north wall leading on to the upper landing of the great staircase. The ballroom also has a bay window looking towards the south-east and is flanked on that side by the small enclosed Pheasant Court. They are good examples of new uses for rooms of earlier date and purpose.

There are a number of important seventeenth-century long galleries, of which the principal, apart from that at Knole, must be those at Hatfield House, Hertfordshire (1612); Blickling Hall, Norfolk (*c.* 1620); Ham House, Surrey (remodelled in 1639); the superb garden-front gallery on the first floor of Sudbury Hall, Derbyshire (*c.* 1676); the 115-ft long picture gallery at Althorp, Northamptonshire, remodelled from the Elizabethan one and a grand setting for a reception given to William III in 1695; and finally, the smaller galleries at houses such as Easton Neston, Northamptonshire, arranged on the main axis of the house from front to back.

At Hatfield, Robert Cecil, 1st Earl of Salisbury, made his long gallery as long as he could. It is a wonderful Jacobean space, with a length of 180 ft, set on the centre of the south front over a loggia and having nine windows, the middle one being behind the frontispiece. The loggia was originally open, in the Italian Renaissance style, but the windows were added in about 1830, a black-and-white marble floor laid, and it became the Armoury. The gallery was finished originally with two pillars at either end with a space beyond them forming separate lobbies. The panels were removed by the 2nd Marquess of Salisbury in the 1860s when he covered the white plasterwork ribs of the ceiling with gold leaf. This opulent trim, which suited the age in which he lived, was to gild a proud house for a visit by Queen Victoria. When she announced her visit the Marquess also amended the approach to the house, finishing the work just in time.

33. The long gallery c. 1676, at Sudbury Hall, Derbyshire, showing Robert Bradbury and James Pettifer's enriched plaster ceiling.

The grandest of the mid-seventeenth-century interiors in England, in the style of an Italian *salone*, is the Double Cube Room at Wilton House, Wiltshire. Its builder, the 4th Earl of Pembroke, who had succeeded in 1630, was often the king's host at Wilton. John Aubrey in his *Natural History of Wiltshire* (which was edited in 1847 by John Britton) noted that it was Charles I: 'that did put Philip, Earle of Pembroke upon making this magnificent garden and grotto and to build that side of the house that fronts the garden, with two stately pavilions at each end, all *al Italiano...*' Aubrey added that the king intended Inigo Jones to be the architect for the earl, but Jones was engaged at the Queen's House at Greenwich and so recommended Isaac de Caus, a Huguenot, versed in hydraulics, geometry and perspective. The long and complicated story of the rebuilding of the south front of Wilton 'burnt ann. 1647 or 1648, by airing of the rooms' has been told elsewhere.[11] The rehabilitation of the wing was carried out under the careful supervision of Jones's nephew by marriage, the very competent John Webb (1611–72), but surely with 'the advice and approbation of Mr Jones' who was by then seventy-three years of age. Whatever the art-historical niceties of the 1650 reconstruction at Wilton, the result was a splendid group of richly carved and gilded rooms with painted ceilings, which included the Double Cube Room (60 ft long by 30 ft wide by 30 ft high), flanked by the Single Cube Room of 30 by 30 by 30 ft.

Palladio had given seven ratios for the proportions of rooms[12] in his *Quattro Libri*, with the square and two squares, as at Wilton, being the most basic. Compromise on the exact measured alignments of windows and chimneypiece in these rooms at Wilton had to take place to incorporate pre-existing structures, but their slight asymmetry contributes to the richly overpowering and theatrical effect, even if much of the decoration (described below in the section on walls and ceilings) is undeniably coarse. In fact, in a critical description of Wilton in the late 1750s Sir William Chambers dismissed the many gilded wood swags of fruit as 'vast lumps of wood not unlike bunches of turnips',[13] but they well define the spaces, even if some style is lacking.

FLOORS

The most significant development in flooring in the seventeenth century was the adaptation of pattern-book designs for floors in rooms that were to be paved in stone or marble, or inlaid in wood in intricate parquetry patterns. Both Sebastiano Serlio's treatises on architecture (from 1537 onwards) and Palladio's important *Quattro Libri* (1570) became better known

34 (opposite). The Double Cube Room completed c. 1653 at Wilton House, Wiltshire, showing the ceiling paintings by Emmanuel de Critz with those in the cove by Edward Pierce. The canvas paintings are mostly by Van Dyck.

in England through English translations, which were made in 1611 and 1663 respectively. Two of Serlio's ceiling patterns from Book IV of his *Architettura* (1559–62) were often modified as floor patterns. Their arrangement of interlocking frets, crosses and octagons and some of the other designs were also taken over in 1615 by Walter Gedde. Whilst his book was titled, at length: *Booke of Sundry Draughtes, Principally serving for Glasiers: And not impertinent for Plasterers, and Gardiners: besides sundry other professions*, many of his designs were too complicated to realize, as floor patterns. No known floor survives based on them, but his book became well-known as a useful source of ideas.

In 1670 Godfrey Richards translated into English the French edition of Palladio's *Quattro Libri* (1570) by Pierre Le Muet. At least his little work, as the title-page shows, only contained Palladio's 'First Book', which dealt with the architectural orders. To this, Richards, from his bookshop near the old Exchange in London, added 'diverse other designes necessary to the art of well building', including designs for doors, floors and frames of houses.[14] The book went through four more editions in the seventeenth century alone and at least six in the eighteenth century. In the 1683 edition two plates were given of parquetry floors in the French manner at Somerset House, London, where Henrietta Maria, wife of Charles I, had lived as Queen Dowager on returning from exile in France in 1660. She had presumably become familiar with parquet floors at Versailles and elsewhere and wanted them laid in London. The joiner Henry Harlow installed parquet flooring of cedar inlaid with walnut at Ham House, Surrey, in 1673–4, both in the queen's closet (where the Duke of Lauderdale's coronet and cipher is incorporated in the floor of the arched recess) and in the queen's bedchamber. The queen in question was Catherine of Braganza. He made a standard charge of 16s a yard, rising to 35s for ornate sections.

Parquetry involves inlaying various coloured woods, or slivers of the same wood, into shallow grooves cut in a contrasting wood surface such as a floor. In furniture it is known as 'inlaying'; this differs from 'marquetry' in which a pattern is assembled by using thin veneers of wood, which are then glued to the surface of the carcase. Throughout the seventeenth century many wood-plank floors were laid, in oak, deal and rarely, as at Canons Ashby, Northamptonshire, in sycamore. Frequently, the ravages of wear, woodworm and fires have destroyed much, but there are well-preserved, wide floorboards at Knole in Kent and one 22-in-wide board in the long gallery floor at Haddon Hall, Derbyshire, has the date 1662 burned on its under surface. Hard plaster floors (*glacis*) are to be found at Bolsover Castle, Derbyshire, dating from the 1620s.

35. *Detail of the section of friezes by Sebastiano Serlio, from Book IV
of* Architettura, *1559–62, used as patterns for floors and other decoration.*

One of the most significant sources for seventeenth-century architectural patterns was also issued in France: Daviler's *Cours complet d'architecture*, published in two volumes in 1691. Charles Augustine Daviler (1653–1700) had worked under Jules Hardouin-Mansart (1646–1708) at Versailles and elsewhere. He discusses paving, somewhat fulsomely, in his *Cours* and two dense plates show many intricate patterns such as *pavé antique, carreaux triangulaires*, and *carreaux octagones*. The last became a common pattern for marble and stone floors in eighteenth-century England. Daviler thought 'Dutch' earthenware tiles most suitable for small 'cabinet' rooms, grottoes and bathrooms, whilst hard plaster floors could be coloured with oil colours or *scagliola* (artificial marble) and laid in areas of light use. Although he regarded parquet as the most beautiful way of flooring bedrooms and 'cabinet' rooms, he decreed that stone flags, laid in square or lozenge shapes, were best for churches, kitchens and refectories. Variations in shape included triangular, hexagonal or octagonal stone slabs laid with small squares for use in halls, passages, landings and dining-rooms. If patterns were created in various marbles (as in his Plate 203), Daviler suggested that they correspond with the compartments of the ceiling or vault above and be of similar hardness to each other. There was Gallic disapproval, for this last reason, of putting stone and marble together, or of using either porphyry or granite with soft marbles.[15]

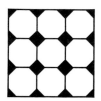

Fig. 7. *Design for a marble floor drawn from Daviler,*
Cours complet d'architecture, *1691, Plate 2.*

The circular pattern given by Daviler in his Plate 203, 'Rose de compartiment variée de sept façons', corresponded to the floor of the mid 1550s at Philibert de l'Orme's chapel in the Château d'Anet. The circle was the perfect figure, according to Renaissance thinking, and therefore it was the most suitable for a dedicated chapel. The marble pavement was made entirely of arcs of circles, corresponding not only to the coffering in the dome but to a design found in ancient Roman mosaics.[16] Inigo Jones used the pattern again in the hall of the Queen's House at Greenwich, and in 1636–7 the mason Nicholas Stone supervised the laying of the marble floor there. The entrance hall at the Queen's House is a 40-ft cube of two storeys, with a gallery supported on great console brackets at first-floor level. The marble 'rose' circle, pictured later by Daviler, is surrounded on four sides by more corner circles and rectangular borders in a diamond black-and-white pattern, which is continued in a simpler pattern in the loggias. It follows the ribs of the ceiling pattern.

One of the most lavish uses of marble outside London was in the Keep (called the 'Little Castle') at Bolsover, Derbyshire, laid about 1614. Bolsover Castle, as I have noted, was started in November 1612 by Robert Smythson for Sir Charles Cavendish. As Robert died in October 1614, most of the work in the Keep must have been supervised by his son, John Smythson. On the first floor there is a marble closet (as well as many elaborate hooded marble chimneypieces). Its floor is of chequered black-and-white marble and the rib vaults of the ceiling are also covered in marble, a most unlikely material for an area likely to be under stress and tension, but one suited to the Mannerist oddities of hill-top Bolsover.

When the indefatigable traveller Celia Fiennes visited the newly built Newby Hall, Yorkshire, in 1692 she observed that there were two dining-rooms and two drawing-rooms, of which 'one for the summer' had 'a marble floor'.[17] She also noted Pratt's Coleshill House, Berkshire, and Burghley House, Lincolnshire, as having rooms paved with black-and-white marble. She remarked that the marble about the house at Chatsworth was 'finely polished like a looking-glass' and that its stairs were of stone 'cut out of the hills ... above the house', that is at Sheldon Moor, five miles away. In the chapel at Chatsworth, the pavement, c. 1688, and still in situ, was of 'black-and-white marble vein'd, lay'd longwayes in large stones all of the same', and twenty loads of alabaster came from near Tutbury, Staffordshire, for the towering altarpiece designed by Caius Gabriel Cibber and carved (with the exception of Cibber's figures of Faith and Justice) by Samuel Watson (1663–1715). It was completed by the summer of 1691: George Vertue noted later that 'the ornaments carvd in wood & foliages [were] by Watson, sculptor in Wood & stone'. Watson came from Heanor in Derbyshire but had trained under Charles Okey, the London carver; he spent most of his working life at Chatsworth in the capacity of the 'house-carver'. His contemporary, John Selden (d. 1715), occupied a similar position at Petworth.[18]

The rebuilding of Belton House, Lincolnshire, had been started by Sir John Brownlow in 1684, as a small version of Sir Roger Pratt's Clarendon House in Piccadilly, which was influential in its plan, although it was demolished a year or so before Sir John commenced his work. He finished with a house which more than befitted his position as High Sheriff (although it lacked richly painted decoration) and which provided a worthy setting for the reception of William III. The chapel occupying the north-east wing of the house as a double-storeyed room, has a black-and-white marble floor, supplied by William Stanton in 1688, and seemingly the one still *in situ*.

SCREENS
AND PANELLED WALLS

The medieval and Tudor arrangement of the hall and its screen was slow to die away and at the start of the seventeenth century the screen was still an object covered with richly carved ornament and heraldic displays. In Joseph Nash's watercolours of the 1840s, as well as the four volumes of his *The Mansions of England in the Olden Times* (1839–49), there are many romanticized views of lost interiors, such as the great hall of Crewe Hall, Cheshire (1616–32), with its screen covered in open-work strapwork ornaments, terminal caryatids and fantastic details, all of which could be culled from the Flemish pattern-books. Whilst Crewe Hall was almost gutted by fire in 1866, Nash showed much that does still survive in other houses, such as the screens at Hatfield House, Hertfordshire, Audley End, Essex, and Knole in Kent.

At Hatfield House, the screen and the carving of the open-well staircase (noted below) were the work of the carver John Bucke, and both were originally painted in 1611 by Rowland Bucket. This interior must have been brilliant with colour for Bucket covered the screen with 'Armes, gilding & personages' and there are ten cartouches on the lower stage alone. In addition, there were wooden friezes in every room, picked out in paint and gilding. But a pause in work came when Robert Cecil died in May 1612, 'without having slept for more than a few days in the building on which he had lavished so much trouble and so much money'.[19]

The Audley End screen, *c.* 1605–10, is one of the grandest in an English house, with open-work carving in the upper part concealing a gallery. It is remarkably fresh in appearance, owing, perhaps, to the fact that in about 1740 the screen (as well as the roof timbers of the hall) was covered in white paint to represent stucco, which was not removed until *c*.1825–30. The screen originally had two openings but was amended, seemingly not long after its erection, to give the present central one, which had a pair of doors. This may have been done to give a more imposing entrance to the hall but it has been noted that one opening was common to many Elizabethan and Jacobean screens.[20]

36. The Oak Screen in the great hall, c. 1605–8, at Knole, Kent,
probably carved by William Portington, the master carpenter to James I.

The Knole screen, *c.* 1605–8, was probably carved by the king's master
carpenter, William Portington, although the surveyor, John Thorpe, well
versed in foreign patterns, may have had a hand in the design. The exact
facts are not revealed by the accounts but the screen, some 25 ft high overall,
is stylistically based on the Flemish engravings of Wendel Dietterlein and
Marten de Vos. This is particularly so in the pairs of caryatids and panels
of elaborate grotesque ornament, perhaps adapted from the second enlarged
edition of Wendel Dietterlein's *Architectura*, published at Nuremberg in
1598. The Sackville arms are placed at the centre of the cresting, which
rears itself at each end to die into the walls in a flourish of pierced scrolls.

Throughout the seventeenth century it was common to line rooms with
wood wainscoting. Reference to a simple diagram will make discussion of
its component parts more intelligible.

In rooms under ten ft high, two heights of panel were used; if 11–12 ft and over, three panels. In proportion the frieze rail (F) had the same breadth as the stiles (A), and the middle rail (E) was commonly twice the breadth of the stiles; the lower and upper rails (C and G) were also of the same breadth as the stiles. In the late seventeenth century skilled joiners started to bevel the edge of the panels (I, K and L) to leave a raised 'table' in the middle. The oblong panels were usually 4–5 ft in width, and as tall, and were dignified with the simplest of mouldings. Further overlaid soft-wood enrichments were the province of the carvers.

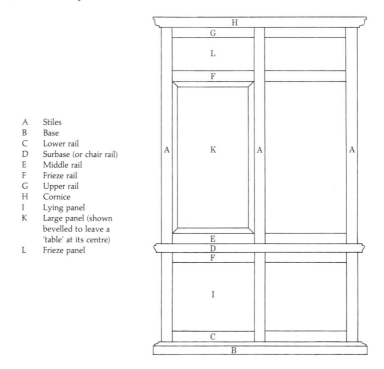

A	Stiles
B	Base
C	Lower rail
D	Surbase (or chair rail)
E	Middle rail
F	Frieze rail
G	Upper rail
H	Cornice
I	Lying panel
K	Large panel (shown bevelled to leave a 'table' at its centre)
L	Frieze panel

Fig. 8. *Wainscoting, after Joseph Moxon,* Mechanick Exercises, *1694.*

The wood used for wainscoting varied with the patron's ability to pay and his joiner's competence to work whatever was chosen. Oak was in frequent use but, in many City Company Halls and Oxford and Cambridge colleges, cedar and walnut were used with great competence. The wood was usually cut to show the attractive radiating medullary rays of the tree, so that the largest amount of grain was displayed. Wainscoting provided a handsome setting for paintings and was usually given an enriched cornice.

37. *The dining-room at Dunster Castle, Somerset, with its plaster ceiling, dated 1681.*
The 'fielded' or bevelled panelling shows the portraits to advantage.

In 1669 Robert, Lord Brooke, owner of Warwick Castle, one of the finest medieval structures in England, decided to create an impressive range of state rooms, including a Cedar Room. He entered into agreement with the Warwickshire joiner, Roger Hurlbutt, to wainscot the great hall, and Roger's brother, William, was sent to look at Kingston Lacy, the Dorset house that Sir Roger Pratt had designed for Sir Ralph Bankes; at William Hurlbutt's return in 1670 he received the first payment for altering rooms of the castle. The agreement is presumed to cover the whole range of state apartments to the south-west of the great hall; these are now known as the Cedar Drawing Room, the Red and Green Drawing Rooms, the State or Queen Anne's Bedroom and the Boudoir. The so-called Italian Room was also refitted at the same time.

In 1671 over 57 cwt of cedar boards were brought from London to the castle. William Hurlbutt, over the next few years (he received a final payment in 1678) supervised various jobs, including the cutting of 19,628 ft of timber at 2s 2d per 100 ft by his sawyers, and the transportation of the boards from London. The cedar wainscoting was set below elaborate plaster ceilings and survived the Warwick Castle fire of 1871. At Ham House, Surrey, the joiner Henry Harlow supplied panelling in 1673 for all the new rooms; shelves with cedar mouldings; and the furnishings for the chapel, as well as being versatile enough to install the new oak sash-windows.

Celia Fiennes described the hall at Chippenham Park, near Newmarket, in the early 1690s as:

'wainscoted with Walnutt tree, the pannells and Rims round with Mulbery tree yt is a Lemon Coulleur, and the mouldings beyond it round are of a sweete outlandish wood not much differing from Cedar, but of a finer graine...'[21]

Sometimes use of a heavy, expensive timber such as oak was avoided by obtaining fir and then painting it. John Evelyn noted that in 1677 at Euston Hall: 'the wainscott, being of fir and painted does not please me so well as Spanish oak without paint.'[22] It was a case of a long purse or of compromise.

The fir, or deal, came to England as part of the extensive Norwegian timber export trade. The effects of exotic timbers could be obtained by painting the wood in various ways. The architect, Captain William Winde (d. 1722), who was remodelling Castle Bromwich Hall, Warwickshire, for his cousin, Lady Mary Bridgeman, wrote to her [23] in September 1690, that the best wainscoting was made of Danish oak, which did not easily warp, but that the greatest difficulty was in transporting it to the site. Winde's advice was always precise, if occasionally late in arriving, and many patrons involved in building must have received similar information from their architects, and master joiners too, if equal to their jobs.

The craftsmen who were able both to pierce wood and to fashion it so that it resembled other materials and natural forms were the carvers. They were often skilled joiners who had specialized further, in that carvers had no trade guild of their own. They became adept at carving in both wood and stone, but surviving accounts are not always informative about the kinds of materials used.

Carving in wood in the last thirty years of the seventeenth century is associated in particular with the achievements of Grinling Gibbons (1648– 1721), born in Rotterdam of English parents.[24] He was in England by the mid 1660s and was discovered carving a panel by John Evelyn, who introduced him to the king and to Sir Christopher Wren. His principal carved works in wood may be seen in various rooms at Windsor Castle, Hampton Court, St Paul's Cathedral and Petworth, Sussex. Working at Windsor under the supervision of the talented architect Hugh May (1621– 84), Gibbons and Henry Phillips (fl. 1662–93) – whom Gibbons was to

38 (left). *The limewood carving by Grinling Gibbons, c. 1692, surrounding a portrait of the 'Proud' 6th Duke of Somerset, builder of the house, at Petworth House, Sussex.*

39 (right). *Detail of the limewood carving. Horace Walpole described this masterpiece as 'the most superb monument of his skill'.*

succeed as 'Sculptor and Master Carver in Wood' to the Crown in December 1693 – decorated the walls from chair-rail to cornice with dextrously carved soft-wood representations of flowers, fruits, shells and other ornaments.

The principal wood favoured by Gibbons and most carvers was lime (although oak, box and pear were used), laminated with glue into two or three layers. The grain needed to be carefully observed as it was worked and heightened with a wide variety of gouges, veiners, chisels, points and fine saws. The pieces were assembled into a final pattern by pinning them with glue and steel pins. These pins have, in many cases, rusted over the years and woodworm has taken an even more savage toll on the delicate panels. However, enough pieces survive in reasonable condition to demonstrate that the art was a popular and considerable one, akin to the three-dimensional realization of a Dutch still-life painting of flowers by an artist such as Justus van Huysum the Elder.

The Carved Room at Petworth, Sussex, was originally two separate rooms, which were made into one in about 1794–5. The blending of local with London talent combined the work of men whose usual occupation was domestic building with the achievements of those who enhanced great houses. Grinling Gibbons received £173 for statues in March 1692 and on 10 December in the same year, 'for Carveing, £150'. On hand, and carving with almost equal skill, was the resourceful Petworth carver, John Selden. His main achievement can be seen in the Marble Hall, with its niches, carved coat-of-arms and supporters, and in the chapel, where life-size angels hold back draped wood curtains around the family arms. These carvings are spirited and expressive enough to be by Gibbons but the documentation does not, alas, provide a certain attribution.

Gibbons,[25] with the aid of an accomplished team of assistants, turned more and more in his own late years to working in marble and being a provider of lavish funerary monuments.

Other skilled woodcarvers worked in the late seventeenth century at Burghley House, Lincolnshire, Chatsworth, Derbyshire, and at Belton House, Lincolnshire. The woodcarvers at Burghley House were Jonathan Maine and Thomas Young; Maine was a very competent craftsman from Oxford, with a long list of good work to his credit, including woodwork at Trinity College, Oxford, and at St Paul's Cathedral. Maine and Young received over £402 in the years 1682 to 1687, and this implies that much of the wainscoting and carved work at Burghley is by them; Gibbons only received £50. Maine and Young's wainscot panels and carved wood overdoors are topped by flamboyant painted ceilings. John, the 5th Earl of Exeter, who was engaged in altering and repairing Burghley House in the late seventeenth century, was the brother-in-law of William Cavendish, the 1st Duke of Devonshire, who was doing the same sort of decorations in the rebuilding of Chatsworth. They shared craftsmen, particularly the painter Antonio Verrio, and the carver Thomas Young, who joined up with William Davis and Joel Lobb to do more carved work in the new state rooms of the duke's fine house.

It has been suggested that the long mirror in the great dining-chamber at Chatsworth was so placed, presumably at the suggestion of the duke or his architect, to reflect the enfilade of oak-wainscoted rooms, enhanced with rich soft-wood carvings over the doors, stretching westwards along the south front, thus 'repeating' them, as images to the east. This would give the illusion of a saloon with matching apartments, although in reality these could not be built because so few Baroque rooms could be squeezed into the limited space of the main front of Elizabethan Chatsworth.

40. *Overmantel in the State Music Room, 1692–4, at Chatsworth, Derbyshire, carved by a partnership of four carvers, including the house carver, Samuel Watson.*

A house with which Grinling Gibbons has been long associated, with little archival evidence, is Belton House, Lincolnshire, built for Sir John Brownlow (1685–7). The wainscoting there is conventional in form but is in red cedar and deal, the latter grained to resemble oak. There are at least two different hands at work in the several carvings. The limewood carvings in the Marble Hall include work over the two fireplaces. That to the right is probably the work of the otherwise unknown carver, Edmund Carpenter, who was paid £26 10s in 1688 for overmantels, including 'varieties of fish and sheals/with birds, foulige, fruit & flowers'. The carving over the left overmantel is more finely executed and may be worthy of the traditional family ascription to Grinling Gibbons. The builder's nephew, also Sir John, was created Viscount Tyrconnel in 1718 and a 1738 inventory of his London house lists 'A fine piece of carving in a panel by Gibbons', which may have come to Belton. There is more carving of high quality in the gallery to the chapel and some by Carpenter at the east end of the saloon (although, again, that at the west end is richer and bolder). Interestingly, in the 1698 Inventory, this last room is described as the 'White Varnished Drawing Room'.[26]

Wood panelling was used in most smaller houses as the most appropriate lining to make rooms look rich and warm. At the small Townend House, Troutbeck, Cumbria several of the rooms were panelled by the Browne family and many useful inscriptions and dates were carved thereon. For example, a small room on the first floor has an inset cupboard with the initials 'GB: B.B 1670' – and there are further cupboard recesses with other Browne family initials and dates ranging from 1626 to 1687.[27] It was a suitable and practical lining to insulate further the thick stone walls from the rigours of a harsh northern winter.

Something of the intimate scale given to a small room by simple panelling can also be seen in the drawing-room of the 1640s at East Riddlesden Hall, Yorkshire. It lies at the west side of the house, which has a two-storeyed great hall, and is adjacent to the large kitchen. The fireplace is dated '1648' and perhaps gives a terminal date for the room, done as part of the rebuilding of a medieval house by the staunch Royalist, James Murgatroyd (d. 1653).

PAINTED WALLS
AND CEILINGS

The standard of decorative painting in the seventeenth century was laid down in splendidly grand form by the nine great canvases Sir Peter Paul

Rubens painted, 1629–34, for Charles I. Representing an 'Apotheosis of James I', they were inserted between the mighty gilded wooden ribs of the ceiling of Inigo Jones's Banqueting Hall, part of the royal palace of Whitehall, and they were intended to complement it as a setting for the performance of royal masques. The complex iconography of these and other scenes, [28] often quite unsuitable for a domestic interior, is not our concern here, but many decorative paintings in seventeenth-century England contained similar statements of the divine right of kings or praise for the achievements of lesser patrons.

The paintings by Rubens for the Whitehall ceiling were done in oil on canvas in his studio at Antwerp and did not reach England until October 1635. There is a tradition that the walls of the Banqueting House were to be painted by the best-known of Rubens's pupils, Anthony van Dyck, and one of his oil sketches for the scheme survives. Nothing came of the idea, but a number of other artists had agreed to work under Inigo Jones's supervision at the Queen's House in Greenwich. These were Orazio Gentileschi, Jacob Jordaens and, again, Rubens.

The Queen's House hall ceiling (now at Marlborough House, London) by Gentileschi, painted a little after 1626, shows a disposition of twelve females, including the Nine Muses, floating with quiet detachment around the edge of the circular canvas. Jordaens's work at the Queen's House, 'The Story of Cupid and Psyche', 1639, is interesting in that instructions for its painting survive and care was taken not only to specify strong new cloth but also to indicate where each figure should be placed in the composition, and to warn the painter to observe the direction in which the 'lights doe seem to strike on ye payntings, so as the shadowes may bee given accordingly.'

This care was necessary because, unlike Gentileschi, Jacob Jordaens did not come to England. He was asked to do the work in Antwerp by Sir Balthazar Gerbier who, as a good diplomat, hid the identity of his royal patron to keep the cost down. Gerbier had been hoping that Rubens could paint the ceiling (which, in view of the foreshortening, was difficult technically and therefore costly), but the artist's death in May 1640 put an end to the plan. At least eight of Jordaens's paintings finally reached England but they were sold at the king's execution in 1649 and their present whereabouts are unknown.

The Baltic German painter, Francis Cleyn, was in England and ready to serve Charles I by the 1620s. His first big commission was to paint the ceiling of Henrietta Maria's 'cabinet' at Old Somerset House, but his only surviving paintings are at Ham House, Surrey. He filled his ceilings there with grotesques in the Roman manner of Raphael. He also designed cartoons for many tapestries which were to be produced at the royal Mortlake factory.

Apart from the names of many foreign painters, much of whose work has disappeared, those of three English painters appear frequently in the royal accounts: the Sergeant Painter in the king's service, John de Critz, Matthew Gooderick, active from 1617, and the elder Edward Pierce (or Pearce). Inigo Jones knew and used all of them, but little of their domestic work survives. Matthew Gooderick may have done the rich little 'Painted Bower' at Castle Ashby, Northamptonshire, for the Keeper of the Great Wardrobe, Spencer Compton, 2nd Earl of Northampton. Their representations of Raphaelesque 'grotesque' were in demand and form a prominent element in the decoration of the Single and Double Cube rooms at Wilton House, Wiltshire.

The cove to a ceiling, based in form on the *volta a conca* of Palladio, was one of Jones's most striking innovations in English architecture. Its depth could be further suggested and enhanced by painting it and the best examples of this are found at Wilton. Gooderick seems to have painted the cove in the Single Cube Room but the one around the Double Cube Room is normally credited to Pierce, as its style is consistent with a book of decorative friezes he had issued in 1640 suggesting that they would be of use to plasterers, as well as to painters. The cove of the Double Cube Room is painted with coarse, overpowering swags of fruit and vegetables, fit in size only for a giant's table and held up by muscular and untiring *putti*. There is a theatrical aspect about it all that matches the paintings in the three central compartments of the main ceiling, *c.* 1651, depicting scenes from 'The Legend of Perseus'. Both the seventeenth-century chroniclers John Aubrey and John Evelyn gave Emanuel de Critz as their creator.[29] As the younger son of the Sergeant Painter, de Critz was regarded as the best painter in London, with Venetian influences strong in his work. Nevertheless the paintings are not well accomplished and the steep perspective of architectural forms and foreshortening are strained attempts to do what Rubens did much better.

In the Hunting Room at Wilton House Pierce painted eighteen panels of European, African and Asiatic hunting subjects (*c.* 1654), using the suites of etchings by Antonio Tempesta of 1602 and 1624 as his source. The figures, in tall black hats on prancing horses, release falcons into the stormy skies, or stand, near naked, in waist-deep silvery waters, netting fish. The distant landscapes in the panels are all well realized, in oil on wood, and were noted as Pierce's work by John Evelyn (*Diary*, 20, vii, 1654).

In the first half of the seventeenth century there is much good anonymous work, of which the principal scheme is in various rooms of Bolsover Castle, Derbyshire, c. 1620. In the Elysium Room pagan deities prance at the edge of an Assembly of the Gods and, in the Star Chamber, large figures of Aaron, Solomon, David and Moses appear with the Tablets of the Law (dated 1621). The work, (oil on wood, canvas or plaster) is in five rooms and is based on a variety of engravings; those in the Elysium Room, for example, use as their source an engraving by Cornelius Cort, after a design by Primaticcio for a ceiling at Fontainebleau. At Royston, Hertfordshire, the house called Thurnalls has several rooms on its first floor filled with grotesque paintings and figures of biblical subjects, which incorporate the initials A/T.M, for 'Thomas and Mary Archer', and the dates '1635' and '1636'.

A useful reference to the vivid style and bright colours of interior painting in the 1660s occurs in accounts and instructions in the correspondence of John Cosin, Bishop of Durham, for work in the chapel at his palace of Bishop Auckland. The painter, John Baptist van Ersell, was instructed[30] to do work in 1664 on the 'middle rooffe of the middle Ile of his Lordshipp's Chappell at Auckland'. The groundwork of the whole roof was to be painted blue and the coffering in yellow 'mixed with black stroakes, to showe like teeth'. The painter was also to colour the 'carved martyrs' and cherubims' heads, which are fixed to the roof ... with proper coullours and shall guilde with leafe gold the carved work ... in proper places only'. He was further instructed to paint two sides of a wall by the east window, and the chairs and desks in stone colour. The carpenter's work was to be painted in a walnut-tree colour, handsomely veined with fruit down the pilasters: 'the freeze blew with large gold letters'. Regrettably, it has all gone, but work by the grander painters[31] survives in reasonable quantity in many parts of England.

One of the leading painters to work in England was the Italian from Lecce, Antonio Verrio (c. 1639–1707), who arrived in London in about 1672 and stayed in England until his death. It might fairly be said of Verrio that he introduced late Baroque painting on the grand scale to England. About half of his twenty-nine recorded English commissions were painted in oil on plaster, with the remainder done in oil on canvas, or on wood. This approach was, of course, very different from the true fresco techniques of Verrio's native Italy, which involved an artist applying his colours on wet *intonaco* as soon as it had been prepared. The colours were absorbed by the wet plaster and the ensuing chemical reaction caused them to become integrated with the plaster itself.

One of Verrio's earliest English patrons was Charles II, who was busy providing new state rooms at Windsor Castle with his architects. The castle's dramatic hilltop site afforded scenic and picturesque possibilities beyond those of any other royal palace in England, or even in the France of the king's rival, Louis XIV. The architect, Hugh May, was careful not to disturb the general external character of the medieval buildings, but lavished attention on the interiors. In the 1670s, the king was to spend at least £190,000 on the new works at Windsor. Under May's direction, Verrio and his assistants painted some twenty ceilings, three staircases, the chapel and the hall.[32] Most of these decorations (shown in engravings in Pyne's *Royal Residences*, 1819) were swept away in the work Sir Jeffry Wyatville did for George IV in about 1824, and only three ceilings now exist in their entirety, relics of the grandest of Baroque interiors.

The entrance to the royal apartments was made from two staircases, named after the king and his queen. The Queen's Great Staircase was built first and stood in a painted hall; as the first grand painted staircase erected in this country, it must have made a tremendous visual impact on visitors entering it from the low, columned vestibules. On its walls, in about 1678, Verrio and his team painted the stories of Phaeton's sisters changing into trees and Cygnus being changed into a swan. There were eight figures in niches, made of copper and gilded by René Cousin and, in the dome far above, Apollo was depicted granting permission to Phaeton to drive the fiery chariot of the Sun across the heavens.

The later of the two blocks May built at Windsor contained the King's Staircase, the Chapel Royal and St George's Hall. Again, the roof of the King's Staircase was domed. On its walls 'The Four Ages of the World' were painted and many prancing giants battled in the bright frescoes overhead. The King's Chapel was adorned with Verrio's paintings on ceilings, wall and altarpiece; Gibbons's carvings done in 'white natural wood without varnish'; and much gilding. The rich effect was enhanced by unseen music from organs behind the altar, which delighted at least one attentive visitor, the diarist John Evelyn.

The Catholic court of James II, on which painters such as Antonio Verrio depended for patronage, was short-lived. James II's reign, however, had brought with it his own fearless demands for a splendid Roman Catholic chapel. Begun in 1685, so swift was its building and decoration that it was in use by November 1686. Erected near to Inigo Jones's Banqueting House, it vanished in the great fires of 1691 and 1698, which reduced the Palace of Whitehall to ruins. The Banqueting House was saved, owing partly to its massive construction and partly to the special exertions at the time.

One of Charles II's courtiers was the Catholic William Herbert, created 1st Earl of Powis in 1674. At his splendid house, Powis Castle, near Welshpool (just across the Welsh border, but included here for the splendours of its Baroque decoration by leading craftsmen), the earl was active in building from the late 1660s. The staircase ceiling at Powis was probably painted near the time of the creation of the earldom, as it includes the earl's coronet and arms and the monogram of Charles II. It is attributed to Verrio and must therefore be amongst his earliest commissions in England.

Owing to the intrigues of Titus Oates, the earl fell from favour in 1678 and was imprisoned in the Tower until February 1684/5. The staircase walls were still not painted as the earl (made a marquess in 1687 and a duke by James II) fled abroad with his Catholic king, to die at St-Germain-en-Laye in 1696. The 2nd Duke of Powis also fled abroad and the Powis estates were granted to one of William III's followers, the Earl of Rochford. In 1701, the king gave the duke permission to return to England, but, short of money, he did not return to Powis Castle until 1704. A year later Gerard Lanscroon finally painted the staircase walls, below Verrio's ceiling of thirty years earlier.

Verrio was, of course, helped in his commissions by many assistants, mostly French or Flemish, and some were listed in a warrant of 1678 exempting them, as 'Popish recusants' from all molestation. The principal member was the gilder, René Cousin, but there were also grinders of colours, a stonecarver, painters (including one of flowers), apprentices, servants and several wives and children. With the flight of James II in 1685, Verrio's team took on two significant private commissions, painting six rooms and the staircase ceiling at Burghley House, Lincolnshire, and then undertook similar work at Chatsworth, Derbyshire. At Burghley, Verrio was receiving in payment a regular £200 every three or four weeks, in addition to keep for his party, schooling for his children and stabling for his horses.

Before painting could commence, the surfaces had to be primed with a size or thin paint to prevent undue absorption. The extensive Verrio archive at Burghley House records that for the painting of the Second George Room (then the drawing-room), John Collins, on 5 August 1691: 'Rec'd then of Sigr. Verrio three pounds six shillings in full for double priming the Drawing Room att 8d the yard.'

The State Bedchamber or the First George Room (1690) is representative of the superb work in all the state rooms – great wainscot panels, carved wood overdoors and a flamboyant painted ceiling representing the chasing away of Night by Morning. It was worked on for over nineteen weeks.

The painting of the Second George Room was also in progress before 1691. After the processes of Collins's double-priming and Verrio's painting it was gilded by René Cousin.

Finally, came the creation of the Fifth George Room, saloon, or the Heaven Room, one of the finest painted Baroque rooms in England. On the ceiling of the Heaven Room an 'Assembly of the Olympians' is attended by spirited creatures of the zodiac. The walls, painted with a colonnade of Corinthian columns and a rearing pediment strung with garlands of exotic flowers, are peopled with a host of aerial and over-muscular figures. A horse with a red-robed rider gallops down from the cornice, and on the north wall Neptune almost leaves his court, striding towards the onlooker with burning eyes, and backed by sharp trident and swirling dark cloak. Most dramatically, the east wall has a lively representation of Vulcan's forge, with a self-portrait of Verrio himself seated nonchalantly among the attendant Cyclops. The colours for the artist's palette are sent down on a bright, arching rainbow. The many accounts for this great room, completed in 1696, show that Verrio received a weekly sum, with many advances and extras for colours, oils, pencils, brushes, board for assistants, or for the services of his specialists. Cousin's bill for gilding included a charge of £37 0s 10d for 4,446 sheets of gold leaf, of which 1,030 were used on the cornice alone. The bills in later commissions were often mixed with those for living. Verrio's bill of 1696 for colours used at Lowther Castle, Cumbria (work now no longer extant) was mixed in with payments for caviare and a request for more anchovies.

Apart from the Lowther commission in the far north-west, Verrio's other main work of the 1690s was at Chatsworth. He left Burghley to paint the walls of the great stairs at Chatsworth with the Triumphs of Ceres, Cybele and Bacchus in monochrome and then, on the ceiling, depicted Cybele in her chariot, attended by Ceres. In the great chamber, or state dining-room, he painted the ceiling, and amid the painted work in the chapel by his talented French contemporary, Louis Laguerre, he painted Cibber and Watson's altarpiece. Finally, in the gallery (now the library) Verrio provided medallions of Apollo, Mercury and Minerva presiding over the Muses, set as canvases into the compartments of the richly plastered and gilded ceiling by Edward Goudge.

Louis Laguerre (1663–1721) started life with the double advantage that his godfather was Louis XIV and that he was born at the king's palace of Versailles, where his father was keeper of the royal menagerie. Laguerre was in England, fresh from his rigorous training at the Académie, by 1684 and became an assistant to Verrio at Windsor Castle. Thereafter, as he also

41. The chapel ceiling at Chatsworth, Derbyshire; oil on plaster, painted by Louis Laguerre, 1689–93, depicting 'Christ in Glory'.

became a master painter, he was soon required at many great houses including Chatsworth, Burghley, Marlborough House and Blenheim Palace. His first large commission was at Chatsworth, where for eight years (1689–97) he painted the chapel, hall and most of the state rooms along the south front. Whilst less competent than Verrio, Laguerre was not afraid of a large scheme, such as the hall at Chatsworth, but it is not easy to isolate his work from that of his assistants. Moreover, when his painting of the ballroom at

42. *A wall of the King's staircase at Hampton Court, Middlesex.*
Painted in oil on plaster by Antonio Verrio, c. 1700, the scene shows Hercules
and Romulus pressing the claims of Alexander the Great and the twelve Caesars
to be invited to the heavenly banquet of the Saturnalia.

Burghley House is compared with Verrio's lively compositions in the other
state rooms there, his work looks very sombre. One of Laguerre's liveliest
works, the staircase walls and ceiling at Petworth House, Sussex, painted
after the fire of 1714, shows him in good form.

Late in his life, and perhaps at the intervention of the Earl of Exeter,
Verrio returned to William III's service at Hampton Court (as did Louis
Laguerre, though in a lesser capacity). Verrio was at the royal palace by
the autumn of 1699 to paint the Great, or King's Staircase, with a complicated allegory associating the Emperor Julian the Apostate and his *Satire
of the Caesars* with his royal patron, William, the upholder of Protestantism
and freedom. On the wall Julian, seated within an open colonnade, is seen
writing his book at Mercury's dictation. Above, there is a 'Banquet of the
Gods' and below, Hercules and Romulus are shown pressing the rival claims

of Alexander the Great and the twelve Caesars to be invited to the heavenly feast. The colours are garish and what might have been Verrio's masterpiece became a crowded daub. Payments were delayed for it and by 1705, with his eyesight almost gone, Verrio retired quietly to a house at Hampton Court, on a royal pension of £200 a year. He died there on 15 June 1707: his burial place is unknown and therefore his memorial lies in his paintings and in the well-known lines about him in Alexander Pope's *Epistle to . . . Richard, Earl of Burlington* (1731)

> On painted Cielings you devoutly stare,
> Where sprawl the Saints of Verrio or Laguerre,
> On gilded clouds in fair expansion lie,
> And bring all Paradise before your eye . . .

In fact, the dominance of Verrio and Laguerre in the decoration of walls and ceilings caused even first-rate plasterers such as Edward Goudge to lament the suppression of their trade during the last years of the seventeenth century.

Finally, I should mention the way in which paint was used to simulate other materials. Again, Captain William Winde's work for Lord Craven at Combe Abbey, Warwickshire, produced a useful statement from him in 1686. The painter George Holmes submitted a long bill and it followed closely 'Captain Winde's directions for painting at Comb Abbey, 17 August 1685'.

A   for the bedchambers, white and veind, and mouldings plaine at 1s.10d. per yard.
B   for the hall, wainscott colour at 13d per yard.
C   for the greate stayre case, by the hall cedar colour at 13d per yard.
D   for the little stayre case, white and vein'd, at 1s.10d per yard.
E   for the greate roome above stayres, marble colour at 2s.4d per yard.
F   to be used as Mr Holmes thinks fitt, Lignum Vitae colour at 18d per yard.

Winde further noted that for 'C', the great staircase, the mouldings round the panels and also on the rails were 'to be guilded with gould'. This was a long-seated practice; as early as 1637–8 Matthew Gooderick gilded mouldings on the simulated walnut of the staircase-landing doors at Ham House, Surrey (see p. 116).

In a letter to Lady Mary Bridgeman of August 1700 Winde gave advice on the different shades of paint (A, B and C) that were available for use on wainscoting:

A is a dark wallnut tree & will requier a glossey varnishe and is very proper in Light chambers – B is properest for a Bedchamber . . . it represents a Light wallnut tree color – C is a wainscot color muche in voge ... ye use at present is a flate color that of torteschall & the mouldings being vayned marble...

A few years later than the work at Combe Abbey, the dado, soffits, doors and windowcases of the Cedar Staircase at Dyrham Park, Avon, were grained, c. 1692–4, to represent the North American or West Indian cedar used on the treads, risers and balusters. Samuel Hauduroy also 'painted' the Balcony Room of this house in 'marble' with the fluted pilasters in porphyry. Traces of his original marbling have been discovered under nineteenth-century graining but the gilded enrichments in this room are much as when first done.

PLASTERED WALLS
AND CEILINGS

The Jacobean style of plasterwork of the early seventeenth century in England, with its shallow interlocking ribs and low-relief ornament, often of vine motifs, was largely derived from vigorous Elizabethan plasterwork, which had also often been modelled *in situ* working from the scaffolding. The influence of many Continental engravers is discernible in a growing use of strapwork and arabesque, cartouches and mythological panels. Architectural books, with crude wood-cuts, made their appearance regularly and no gentleman could neglect studying them in selecting the decorative motifs for his plasterer to copy. They and their artisans could turn to the books issued by Jan Vriedeman de Vries (1563), Abraham de Bruyn (1584) and Wendel Dietterlein (1598). The issue of the 1611 edition of King James's Bible led to an increasing adaptation of well-known biblical themes and texts, while allusions to Classical knowledge were prompted by Robert Peake's 1611 English translation of the Dutch edition (1606) of Serlio's *Architettura*. Modellers of the time also used engravings in herbals and emblem books as sources for ornament. Whatever they found they set out on ceilings that had been carefully marked out into the relevant compartments.

Two of the most accomplished of the early-seventeenth-century plasterers were Richard Dungan and James Lee. Dungan worked at Knole, the Kent house of the Sackvilles, and at the Tudor palace of Whitehall (1606–9), while Lee was employed at Hatfield House, Hertfordshire, by Robert Cecil, 1st Earl of Salisbury. The work at Knole for Thomas Sackville, 1st Earl of Dorset, consists of geometric patterns of interlaced ribs with stylized, separately moulded flowers set in the spaces between them. It provides the

43, 44. *Detail of a plaster overmantel, c. 1620, at Boston Manor, Brentford (above), based on an engraving of 'Andromeda' by Abraham de Bruyn, 1584 (below).*

supreme example of plasterwork from the early years of the seventeenth century, as Lee's ceilings at Hatfield, presumably of a similar style, have disappeared. The earl's account book[33] records large payments to Dungan from 1605 to 1607 for 'ffresse and plaistering work', the carriage of plaster of Paris and 'for fretts & Other worke done at Knoll'. It seems probable that the flat interlaced ceiling snaking above the painted staircase and those in the Cartoon Gallery, the ballroom, the King's Room and the Reynolds Room are by Dungan.

A popular source of inspiration for modellers was Geoffrey Whitney's *A Choice of Emblems*, issued in 1586, its wood engravings being used as a basis for many kinds of decoration. Edward Stanyan followed Henry Peacham's emblem book, *Minerva Brittana or a Garden of heroical devises* (1612), in his twenty-one panels in the long gallery at Blickling Hall, Norfolk, which are naïve and lively in their miniature perfection. Stanyan executed his work in the period from August to December 1620 and charged £95 19s. The overmantel at Boston Manor, Brentford, 1620, by an unknown plasterer, is based on an engraving of 1584 by Abraham de Bruyn. It follows closely the disposition of ornament, although the central panel of Andromeda has been changed. The use of emblem books made a welcome change from the assumption that all that was good could only come from Serlio or Palladio.

At Bolsover Castle, Derbyshire, the unusual plasterwork in the Star Chamber has a central device which betokened interest in another form of expression – the emotional poem, printed in a diamond shape.[34] Further north, at Sheriff Hutton Park, Yorkshire, John Burridge and Francis Gunby, plasterers from York, made such diamond devices on the ceilings, and Burridge set his plaster foliage within the precise geometry of the ribs of the Bird and Baby Room and the Oak Parlour (*c*. 1620).[35] The human figure in stylized form joins the spirited representations of birds and beasts on the ceilings at Lanhydrock, Cornwall, while the twenty-four sections of the long gallery ceiling, *c*. 1640, illustrated events of the Old Testament from the Creation to the burial of Isaac.

Henry Peacham's recommended imitation of 'the Antique', which he defined as 'an unnatural or disorderly composition for delight's sake, of men, birds, fishes, flowers etc., without (as we say) Rhime or Reason, for the greater variety you show in your invention, the more you please' is found in Lanhydrock and in a number of houses in the West Country. Some of those, for example, in the High Street at Barnstaple or at Forde Abbey in Dorset are as interesting as any in Britain. Other similar lively work is found at Herringston and at Golden Farm, near Wiveliscombe, Somerset. Some of these ceilings were probably by John and Richard Abbott, members of a family of Devon plasterers, whose descendant, John Abbott II (1639–1727), invented the ideas and put down a great variety of his sketches in a notebook. This, together with some of John's tools, has survived[36] and gives a unique idea of the activity of a provincial Carolean plasterer and the influences that formed his vigorous style.

45. *Detail of the heavy naturalistic plasterwork, c. 1657,*
in the dining-room at Forde Abbey, Dorset,
possibly by Richard Abbott of Barnstaple.

One of the characteristics of such a provincial plasterer's activity was his frequent use of pendants. At Lanhydrock they are unusual: small, sculptured figures are encased within a framework built on metal armatures, one of which terminates in a hook to support a lamp. Pendants of this elaborate kind and date – the 1630s – are a development from the flat medieval roof boss which hid the intersection of ribs, and they can be seen at the two Northamptonshire houses of Rushton Hall and Canons Ashby. Pendants are also found extensively in Scottish houses, such as Glamis Castle and Auchterhouse, by Dundee. The succeeding years saw the pendant gradually decline in favour as a decorative motif and, by the outbreak of the Civil Wars in 1642, it had gone altogether. A late example may be seen at Nettlecombe Court, Somerset (c. 1645), and there are, of course, a few from the eighteenth century, principally those in neo-Jacobean style at Audley

46. *A pendant on the long-gallery ceiling, c. 1640, at Lanhydrock, Cornwall.*
The pendant terminates in a hook to support a lamp.

End, Essex. Pendants also reappeared in 'Jacobethan' work of the nineteenth century, as misunderstood and bewildering as the outmoded style itself.

Styles and moods could not easily continue in a ferment of activity while the Civil Wars were taking their toll, but building and decoration did not cease altogether. It was not a time for lavish display and ostentation but for repairs, for quiet consolidation and, if one were lucky, for travel: Roger Pratt spent the Civil War years mostly in Italy, collecting his library and studying the buildings of what he was later to call 'the best authors of Architecture, viz., Serlio, Palladio and Scamozzi'.

At the cessation of the war in 1649, building once more stirred slowly to life. The south-front rooms at Wilton House were already under way

47. *The saloon ceiling plastered by John Grove senior, c. 1660, at Coleshill House, Berkshire. The house was destroyed by fire in 1952 but details of its plan and decoration are still vital to an understanding of seventeenth-century architecture.*

and Pratt returned from the Continent and started Coleshill House in Berkshire. There were similarities between the ceilings at Coleshill and that in the hall of the Queen's House at Greenwich, and further touches of Italy could be discerned in the heads of Roman emperors[37] in the niches and in the stiff swags and twenty shields in the cornice of the Coleshill saloon. Close parallels can be observed with the essentially English ceilings at Thorpe Hall, Northamptonshire, a house designed between 1654 and 1656 by Peter Mills, a leading London architect, who was acquainted with Pratt. With Wren and Hugh May, Mills was appointed a surveyor to supervise the rebuilding of London after the Great Fire of 1666.

There was still a stiffness in the plasterwork of the first half of the seventeenth century, although there were many exuberant outbursts, such as the ceilings of the mid 1650s at Forde Abbey, Dorset. The beasts, caryatid figures and emblazoned heraldic shields of these years betrayed a preoccupation with pattern-book and lineage. Whilst the influence of Roger Pratt was encouraging a concern for Classicism, he was quick to point out that it was not always necessary 'to proceede to a rash and foolish imitation' of Italian models. John Webb received some building commissions from Commonwealth leaders – his Gunnersbury House, Middlesex, and Amesbury House, Wiltshire, were being constructed by 1658 (in a Jonesian style but of a most original plan, both now gone) – but elaborate commissions for plasterers had to wait for the restoration of the king and the return of the court from its exile abroad.

An age of grandeur began with the king's return in 1660, when there was much for craftsmen to do in the royal palaces, neglected over long years. Stylistic constraints of the previous sixty years were thrown off and none was more active at this than the artificers of the Office of Works, which included the teams assembled by John Grove (c. 1610–76), its Master Plasterer. Grove's plasterwork at Coleshill House, c. 1660, was to set the standard for fifty years. At his death in 1676, John Grove's son, also John, succeeded him and was to serve the Surveyor, Sir Christopher Wren, and the Office of Works for a further thirty years until his own death in 1706. Their work was of unvarying quality, made from good, well-tried materials, beaten at least six times before use. Then it was set out in many forms with unerring accuracy, but seemingly in a free, abandoned, naturalistic style, amid the precisely moulded profiled ribs. No one has ever plastered a ceiling better than the Groves: ripe fruit, summer-lazy open flowers and curling fronds crawled across the vast lime-washed expanses of ceiling, which had been rendered completely flat by a process of 'floating', charged at a few pence a yard, and meticulously tested for flatness with a twelve-foot wooden rule.

Two London plasterers of this period – the 1660s – whose work was similarly accomplished, were Robert Bradbury and James Pettifer. We know Pettifer trained under the London plasterer Arthur Toogood, who was Master of the Plaisterers Company in 1663. Their best work outside London is at Sudbury Hall, Derbyshire, where they plastered ceilings in 1675–6. These are densely and richly decorated and deserve close attention. The house was begun for Mary Vernon in the reign of James I, but was far from finished when she died in 1622. It then stood empty as a partly completed shell until after the Restoration, when Mary's great-grandson, George Vernon, completed it. In doing so, he had the good sense to use excellent carvers, plasterers and painters.

In 1675–6 Bradbury and Pettifer provided the ceilings of the drawing-room, the parlour, the staircase hall, the well, the Queen's Bedroom and that of the 138-ft long gallery. They charged at the rate of 6s a yard and whilst to some eyes their decorations are florid and all-enveloping, the exuberantly fashioned ornament was at least confined to the spaces provided in the design. Just enough was allowed to stray beyond the limits set down by the moulded ribs to give a natural effect. In fact, the delicate swirling work, most of it moulded but carefully arranged so that it appeared to consist of many different parts, was positioned with such skill that Laurence Turner wrote in his book on decorative plasterwork in 1927 before the discovery of the accounts, 'the four well modelled amorini in the corners of the [staircase] cove [are] evidently by an Italian modeller, for no English plasterer could have developed so suddenly the ability to model the human figure ...' In the seven compartments of the long gallery ceiling and its frieze, there are curling flowers and foliage, shells, emperors' heads, horses galloping from cornucopias, and dragons and wild boar in unlikely proximity to each other.

The long years of apprenticeship undertaken by all craftsmen produced many competent plasterers able to work in a way similar to Bradbury and Pettifer. One such was Samuel Mansfield of Derby, who did other ceilings at Sudbury. Another was James Petiver (d. 1689), possibly, the father of 'James Pettifer', the Sudbury plasterer who went on to work for Sir Christopher Wren as late as 1702 in the City churches of St Bride's, and St James's, Piccadilly. When Lord Brooke created the state rooms at Warwick Castle his comptroller was paid, in 1671, for coach hire and gifts on a visit to London to view 'ffrettworkes' or decorated plaster ceilings. A few pages before the end of the 1669–71 account-book[38] (that for 1672–6 is, alas, missing), there is the entry: 'Mr Petiver & Mr Pelton for their draught and Estimate about the Frettworke 001.05.00.' It may be assumed that they are the artists of the deeply recessed ceilings surviving in the Cedar Drawing Room and the Blue Boudoir at Warwick Castle. Lord Brooke died in 1677 just as his series of state rooms was being completed.

The London plasterers, able to work for the Office of Works and constantly to improve their skills in a variety of demanding tasks, included several of outstanding ability. Two such were Edward Martin and Edward Goudge. Martin had been apprenticed to his father John in 1648 and whilst he seemed to get into trouble with the officers of his Worshipful Company for bad workmanship in his early years (along with James Pettifer who had worked at Sudbury), he excelled when occasion demanded.[39] This can be seen in his ceilings at Arbury Hall, Warwickshire, and Burghley House, Lincolnshire, and despite Martin's disagreements he became Master of the Plaisterers Company in 1699.

Sir Christopher Wren may have had a little to do with the Arbury ceiling as he wrote in 1674 to Sir Richard Newdigate about the doorway to the stable building there, and Martin had been working for Wren from 1671 in the City church of St Nicholas Cole Abbey, Queenhithe. Martin agreed in January 1678 to do the chapel ceiling at Arbury (together with one in a closet) for the sum of £48 'besides comeing and going and goat's hair'. The Arbury chapel ceiling, perfect in the small space of the Carolean chapel, shows the technical advances made by plasterers at this time in moulding ever-deeper ribs and applying decorative foliage to them. The Burghley ceilings (1682–3) are again deep and rich with mounds of applied foliage, finished in white limewash and presumably containing the fine white goat's hair which gave tensile strength to the mixture, but which was an expensive alternative to the more usual ox or horse-hair.

Edward Goudge may have had an early connection with the architect Nicholas Hawksmoor (c. 1661–1736). George Vertue wrote that Goudge did 'some frettworke ceilings' at Justice Mellust's house in Yorkshire. This was probably Samuel Mellish of Doncaster, Deputy Lieutenant for Yorkshire, who died in 1707. Vertue further indicated that Hawksmoor[40] was 'Clerk to Justice Mellust' and it seems probable Goudge introduced him to London circles.

It is, however, with the gentleman-architect Captain William Winde that Goudge's name is generally connected, and we owe it to Winde's letters, on occasion, to indicate the works by Goudge. Writing on 8 February 1690 to his cousin, Lady Mary Bridgeman, Winde stated:[41] 'Mr Goudge will undougtedly have a goode deall of worke for hee is now looked on as ye beste master in England in his profession as his worke att Combe, Hampstead, & Sr John Brownlowe's will Evidence.'

This letter, which I found in 1952, was the only evidence that Goudge was the plasterer at Belton House, Lincolnshire, until the discovery recently of a payment of £100 to him in 1687 (perhaps one of several) in the Belton archives. Winde may have been involved in the design of Belton because most of his favourite craftsmen, such as Goudge and the carpenter Jonathan Willcox, worked there. But his name does not appear, only that of the mason-contractor, William Stanton, better known for his marble funerary monuments. The Belton ceilings, particularly those in the staircase well and the chapel, are of very high quality. A drawing by Goudge in the Bodleian Library, Oxford, for the dining-room ceiling at Hampstead Marshall, Berkshire (1686), shows in an inscription that the design was accepted by William Winde. Winde was to state a year or two later, in a letter of July 1688 to Lady Bridgeman, that the plasterer made all his own designs and had been employed by him for six or seven years. Although Winde's supervision of much work[42] for the Earl of Craven at Hampstead Marshall,

*48. The staircase ceiling at Belton House, Lincolnshire, plastered by Edward Goudge,
c. 1687, for Sir John Brownlow, whose crest is in the four corners.*

Combe Abbey and elsewhere was very lax (and in any case has now largely
disappeared) he probably used Goudge on most occasions, perhaps even
at Dunster Castle, Somerset.

In the 1680s the owner of Dunster Castle was Colonel Francis Luttrell.
Both he and Winde fought at the Battle of Sedgemoor in June 1685 and
through their respective army careers they may have known one another
in earlier years. The dining-room ceiling at Dunster is incised with the date

*49. Detail of the dining-room ceiling at Dunster Castle, Somerset,
showing the date 'MDCLXXXI' (1681); probably plastered by Edward Goudge.*

'1681' in Roman numerals. Its authorship must remain speculative but it
seems at least probable that Winde and Goudge were involved. There is
also the Dunster staircase (noted below), which is very reminiscent of the
work of the younger Edward Pierce, another of Winde's craftsmen and son
of the painter who had worked in the Double Cube Room at Wilton House.

I can only give a few mentions of late and lesser seventeenth-century
plasterwork. Sir Roger Hill, High Sheriff of Buckinghamshire, began to
rebuild his house, Denham Place, in 1688. He had William Stanton, fresh
from his work at Belton, to supervise although in the end he received very
little for his pains – £214, compared with some £5,000 at Belton. The
London plasterer William Parker was also employed, and he and his patron
were obviously lovers of the drawings of Francis Barlow (as engraved by
Hollar) executed for his *Several Wayes in Hunting* (1671). The drawing-room
frieze provides as charming a decoration as can be found anywhere in the
British Isles. Parker was no mean performer and imbued the cupid in the
centre of the Tapestry Room ceiling with a freedom only recaptured by
the Italian *stuccatori* forty years later. At Denham he received a little over
£273 for his ceilings. Fortunately the precise record survives,[43] without
which it would be impossible to know the work was Parker's. It is tempting
to ascribe to him the 1691 ceiling at Fawley Court, Buckingham, but this
is the stuff of attribution. Plasterwork research is bedevilled by attributions
in the plethora of surviving anonymous and unsigned ceilings.

A local 'vernacular style' may be found, for example, at Eye Manor, Herefordshire, Clarke Hall, Wakefield, and Astley Hall, Lancashire. The great hall and drawing-room ceilings at Astley are fantasies: the plaster figures intertwine with great scallop shells, palm-branches and lively festoons in a flamboyant display suggestive of the rim of a giant Dutch silver salver rich with heavy *repoussé* work. The idealized flowers and gingerbread-styled motifs that appear at Clarke Hall are probably the work of a local plasterer. The ceilings at Eye Manor have some similarities with the plasterwork at Holyroodhouse, the royal palace in Edinburgh. This has led to the suggestion that the same plasterers were employed. Reference has also been made[44] to the panels of scrolling acanthus at Eye Manor which have some parallels with those in *The Art of the Plasterer*, a book reissued in about 1680 by the younger Edward Pierce.

Whilst London plasterers may have been involved at Eye Manor, they were certainly employed at Holme Lacy, the Herefordshire home of the Scudamore family. The master mason at Holme Lacy was Anthony Deane, who contracted to build the house in 1674 to the approval of the architect, Hugh May. Deane also acted as mason at Horseheath Hall, Cambridgeshire, building to the designs of Sir Roger Pratt, who undoubtedly employed London craftsmen. Whether John Grove, or George Dunsterfield and John Houlbert (the London plasterers working at Holyroodhouse in 1675–8) ever travelled to work at Holme Lacy we shall, perhaps, never know. All we have is competent London-style ceilings of some quality.

The last years of the seventeenth century had allowed, through the combined development of taste and technique, a finer plasterwork to appear in England than ever before. Many plasterers, however, were not able to rid themselves of stiff geometric borders and a hesitation at handling lifesize figures. On 25 March 1702 'the beste master in England' in his profession, Edward Goudge, wrote[45] to Sir Thomas Coke about other elements that were adversely affecting his trade: 'for want of money occasioned by the War, and by the use of ceiling painting, the employment which hath been my chiefest pretence hath always been dwindling away, till now its just come to nothing...' There is no more known work by Goudge after this and the date of his death has not yet been traced.

WINDOWS

Two most significant developments in the construction of windows occurred during the seventeenth century. Firstly, there was the adoption of a timber,

50. The drawing-room at East Riddlesden Hall, Yorkshire,
showing a stone mullion and transom window and wood panelling, c. 1648.

rather than a stone, frame (although the latter remained in use) and, more importantly, there was a fashion, after the Restoration, for a vertical sliding sash-window, in which, by use of weights working on pulleys and cords as counter-balances, the window stayed open at any selected position. It is useful to bear in mind that whilst windows admitted light, the patron, pacing the long walks through his Baroque house, could also gaze out through them at a contrived formal landscape, running away in straight lines and radiating rides as far as the eye could see. It was no accident that the views matched the position of the windows, and that many of these were built out as bays from which to appreciate the scene more fully. And if, during cold dark days, there was no wish to look out at grey misty reaches of sheep-dotted pastures, then swinging shutters hid all from sight.

The grandest type of stone window was the three-light form, with the larger central opening arched; it was known as the 'Venetian window'. Palladio used it on the grand scale on the façades of the basilica at Vicenza and it was, in its form, derived from antique Rome and was later illustrated in Serlio's fourth book of his *Architettura* (1537). It was a form that bridged the void between precise columns and it could easily be glazed. When Inigo Jones introduced it to England towards 1620, however, he based his drawings on those in Scamozzi's *Idea della Architettura universale* (1615).

Writing later, in 1756, Isaac Ware says that Venetian windows are of a kind 'calculated for shew, and very pompous in their nature; and, when executed with judgment, of exteme elegance' (*A Complete Body of Architecture*). A superb example is in the centre of the south front of Wilton House, Wiltshire, designed by Isaac de Caus in the late 1630s. Although enthusiasm for the Venetian window in the work of Jones and his contemporaries was short-lived it was, however, an appropriate motif for resuscitation in the early-eighteenth-century Palladian and Jonesian revival.[46]

At the opening of the seventeenth century, glass for use in any kind of window was usually only available in small pieces, which were set into patterns and held by lead 'cames'. The patterns themselves were set out in 1615 in Walter Gedde's *A Book of Sundry Draughts principally serving for Glasiers*, but although they may have looked attractive the windows were never easy to open and were easily damaged by strong winds. This may have led, in part, to consideration of timber-framed windows, which slid upwards, one part over the other. Such windows were known in England from the late sixteenth century, if allusions to them by Shakespeare can be accepted. Dr. H. J. Louw, in a detailed survey of the origin of the sash-window,[47] has written: 'Could Shakespeare have used the phrase "Ere I let fall the windowes of mine eyes" if he had not been familiar with vertically sliding windows?'

Looked at with other literary references it is clear that the 'drawing windows' listed in inventories were shutters made to slide, consistent with drawing the curtains,[48] and that the sliding vertical window was not a true sash-window. Sliding windows only came to be drawn and used prominently in houses after the Restoration.

Within a year or two of 1660, when the court had settled back to a normal, if more progressive, routine, 'shashes', 'shassis' or 'shashis' windows were in use and are mentioned in the royal accounts for 1662. The French word for any frame, particularly those for windows, is *chassis* from which the English 'sash' derives. These windows had a combination of glass and oiled paper for better weatherproofing. Sir Roger Pratt in his notes 'of the most noble Houses of France ...' wrote: 'Their glass is for the most part placed on the inside of their walling, and another glasing or paper etc. on the outside again which they call "Chasses".'[49]

Little is known of the details and appearance of 'shassis' windows of the 1660s, but much more of the new counter-balanced windows, introduced by the early 1670s. John Maitland, 1st Duke of Lauderdale (1616–82), who was both intelligent (he was a master of Latin, Greek and Hebrew and had an exceptional memory) and knowledgeable about Continental practices, was soon involved with building. This included the remodelling of Ham House, Surrey, two other London residences, and three Scottish castles – the duke was Charles II's powerful Secretary for Scotland. Some twenty-six sash-windows were installed at Ham House during 1673[50] by the joiner Henry Harlow, under the direction of the gentleman-architect, William Samwell (1628–76). The windows were operated by brass pulleys set within boxes at the side of the oak frames. A central mullion gave greater strength and rigidity although the panes were small – sixty being a typical number in the garden-front windows – and 'white inside glass' was installed to keep out draughts. This early form of 'double-glazing' was also noted by Celia Fiennes at Ashtead Park, Surrey, in about 1700: 'all the windows are sarshes and large squares of glass, I observ'd they are double sashes to make the house warmer for its stands pretty bleake . . .'

In the Duke and Duchess of Lauderdale's Privy Garden lodging in Whitehall, part of the royal palace, Thomas Kinward, the Master Joiner of the Office of Works (whom Dr Louw credits with the introduction of the sash-window to England, from where its use spread to France and Holland), installed double sash-windows in the duchess's dressing-room. The accounts for this were signed by the Surveyor, Sir Christopher Wren, who also introduced sash-opening to the windows of the royal palaces at Whitehall, Hampton Court and Kensington, building, or re-building, in the years 1685 to 1696. Those at Chatsworth and some other houses had gilded glazing bars.

DOORS

When Sir Balthazar Gerbier wrote his *Counsel and Advice to all Builders* in 1664 he stated: 'the wideness of the door must serve for two to pass at once, that is to say the doors of Chambers of a pallace . . .' adding that the height of the door should be double its width. In other lesser rooms the door should be of sufficient height for a man 'of compleat stature' to pass through with a hat upon his head.[51] The door itself was divided into as many as ten panels of varying size, although the six-panelled door was the most usual by the end of the seventeenth century.

The staircase at Ham House, Surrey, was constructed in 1637–8 and on the landings there are handsome doors and doorcases. They were the work of the joiner Thomas Carter, whose bill included charges for five doors and doorcases. The woodwork was painted and 'veined' to simulate walnut and the mouldings were picked out with gilding by Matthew Gooderick, whose work I have noted earlier at Castle Ashby, Northamptonshire. His activities at Ham House gave the simple plane of Carter's doors – two to each frame – an elegance that is their prime characteristic, a tribute to Gooderick's considerable ability.

In 1658, during the quiet late years of the Commonwealth, Peter Mills designed Thorpe Hall, Northamptonshire, for Oliver St John, Chief Justice to Oliver Cromwell.[52] The doorcases at the house – of which a drawing of one survives – were probably executed by the joiner Thomas Whiting and

51. *Drawing in pen, ink and wash of a 'Door case in ye Great Parlor' at Thorpe Hall, Northamptonshire, c. 1658 (Victoria and Albert Museum, London, No. 1833–85). The doorcase itself is now at Leeds Castle, Kent, installed c. 1920.*

by Richard Cleere, the carver who worked for Wren on the Great Model of St Paul's Cathedral. They were to work in the early 1660s at Cobham Hall, Kent, under Mills's supervision, and architects usually stayed with reliable craftsmen they knew. The doorcase and panelling from the great parlour (or library as it was later called) at Thorpe Hall were removed *c.* 1920 and inserted into Leeds Castle, Kent.[53] This door has ten panels and the architrave of the doorcase is richly carved over its formal architectural proportions. The architrave was a good position for carving, but this is also found around framed panels and overdoor pictures, or flanking a bracketed pediment. Additional emphasis was given to the door by flanking it with panelled or fluted pilasters. These appear alongside the doors to the Double Cube Room at Wilton House, Wiltshire, where a rich and monumental effect was needed to stand out against the white and gilded panelling, gilded soft-wood swags, great paintings by van Dyck and the overbearing cove and ceiling paintings, redolent with mythological story.

I have mentioned the richness of the plasterwork on the ceilings at Sudbury Hall, Derbyshire, and this is repeated on the soffits of the staircase landings and high in the stairwell itself. There are two doorcases, *c.* 1676, on the landings, each with two ten-panelled, bevelled doors. They are the work of Edward Pierce the younger, the talented London carver in wood, stone and marble who was capable of erecting a whole building himself. The carved pediments are on broken entablatures with sprays of olive and palm in a central panel. The architraves have Corinthian pilasters finishing in scrolled ends at each lower side. Whilst the doorcases sit together a little awkwardly, at right angles in the corners of the landing, there is no denying the style and balance they give to an already rich setting.

Sir William Winde's letters to Lady Mary Bridgeman and to William, Lord Craven, in the 1680s and 1690s are again illuminating on the current decorative practices.[54] Symmetry was ever a concern and the long vistas in houses such as Petworth, Sussex, are given additional emphasis by a series of open doors. In October 1688 Winde advised Lady Bridgeman that for the four doors at the sides of the hall at Castle Bromwich Hall, Warwickshire, 'I would willingly have the matter ordered soe that they may be all allike, & of one and ye same dimension.' Most of Winde's designs in marble and wood were executed by the carpenter Jonathan Wilcox, the joiners John Sims and Robert Aiscough and the London carver Edward Pierce the younger, whom I have noted working at Sudbury Hall, Derbyshire. He was also to provide the carving on the great staircase itself, in the new foliated style introduced in the 1670s.

It was common in lesser gentry houses for the door to be framed to match the panelled wainscoting, but to have similar, smaller panels. A design much used in farmhouses was a door formed of three or more timber planks, of varying width, cut and used vertically to fill the opening, with cross battens on one side. These were fixed to the planks by heavy iron studs and two long iron hinges ran horizontally across two thirds of the

52. *The doors at the top of the carved staircase at Sudbury Hall, Derbyshire*
were carved by Edward Pierce the younger, c. 1676.
The staircase has balusters of foliated panels also carved by Pierce.

door. The head of the door often copied Tudor patterns in stone, having a four-centred arch with moulded jambs and simple sunk spandrels.[55]

CHIMNEYPIECES

At all periods the design of chimneypieces was affected by the availability of suitable materials. Alabaster and marble were worked by masons who sought contrasting effects with the use of black, white and veined marbles. The great panelled marble chimneypieces found in the Jacobean houses of Hatfield, Knole and Blickling were often the work of foreign craftsmen settled in England, such as Maximilian Colt, the Cure family from Holland, and Giles de Whitt. Early in 1601 Lord Cobham was contracting through his steward for de Whitt to make two chimneypieces for Cobham Hall, Kent, and he may well have made the one in the gallery there, a year or so before.[56] They were all as elaborate as great coloured funerary monuments (at which the foreign craftsmen also excelled). In the chimneypiece by Colt in the library at Hatfield House, Hertfordshire, a likeness of the 1st Earl of Salisbury is mounted in a Venetian mosaic of c. 1610, sent from Italy as a gift by the English ambassador, Sir Henry Wotton. The house was then being built under the supervision of Robert Lyminge, or Liminge (d. 1628), who also supervised the building of Blickling Hall, Norfolk, in the 1620s. The best surviving chimneypiece at Blickling, originally painted to resemble different marbles, is in the great chamber of Sir Henry Hobart's house (now the South Drawing Room). It has a Jacobean stone surround and a cast-iron fireback bearing the arms of Queen Elizabeth.

At Knole, in Kent, the woodwork and plasterwork are all of fine quality but the carving reaches its height in the great chimneypieces in the ballroom, the Crimson Drawing Room and the Cartoon Gallery. Some appear to be the work of Maximilian Colt, the Flemish sculptor active in England at the start of the seventeenth century. The style of ornament is close to Netherlandish patterns. One of the three marbles used, the grey, was quarried locally at Bethersden, near Ashford, and is used to good effect in the lintel above the fireplace. Here the 1st Earl of Dorset's arms and Garter (to which Noble Order he had been elevated in 1598) are incised. The work seems to have been done c. 1607, as Cornelius Cuer was paid £26 10s in December 1607 for 'stones for a chimney piece in the Wth drawing Chamber at Knoll'. He was obviously well acquainted with Colt. Black and white marble are used on the overmantel to provide a background for alabaster garlands of flowers and musical instruments.

53 (opposite). Chimneypiece of marble and alabaster
in the ballroom at Knole, Kent, carved c. 1607 by Cornelius Cuer.

In the Crimson Drawing Room the overmantel has Bethersden marble pilasters incised to represent a pattern of strawberries and wild flowers. These flank a central panel where *putti* ride on a pair of sphinxes, holding aloft great trophies of arms. The fireplace opening has caryatids each side with bronze heads and feet. Paired caryatids appear again on the marble and alabaster overmantel in the Cartoon Gallery, as well as in the painted 'grotesques' in its bay windows and the deep recess opposite the fireplace.

Despite this foreign work of consummate quality, it has been asserted that Inigo Jones 'was incomparably the best chimney-piece designer in Northern Europe'.[57] Some of this went hand-in-hand with his concern for the proportion of rooms, in which every decorative feature had to be positioned correctly. Obviously, there was a lesser need for chimneypieces in warmer countries, except as decoration: the chimneypiece was essentially confined in use to the colder lands north of the Alps, and there it was a principal feature of the decorative treatment of the walls of a room. Consequently, there is only one *nappa* or chimney-opening given in Scamozzi's *Idea della Architettura universale* (1615). When Jones did his masterly elevation of a chimneypiece for Oatlands Park, Surrey (now in the collections of the Royal Institute of British Architects), he adopted the broken pediment with its central mask-face from a French source, Jean Barbet's *Livre d'Architecture, d'autels, et de cheminees* (1632). With its engravings by Abraham Bosse, this became a very popular source-book and was re-issued in Paris and Amsterdam in 1641.[58] Both Jones and John Webb used it again as a source at Wilton House, Wiltshire. The Renaissance chimneypiece in Italy and in France had evolved from the overhanging Gothic chimneypiece with its hood (or breast), which could rise even to the ceiling. It was this upper area of display that could be framed by pilasters and have an entablature resting on them or on consoles. It was the place for a panel of painting or sculpture in round, oval, or octagonal shape, or even for a looking-glass.

The use of marble, common in Italy, and found in the French chimney-pieces at the Tuileries and Versailles in the 1660s, was slowly adopted in England. Marble was used alongside stone, alabaster, stucco, and wood for overmantels.

The corner chimneypiece in England was first commented on by John Evelyn (*Diary*, 22 July 1670), who remarked that many of the rooms in Charles II's house at Newmarket 'had the chimnies in the angles and corners, a mode now introduced by His Majesty, which I do at no hand approve of. I predict it will spoile many noble houses and rooms, if followed'. Writing in the mid 1690s, Roger North set out at length his thoughts on

54. *The chimneypiece in the Colonnade Room at Wilton House, Wiltshire,*
designed c. 1650 by either Inigo Jones or John Webb, after a French design by Pierre Barbet.

'Chimnys, Smoaking and Cures'. It is not to our purpose to repeat him but he made several interesting points. Firstly, corner chimneys had continued in use and could be appropriate when standing 'in a waste place, a corner' especially as they could serve four rooms by one stack. To their detriment, they were far from the light, whereas a flat chimney was placed 'in your eye at the entrance and is the best ornament the end of a room is capable of'. According to North, angle chimneys were therefore only suitable for small rooms, such as withdrawing-rooms or closets, and should have overmantels that rose in recessive steps, incorporating displays of oriental flowerpots.

Such chimneypieces became the favoured place for the display of oriental porcelain or Dutch Delft pottery during the reign of William and Mary in the 1690s. Porcelain collecting was one of the queen's passions and the practice of decorating a room with china was given some impetus by designs in the publications of William III's Huguenot architect and designer, Daniel Marot. As Jean Berain's chief pupil, he had fled from France to Holland after the revocation of the Edict of Nantes in 1685, and entered William of Orange's service there. He then spent several short periods in England after William's accession to the English throne, and his engravings of the current French and Dutch styles of chimneypiece were obviously an important factor in the appearance of several chimneypieces at Hampton Court, Kensington Palace and in more distant houses, such as those of Dyrham Park, Gloucestershire, and Beningbrough, Yorkshire. Dyrham was built in 1692–1704, by one of William III's principal ministers, William Blathwayt, who had spent long years as a diplomat at The Hague, as well as travelling in Europe and Scandinavia. Beningbrough was built from 1716 by a York joiner, William Thornton.

One of the most important changes, which led to trimming away the seeming bulk of great Jacobean chimneypieces, was the insertion of mirror glass in the overmantel. Although the innovation started in France in the early years of the seventeenth century, it was not common there until the 1680s and did not feature in engravings until the 1690s. With candle-light reflected in their silvered surfaces, they became a useful feature of a room's decoration. The entire mirrored room remained a Continental feature only.

Elaborate chimneypieces (and there are splendid sketches for them by Grinling Gibbons in the Wren portfolio in the Soane Museum) were intended, of course, for the grand house. They were 'continued' – that is, they had an upper structure of stucco, wood, stone or marble, instead of terminating as in the 'simple' type at a cornice or pediment. (These definitions are taken from Isaac Ware's *A Complete Body of Architecture* (1756).) Much attention to the use of carved and veneered panelling, as at Chatsworth, could make an attractive surround to a simple stone-moulded opening, focusing the eyes but perhaps overwhelming them with decoration in excess. At Ham House, Surrey, there are several of these simple bolection-mould marble and stone fireplace surrounds done in the 1670s. In the Queen's Closet there, the effect is grander as the fireplace surround is of scagliola or imitation marble. This is made from gypsum, earth colours, sand and water and is rolled out like pastry. It is then set as a 'plaster' skim over a hard base, often formed of rubble or brick dust. At Ham it is beautifully inlaid with the ducal coronet and cipher on both hearth-stone and lintel, surrounded by flowers and foliage. On the two jambs classical columns are bedecked with yet more flowers.

55. *The scagliola chimneypiece surround in the Queen's Closet, c. 1678,*
at Ham House, Surrey. The ducal coronets and ciphers,
which also appear on the hearth, belong to the 1st Duke of Lauderdale.

In lesser houses it was the simple surround of wood or stone which was common. In the early-seventeenth-century examples this was often still of four-centred Tudor shape, as was many a doorcase. Gradually the bolection-moulded surround became more common, having a bold outline of double curvature raised above the general plane of its surface. The chimneypiece in the drawing-room at East Riddlesden, Yorkshire, is dated 1648 but is outmoded, having a four-centred stone arch with three pendants above and an inlaid overmantel. A shelf in the modern sense was never used, but there are simple architectural forms of chimneypiece, common at the end of the seventeenth century, in which an elliptical arch and key block were prominent features. The opening could also feature Dutch blue-and-white tiles (as useful for fireplace as for dairy or alcove buffet) and a heavy, moulded iron Wealden fireback could bear the owner's proud arms, to flicker in the firelight.

STAIRCASES

The characteristic feature of a Jacobean staircase was the massive nature of its component parts: the oak newels, balustrade, handrail and string. The newel, or central vertical support, was a ready and prominent area for carved ornament. The style was set by the great staircase at Knole, Kent, which, using the classical orders in correct sequence, was erected for Thomas Sackville, 1st Earl of Dorset, between 1605 and 1608. It is decorated with semi-grisaille paintings of the Six Virtues in panels above simulated strapwork and balusters. Doric columns support the arcade on the ground floor with Ionic at first-floor level. Corinthian pilasters rise above these to the frieze. The staircase was fitted into a square chamber contained within a tower and therefore had to be provided with a handrail on the unenclosed side. This handrail is supported by turned balusters and the two newel-posts between the Classical columns, with counterparts on the side walls, are surmounted by the Sackville supporters of leopards holding shields. Sir Henry Wotton in his *Elements of Architecture* (1624) recommended half-paces, or landings 'at competent distances for reposing on the way'. At Knole the intervals are at nine, seven and nine steps. The breadth of the stair, according to Wotton, was both to 'gratify the beholder' and to avoid encounters.

At Hatfield House, Hertfordshire, each newel or side-post is topped with *amorini* bearing objects such as spheres or lutes and with lions holding shields. The balusters are of the flat form and part of the string is also carved with pierced shapes. There are also a pair of contemporary dog-gates, mounted across the sixth step, in line with the second newel and side-posts. On the newel at the top of the staircase is the carving of a figure with a rake and basket of flowers, said to represent John Tradescant (d. 1637),

56 (opposite). Detail showing part of the staircase, 1605–1608, at Knole, Kent. The newel posts are surmounted by the Sackville supporters of leopards holding shields.

57. Staircase in the great hall at Blickling Hall, Norfolk. The hall dates from the 1620s but was reconstructed in 1767. Watercolour by J. C. Buckler, signed and dated 1820.

who was gardener to Charles I and to Robert Cecil. The Hatfield staircase, *c.* 1611, is the masterpiece of the carver John Bucke, who also carved the screens for the hall. It was originally painted in rich 'heraldic' colours with gilding by Rowland Bucket.

At Blickling Hall, Norfolk, the third of these massive Jacobean staircases, *c.* 1622–7, rises out of the great hall. Decorative oak carvings are reared up on both the newel-posts and the side-posts. While the staircase was enlarged in the eighteenth century, using pine, it still forms, together with those at Knole and Hatfield, an important statement of the Jacobean carver's skill in the robust portrayal of figures and beasts.

There were various ways of filling the balustrade – the space between the newels: at Knole, turned balusters were used and at Hatfield and Blickling, flat carved balusters. A variation of these two forms was to use carved arches between the treads and the handrail and one example of this can be seen at Burton Agnes Hall, Yorkshire. The West Staircase at Castle Ashby, Northamptonshire, *c.* 1635, has a variation of this type of decoration, in the form of open-work cartouches supported by strapwork and scrolling. A similar variation is found at Cromwell House, Highgate, where the staircase, *c.* 1640, in an open well, is relatively narrow and is carried right

58 (opposite). The staircase, c. 1611, at Hatfield House, Hertfordshire, carved by John Bucke, with flat balusters and decorated newel-posts. Note the contemporary dog-gate.

59. *The great staircase at Ham House, Surrey, constructed in 1637–8
with carved and pierced panels instead of balusters, painted to imitate walnut.*

up to the second floor. The panels have pierced decoration of heavy raked
strapwork; a massive handrail is big enough for a parapet, and carved figures
surmount the newel-posts.

One of the best staircases was that erected, *c.* 1637–8, at Ham House,
Surrey. It is an early example of a type of staircase with carved and pierced
panels that was important just prior to, and for fifteen years or so after, the
Restoration. The carved trophies of arms at Ham are unusual. Painted to
simulate walnut, one panel contains the abbreviation 'SPQR' (translated as
'The Senate and People of Rome'), and gun barrels, swords, spears and
drums appear in all the panels. The long landing has doors and cases by
the joiner Thomas Carter. A comparison of the carved baskets of flowers on

the newel-posts with similar ones at Sudbury Hall, Derbyshire, c. 1675–6, shows how little of innovation was to occur in the work of some joiners and carvers in the intervening forty years. Indeed, the staircase at Dunster Castle, Somerset, bears a very close resemblance to that at Ham House, Surrey, but fifty years or so separate their respective creation.

There was, however, progress elsewhere. When Sir Roger Pratt was building Horseheath, Cambridgeshire, 1663–5 (demolished, alas, in 1777), he set out in his notes what was presumably common to all staircases in the newer 'Italian' mood: some detailed consideration of proportions of the component parts. The dimensions of the rails, base and posts were to be taken from the diameter of the balusters. Thus, at Horseheath, the balusters being 6 in, the breadth of rails and base 'being wrought on both sides alike' was necessarily 16 in. The posts were 16 in square and the thickness of the rail between 6 and 7 in. The stair consisted of two flights, the one going, the other returning; between each there was a long landing with a smaller 'hanging' landing in the middle of each flight. It is regrettable that Pratt's important house of Coleshill, Berkshire, was destroyed by fire in 1952. It was fortunately well-illustrated and photographed in 1929, which is some slight consolation[59] at the tragic loss of such a seminal building.

Both Inigo Jones and Sir Roger Pratt, with their Italian training and travels forming important factors in their thinking, were concerned to give good space and light to a staircase. Pratt listed the advantages of 'new designed backstaires', one of the most important being that a 'cupolo' would 'throwe downe light to ye bottome of these staires'. This practice of using an oval lantern for light was to have a far-reaching effect in at least one contemporary staircase, that at Ashburnham House, Westminster, built in about 1662. The staircase uses its space well with the drama building up, in almost Berniniesque style, to a view of the dome through an oval opening. It suggests, however, more knowledge of French prototypes (such as that above the staircase at the Château of Blois) and was designed, possibly, by John Webb, who had considerable interest in French interior design. John, 1st Earl of Ashburnham, descendant from the William Ashburnham for whom the house was built, told Batty Langley that Webb was the architect employed. The plan and section of the staircase appear in Isaac Ware's *Designs of Inigo Jones and Others* (1st edition, c. 1733).

At Coleshill, Pratt decided on a double-flight of stairs, which dominated the staircase hall. The treads were wide and easy, set between great square panelled newel-posts on which a carved lion's head with a ring supported a fruit 'drop'. The balusters were enriched with carved acanthus and along the string, a series of ribboned swags sprang from a cartouche at the centre of the upper gallery, and stretched out to sculptured heads at the corners, before descending in rich sweeps to the foot of the stairs. The carving was done in 1662 by Richard Cleare (d. 1690), a skilled London carver who is best remembered for his work on the Great Model for St Paul's Cathedral, 1673–4, where he cut more than 350 capitals as well as festoons and cherubim's heads. Cleare apparently did his work for the Coleshill stairs in London, for certain 'festoons' were sent down to Coleshill in a basket, with a man who was paid 26s 'ffor his goeing down to set up the ffestoons on the stayres'.[60]

The staircase at Coleshill was in the forefront of the move away from the use of Jacobean pierced panels. These returned, albeit in a different guise, in more naturalistic forms, with great panels of wreathing acanthus and other carved foliage. An early example, c. 1658, is the staircase at Thorpe Hall, Northamptonshire, which rears up between the hall and the library. Its plan was, however, a limited one as it only served the north-east and south-east rooms, and it was not opened out until 1859 by archways and a steep subsidiary flight of steps to other areas. There are two pierced panels to the balustrade of the first flight and to that enclosing the east landing. Similar foliated acanthus panels are found in the staircases at Forde Abbey, Dorset, Tyttenhanger, Hertfordshire, and Eltham Lodge, Kent. At Eltham, the acanthus is separated in each panel by a chubby boy. The carving is from pinewood blocks, some 4 in. thick. Unusual planning by Hugh May gave two landings, one at the west and, at a higher level, one in the centre of the house. It is a small indication of his skill as an architect and user of space to advantage.

Pinewood was originally intended to be painted in white or a light colour and this was done on the staircases at Coleshill and at Eltham (later oak-grained). Though the National Trust was keen to be accurate, it was nevertheless bold in its decision in 1967 to paint in white Edward Pierce the younger's staircase, 1676–7, at Sudbury Hall, Derbyshire.[61] Supportive references to the use of white paint, found in 'scrapes', are made by Celia Fiennes and Captain William Winde. Celia Fiennes, who saw Grinling Gibbons's wood carvings at Windsor Castle in the late 1690s, remarked: 'soe thinn the wood and all white natural wood without varnish', a reference presumably to the limewood favoured by many carvers. Captain Winde, in giving the directions in 1685 for painting at Combe Abbey, Warwickshire (previously referred to), stated that the little staircase should be 'white and vein'd'.

Edward Pierce (c. 1635–95) was the son of Edward Pierce, the London painter-stainer who worked at Wilton House, Wiltshire, and was, according

60. *Part of staircase at Sudbury Hall, Derbyshire, by Edward Pierce the younger,*
c. 1676 (painted white in 1967 on the basis of historical precedents).
Plaster ceiling by Robert Bradbury and James Pettifer.

to George Vertue, 'much esteem'd in his time'. The son also became well
esteemed, but as a mason-sculptor, able to work in wood, stone, marble
and bronze; he is well-known for his fine marble busts of Oliver Cromwell
and of Sir Christopher Wren (both in the Ashmolean Museum, Oxford) as
well as for much carved woodwork in London City churches.[62] Pierce's
carved work on the Sudbury staircase is of a high order and seems to be

*61. French engraving of an acanthus frieze, c. 1670, by Jean Le Pautre (1618–82),
probably used as the source for staircase panels such as those at Sudbury Hall, Derbyshire.*

loosely based on an engraving, *c.* 1670, by Jean Le Pautre, of foliated friezes.
Pierce had known of such engravings for a long time and he re-issued a set
of twelve engraved designs for friezes based on those his father had
published in 1640. Pierce is credited, on the authority of the seventeenth-
century Staffordshire historian, Robert Plot, writing in his *Natural History
of Staffordshire* (1686), with the staircase at Wolseley Hall, Staffordshire
(unfortunately demolished in 1966). The Wolseley staircase was illustrated
in 1929[63] and shows how, following on from Sudbury, Pierce turned
towards the more fashionable acanthus and spiral-twisted balusters. The
newels are still of square, earlier form and he may have amended the
staircase in part only. There was also excellent panelling and carved
doorcases elsewhere in the house. This spiral or 'swash turning' was noted
by Joseph Moxu. in the 1694 edition of *Mechanick Exercises* as a suitable
enrichment and he gave details for turning it on the lathe.

It is not known if Pierce worked for Captain Winde at Powis Castle,
Powys, as he did on many other occasions. It has been assumed that the
staircase there was probably constructed under Winde's supervision in
about 1675, a year after the earldom was created. An earl's coronet appears
on the painted ceiling by Antonio Verrio, noted earlier. The only recorded
mention of Winde's presence at Powis is in a letter of 1697. I am assuming
that he was at the castle at an earlier date and that the woodwork of the

staircase probably dates from the early 1680s. The balusters are enriched at the lower swelling with carved acanthus leaves. A comparison of the Powis staircase with that at Combe Abbey, Warwickshire, [64] which is of 1684 and indisputably by Winde and Pierce, shows an almost identical treatment in the carving of the balusters and rail, which strengthens the attribution.

There are two more staircases with foliated panels which merit mention – that formerly at Cassiobury Park, Hertfordshire, and that at Dunster Castle, Somerset. The Cassiobury staircase, attributed, unconvincingly, to Grinling Gibbons, c. 1678, is rich in carved acanthus, flowers and seed-pods and was fortunately saved when the contents of Cassiobury were sold in June 1922. Part of the staircase is now installed in the Metropolitan Museum, New York. Three principal woods were used at Cassiobury: pine for the handrail and oak-leaf-and-acorn string; solid ash for the balustrade and scrollwork, with pine cone-finials; and oak for the treads, risers and landings, which would suffer most wear. The oak-leaf wreath, 9 in wide, and the acorns on the string, 'were a royalist device alluding to the twenty-four hours which Charles II spent hidden in the Boscobel 'Royal Oak' during the Civil War.[65] The staircase is shown *in situ* in illustrations in *Country Life* for 1910 (17 September).

The Dunster Castle staircase, c. 1683–4, with its carved elm balustrade, rises from the arcaded hall and has considerable similarities to the earlier one at Ham House, Surrey, in the use of military trophies. These are allusive to the military career of Colonel Francis Luttrell, who had married in 1680. In addition, there is a hunting theme in the carving with 'horn-blowing huntsman, accompanied by hounds coursing and leaping together through the rolling acanthus scrolls'. A fistful of carved Charles II shillings, dated 1683/4, along with other Irish and Portuguese coins, is incorporated in the balustrade and gives a date for this good, exuberantly carved staircase.

Finally, a brief note about one of the finest of the late-seventeenth-century staircases, which has a metal balustrade. This is at Chatsworth, Derbyshire, and was wrought by the French ironsmith Jean Tijou, whose son-in-law, the decorative painter Louis Laguerre, also worked in the house. In 1688–9, Tijou was paid £250 for the iron balustrade of the great staircase, but it was not fitted until his second visit to the house in October 1691. During his period at Chatsworth, and in work for the 1st Duke of Leeds at his house at Kiveton, Yorkshire, Tijou trained the Derbyshire smith John Gardom, who did excellent work in the west wing at Chatsworth. The brass vase on the pierced metal newel at the foot of the staircase may be one of an original seventeen supplied by Joseph Ibeck.[66]

62 (left). The staircase, c. 1683–4, at Dunster Castle, Somerset, constructed of carved elm with panels alluding to the career of Colonel Francis Luttrell.

63 (below). Detail of the staircase balustrade, c. 1683–4, at Dunster Castle, Somerset, alluding to an interest in hunting.

Celia Fiennes, who visited Chatsworth in 1697, was much impressed by this staircase, which has stone steps and 'hangs on it self' – it is cantilevered into the wall, or, as she put it, 'the support is from the wall and its own building'.[67]

The way in which servants had access, when required, to the principal upper rooms was by the use of convenient backstairs. These were far simpler in form than the principal staircase. Roger North, writing in the 1690s, declared that a house should have a back entrance and that this should be near to the kitchens, private parlour and backstairs. The ascent to an apartment of state above needed to be easy and unobtrusive, and for this there should be a passage to lead from rooms to the stair 'for the servants in their common offices to pass by'.[68] The examination of the plan of any great house will show these minor backstairs tucked into towers and remote corners of the house, made of oak, elm or sycamore, painted white, or grained and scrubbed and sanded over many years to a silky sheen.

I have made several references to Celia Fiennes in her journeyings to country houses in the 1690s. She was intrigued to see the various state rooms as well as the bathing rooms, water-closets, fountains and 'buffets' (sideboards incorporating cisterns) at houses such as Chatsworth. Room arrangements and facilities were under constant improvement but the low cost of servants hampered the universal application of time- and labour-saving developments. The backstairs gave access for the bringing of hot water (although cold was considered to be of great benefit) and the removal of the contents of close-stools.

The great country house at the end of the seventeenth century was ready for much more refinement in its services. Use made of its series of grand rooms increased with apartments specifically for eating, resting, dressing, taking audience of visitors, making music and reading books.[69] The Baroque rooms at Petworth, Sussex, were visited by the King of Spain in 1703. His progress through them tells us much of the early-eighteenth-century courtly etiquette that influenced such a visit. Charles Seymour, the 6th 'Proud Duke' of Somerset, had married Elizabeth, the young heiress to the vast Percy estates, in 1682. Her fortune enabled him to build at Petworth in a way fitting to one obsessed with lineage and consumed by pride. Nevertheless in his own house, on such an occasion, he took second place to a higher rank. The Spanish king was welcomed to Petworth by Queen Anne's husband, Prince George of Denmark, who escorted him to the entrance of his private apartment. After a time, a bewildering series of calls were paid: by the prince to the king, the king to the prince, and the king, prince and duke to the duchess. After being shown round the house by the prince, all joined together in the saloon for supper. The plan of the rooms, with some apartments more exclusive than others, allowed an elaborate ritual to take place as an ordered and necessary part of power and influence.

—— *Four* ——

THE SPIRIT OF BUILDING
1700–1760

—————— THE HOUSE PLAN ——————

The starting-point of the Baroque in Europe is generally agreed to be Rome in the mid 1620s, developing there for some fifty years. Its bold curved forms soon travelled abroad and quickly found their way into engravings. When Sir Christopher Wren (1632–1721) made his only visit abroad, to Paris in the summer of 1665, he was able to witness the array of magnificent buildings by Mansart and others, to see Guarini's complicated domed church of S. Anne-la-Royale, an example of 'Baroque mathematical ingenuity', the most daring outside Italy, and to meet the aged Italian sculptor, Bernini, who was to provide Louis XIV with a design for the completion of the Louvre. Wren visited fourteen country houses near Paris and acquired so many books and engravings that he said he had brought back 'almost all France in paper'.

The Baroque style for all practical purposes had made its early appearance in England in the plans of Hugh May and others. May's preoccupation was with grand staircases, leading to a sequence of state rooms, the visual trappings of an ordered and precise court etiquette. At Windsor Castle in 1675, May perhaps had this in mind when he designed the vestibules leading to his dramatic painted hall, with its great stone staircase and painted walls rising sheer through three flights. He had also introduced the Berniniesque form of oval room into his plan for Cassiobury in Essex.

In any brief expression of English Baroque, to avoid the pitfalls of generalization, recognition should be given to the group of able men who gathered with Wren to create an architecture that was varied and stimulating, albeit complex. Whilst Wren never engaged much in domestic architecture, the ingenuity he showed in devising the plans of the City churches, in fitting them to awkward sites; and in solving the considerable spatial problems encountered at St Paul's Cathedral, ensured his position at the head of an emerging trio of younger architects: Hawksmoor, Vanbrugh and Talman.

Nicholas Hawksmoor (c. 1661–1736) and John Vanbrugh (1664–1726) were the most original of English Baroque architects; Hawksmoor was Wren's personal assistant, and from 1702 Vanbrugh held the second post to Wren in the Office of Works, as Comptroller, a position wrested from William Talman (1650–1719).

Much of what Talman knew of foreign architecture was gleaned from what his son later called 'the most valuable collection of Books, Prints, Drawings ... as is in any one person's hands in Europe as all the artists in Towne well know'. He had a reputation for being difficult, which accounts for the irregularity of his commissions, but he put together the most talented team of decorative painters, sculptors, carvers and plasterers. Talman was probably involved in remodelling Thoresby House, Nottinghamshire, for the 4th Earl of Kingston (his 'team' definitely worked there) and he was then summoned in about 1686 by the 4th Earl (and later 1st Duke) of Devonshire to remodel part of Elizabethan Chatsworth. Indecision and lack of money dogged his proposals but the south front, which was built, is often described as the first Baroque front in England and was heavily influenced by Talman's study of elevations of buildings in France and elsewhere. It allowed space behind its urn-topped length for a series of grand painted apartments which rivalled those Talman had designed at Burghley House, Lincolnshire, for the duke's brother-in-law, the 5th Earl of Exeter.

Talman was the man of ideas during a period when society was rather uneasily coming to terms with a style which focused attention on the use of irregular forms, and 'movement' in mass, space and line. Its curved extravagances had quickly found their way into many of the engravings Talman possessed. Therefore, it must have been highly exciting for Talman to have a chance in 1698 to design the Baroque elevations for Castle Howard, Yorkshire, for Charles Howard, 3rd Earl of Carlisle, and Talman's disappointment must have been keen when the commission was secured instead by John Vanbrugh. The younger man was then only attracting attention as a popular dramatist and man of the theatre. Suddenly, 'without thought or lecture', as Jonathan Swift put it, Vanbrugh became an architect and Talman's fellow-member of the Kit-Cat Club. Lord Carlisle added further insult when he secured for Vanbrugh the post of Comptroller of the Works in lieu of Talman.[1] Castle Howard was begun in 1701 near the site of the old Howard castle of Henderskelfe.

A year or two later, when Queen Anne conferred the gift of Woodstock Park on the Duke of Marlborough for his military victories over the French, the duke chose Vanbrugh as the architect for his new building – the 'Castle of Blenheim'. Work started above the little river Glyme in 1705 and with the rude disturbance of the earth and stone-strewn site came Vanbrugh's long arguments with, and eventual dismissal by, the irascible and quick-witted Sarah, Duchess of Marlborough. In the designs of both of these houses Vanbrugh owed a great deal to his partnership with the competent professional architect, Nicholas Hawksmoor.

The designs of the English Baroque school had matured quickly with Wren's plans for rebuilding the palace of Whitehall after the disastrous fire of 1698. They show great units placed in dramatic contrast to each other and it is this theme that comes through in Vanbrugh's own work at his early 'great fine houses'. The symmetrical south garden front at Castle Howard falls away equally from the central drum, dome and lantern high above the pedimented centrepiece. On the north side a kitchen and stable

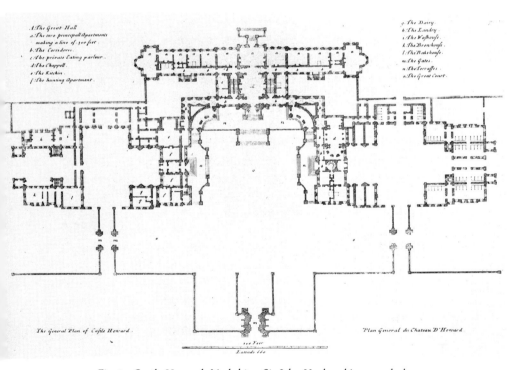

Fig. 9. Castle Howard, Yorkshire, Sir John Vanbrugh's general plan from Colen Campbell, Vitruvius Britannicus, *I, 1715, Plates 63–4. The west wing (right) was not built until 1753–9, and then not as shown in this plan.*

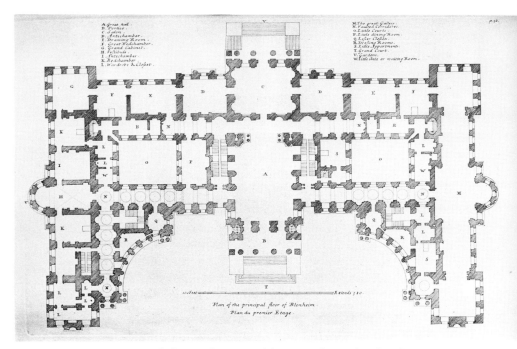

Fig. 10. Blenheim Palace, Oxfordshire. Sir John Vanbrugh's plan of
the principal floor, from Colen Campbell, Vitruvius Britannicus, I, 1715,
Plates 65–6. The Great Hall (A) is backed by a saloon (C).

court were intended to extend the wings to east and west: only the former
close-massed kitchen wing was built. The wings are connected to the main
north block of the house by curved colonnades and that on the north-east
side still houses the private apartments. The north-west wing – a Palladian
form sitting unhappily at the termination of the great Baroque south front –
was added thirty years after Vanbrugh's death by Sir Thomas Robinson.

At Blenheim the Baroque style is triumphant: massive pavilions are
connected by colonnades at either side to the main block with its Corinthian
portico, all built high above a Grand Court. This is flanked by a spreading
Kitchen Court and (to the west) a Stable Court. Blenheim was at once both
a palace and a fortified castle, but was singular enough, like most of
Vanbrugh's work, to have had little direct effect on other contemporary
house plans. Provincial architects and masons relished the chance to emulate
mere parts of it, to rusticate a modest arch, or experiment with the giant
order over more restrained façades. None did this better than the Warwick
builder-architects, Francis and William Smith, in a number of houses of the

1720s and 1730s in the Midland counties, such as Ditchley, Oxfordshire (1725), and the now ruined Sutton Scarsdale, Derbyshire (1724).

Some concern with new plan forms had appeared in 1715 when the Scottish-born architect, Colen Campbell (c. 1676–1729), published the first volume (of an intended three) of his *Vitruvius Britannicus*. It contained the plans and elevations of sixteen houses, including work by William Talman, John Vanbrugh, Nicholas Hawksmoor, Thomas Archer and John James. Significantly, it also included across its thick folio pages crisp engravings of Campbell's design of Wanstead House, Essex (1714–20), then being built for the Child banking family, and the largest Classical house of the early eighteenth century. Wanstead's plan evolved in three stages, with the second chosen for the building. A double-pile rectangle had a hall and saloon on the main axis with six interconnecting rooms on either side. This was modified by a great Corinthian-order hall rising almost to the full height of the great portico, which was flanked by two extended wings; the design included towers on the wings but these were never built. The house gave the powerful and spectacular impression of a Roman temple and, being near to London, was easy to visit and admire. It was, alas, demolished in 1824 but in the hundred years following its construction it spawned many derivatives with grand porticos, such as Wentworth Woodhouse, Nostell Priory and Harewood House, all in the West Riding of Yorkshire, and Prior Park, on the high chalk outskirts overlooking Bath.

More importantly, Colen Campbell used a compressed form of the Wanstead plan in building Houghton Hall, Norfolk, for Sir Robert Walpole from 1722. With its heavy rustication and Venetian windows, Houghton is derivative of plans by Palladio and by John Webb for Greenwich, but is given an extra twist by Campbell's own variations. The plan was similar to that used at Belton House, Lincolnshire (1685–8), and by Robert Hooke at Ragley Hall, Warwickshire (1679–83). Pedimented towers were designed to sit at the four corners in place of wings, as at Wilton House, Wiltshire, a house Campbell much admired. These were built at Houghton, although domes instead of pediments were put on them in the early 1730s by James Gibbs, after Campbell's death.

The plan of Houghton became the standard one in the 1740s and 1750s, with pedimented corner tower-houses and was used, for example, at Lydiard Tregoze, Wiltshire (1743–9), Hagley Hall (1754–60) and Croome Court (1758–63), both in Worcestershire. All of these houses reflected Houghton's overall composition to such an extent that Horace Walpole, writing to his friend John Chute on 22 August 1758, accused George, Lord Lyttelton and his architect Sanderson Miller of having stolen the plan of Hagley Hall

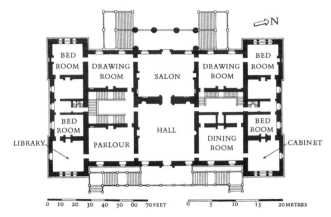

*Fig. 11. Houghton Hall, Norfolk, 1722–35, by Colen Campbell,
from Vitruvius Britannicus, III, 1725.*

from Houghton and was horrified that 'both their eating-room and salon are to be stucco, with pictures'.[2] Chute had an interest in the problem, having prepared Italianate designs in 1752, based on Serlio, which Lord Lyttelton had rejected.[3]

An interest in Palladio's villa plans was shared by several owners and their architects. Lord Burlington used ideas in several of Palladio's drawings in his possession for his villa at Chiswick. Colen Campbell closely imitated the Villa Rotonda at Vicenza when designing Mereworth, Kent, in 1723 for Colonel John Fane, later 7th Earl of Westmorland. When working for the banker Henry Hoare at Stourhead, he also copied the plan and elevation from Palladio's villa at Fanzolo for Leonardo Emo. Yet Campbell only uses the word 'villa' once, in the third volume of his *Vitruvius Britannicus* (1725, p. 8), and he meant it in the Palladian sense of a country estate rather than the house alone.[4] It was a term that had lost its architectural precision and did not gain ready acceptance again until the activities in the 1750s of architects such as Sir William Chambers (1723–96), James Paine (1717–89), Sir Robert Taylor (1714–88), and Isaac Ware (d. 1766).

The principal element of Campbell's Stourhead plan and its later variants was a square, divided both ways into three. The central compartment housed the main staircase and a lesser service one. It was possible to get at least eight rooms round this central core, with natural light fed to the staircase through a top light. Such houses could be compact and small and were suitable as alternative retreats to the great house.

There must be a few last words on the plans for town houses which were obviously restricted in space and were not likely to have spreading colonnades and distant service wings. The pattern for siting houses to achieve 'Uniformitie and Decency' had been set down in the 1630s on land at Covent Garden in London, owned by Francis, 4th Earl of Bedford. The principle was established that this 'new-shaping of London's streets should come under the eye of the King's Surveyor, in other words, Inigo Jones'. The scheme was to include a church and piazza as well as houses, but there is no exact record of what sort of houses Jones built, other than that they were on arches, had steep roofs with dormers and owed not a little to designs by Serlio. Whatever they were, they and the tiny 'piazzas' in front of them have all disappeared, the last of them in the early 1930s.[5]

An admirer of Jones's work and of his drawings was the Bath architect, John Wood the Elder (1704–54). He was concerned to give some character to the simple plan his narrow sites in Bath necessitated when he found himself with sufficient width to develop his ideas. At 24 Queen Square, Bath, the centre house on the north side of the square Wood built in 1730, there was a width of 45 ft. This enabled Wood to place a square vestibule in the front, which gave access to a double reception-room at each side. The vestibule opened through an arch to an inner hall from which the dog-leg staircase ascended. Space and light were provided on the first and second floors by windows in the apsidal-ended half-landings. At the head of the first floor landing there was space for a small ante-room and at each side a fine double-drawing room, 30 ft long. Bedrooms and dressing-rooms were on the second floor and a small staircase led on to the attics. The kitchens and staff accommodation were in the basement.[6]

The fronts of Wood's houses in Bath are of unbroken uniformity, giving style and balance to his achievements. In the King's Circus, 1754–6, a group of thirty houses had to be disposed within a circle, with a diameter of 318 ft. Each segment had three storeys and the party walls were graduated in thickness so that regular apartments could be created within the curved plan. This grand inflexibility was dictated to the sub-leasees who were actually to build the houses. Wood had leased the whole site to himself and did not intend the slightest variation to his design,[7] which, with its 648 external columns and wealth of carved detail, was his final achievement: he died on 23 May 1754, four months after the scheme had been commenced.

Georgian London, as with Bath, had many houses in which economy in frontage was dictated by the width of the strips of land running back from the street. These 'terrace' houses rose sheer from a basement, with one room at the back and one at the front on each floor. A passage and staircase snaked upwards to one side. On narrow sites, some as little as 24 ft wide (those in Bath vary from 20–25 ft in width), few variations to this plan were possible. The solutions resulted in unattractive areas out of sight as, in order to make extra room for the services, it was often necessary to extend the building in a haphazard way at the back. As Sir John Summerson has written:[8] 'The story of the better-class London house is a story of ingenious variation within the inflexible limits of party-walls.'

FLOORS

While the roofing of a house was going ahead the mason and carpenter were considering the stone and timber floors beneath. It is the careful combination of both surfaces that is so characteristic of the early-eighteenth-century house: payments for deals, paving and marble abound in house accounts, and much information can also be gleaned from an examination of the many manuals of practical instruction. In the second edition of *Chamber's Cyclopaedia* it was noted that 'courts, stables, kitchins, halls, churches, &c. are paved with tiles, bricks, flags or fire-stone (sometimes a kind of free-stone), and rag-stone'. The flags were bedded in a lime-and-sand mortar to give a utilitarian surface: there was no attempt at pattern in these floors but the combination of black and natural stone, or, of course, of coloured marbles, lent themselves as readily to pavement patterns as they had done in the previous century. This was so in staircase halls (where the staircase itself was often of stone), chapels, halls and saloons.

Square, octagon and black-and-white chequer patterns in stone and marble, still echoing those designed by Daviler in his *Cours d'Architecture* (1691) were in frequent use.

Marble had one disadvantage in that cool air condensed on it and it was regarded by James Gibbs (in his *Bibliotheca Radcliviana*, 1747) as more suitable for 'Churches, Porticos, common Halls and Passages, than a Library'. Nevertheless, all the leading architects favoured some use of marble in their buildings to give a cool classical appearance, and Sir John Vanbrugh used the marble-cutter, John Thorp, of Bakewell, Derbyshire, to fit black marble squares into the stones of the great hall floor at Castle Howard, Yorkshire, in 1708. James Gibbs also used black and white marble in alternating squares in 1720 in the attractive Octagon he designed for James Johnston at Orleans House, Twickenham. The pattern ends in black marble which provides a successful border for this eight-sided room. At Mereworth in Kent, designed by Colen Campbell, and roofed by 1723, a radiating simple pattern of cut marble follows the circular shape of the central domed hall or 'salon', 35 ft in diameter. However, at Houghton Hall, Norfolk, Campbell used a stone

64 (opposite). The north-east corridor of Castle Howard, Yorkshire, from hall to East Wing, designed by Sir John Vanbrugh c. 1708. Note the carefully cut stone floor, walls and vaults.

65. *Stone and marble floor of the hall, c. 1708, at Castle Howard, Yorkshire,*
laid by John Thorp of Bakewell, Derbyshire.

floor in the appropriately named 'Stone Hall', which is a 40 ft cube. In his description of it, in *Vitruvius Britannicus* (III, 1725, plates dated 1723), he describes it as 'all in stone, the most beautiful in England'.

Sir John Vanbrugh used good cut stone and marble in several interiors. In the precisely formed Temple of the Four Winds at Castle Howard, Yorkshire, which was designed only a year or so before his death in 1726, he specified a marble floor. The temple was, however, not completed until 1736, when Francesco Vassalli stuccoed the interior. The floor pattern is an intricate array of coloured marbles which provides a striking contrast with Vassalli's dramatic black scagliola pilasters, columns, doorcases and window surrounds. Vanbrugh had the hall floor at Grimsthorpe Castle, Lincolnshire, *c.* 1724, laid out in a black oval pattern which repeats that of the ceiling ribs. The paving within the oval itself is finely cut in tapering segments.

One of the most attractive marble floors is that in the mausoleum at Castle Howard, Yorkshire, which Nicholas Hawksmoor had started in 1729, although it was not completed until 1744, eight years after his death. The

66 (opposite). The interior of the Temple of the Four Winds, at Castle Howard, Yorkshire,
with marble floor: stuccoed, and scagliola pilasters by Francesco Vassalli, 1736.

chapel pavement is inlaid with coloured marbles and divided into panels, each with a Greek key-fret border inlaid in brass by the tinsmith Christopher Thompson. These panels decrease in size as they approach the centre of the circle, which contains a stylized flower of twenty-four petals in coloured marbles.[9]

The most active of the eighteenth-century pattern-book plagiarists was Batty Langley (1696–1751), who made a good living from his many practical manuals. He incorporated several of Daviler's plates from *Cours d'Architecture* (1691) into his own *Ancient Masonry* (1736) and pavements and floors are given four plates, as Nos. 449 to 452. He describes one Daviler design as 'an Invention of my own, and which being made with *White*, *Black* and *Dove* colour'd Marble, represents so many Tetraedrons or Pyraments ... which in the Dusk of an Evening appear as so many solid bodies not to be walked on'. One of Langley's engravers who worked on *Ancient Masonry* was John Carwitham and three years later he issued a book entitled *Various Kinds of Floor Decorations ... Whether in Pavements of Stone, or Marble, or with Painted Floor Cloths*. Of the three interiors he illustrated in the twenty-four copper plates, two were of entrance halls, but the elaboration of most of his designs made them more suited to painting than to being realized in stone or marble.

Langley took up Carwitham's publication challenge with alacrity and in 1740 produced twenty-seven designs for marble pavements, for halls, bathing rooms and so on. The plates are dated 1739 and several are identical to those in Daviler and Carwitham. His book had the imposing title, *The City and Country Builder's and Workman's Treasury of Designs*, and Plate 94 gave the most common square and diamond patterns.

Many provincial architects, well grounded in Classical precedents, saw no reason not to imitate their better-known colleagues in the use of stone and marble for flooring. Indeed, many of them, training as masons, had, perhaps, a better working knowledge of their physical properties. Two examples of many are typical. At Crowcombe Court, Somerset, the architects Thomas Parker and Nathaniel Ireson, both active in the county, had their mason set out in the hall, *c.* 1730, the usual black and white diamond patterns in stone. At Nostell Priory, Yorkshire, Colonel John Moyser of Beverley arranged access beneath the *perron* staircase to a stone-floored lower entrance hall, which was underneath the upper hall on the principal floor or *piano nobile*, as in the Palladian villa it copied.

James Paine (1717–89), who established himself as a leading architect but with a good provincial practice, had supervised Nostell Priory's erection, as a young man of nineteen. He used stone and marble in both early commissions, such as the chapel at Cusworth Hall, Yorkshire, c. 1752, and later ones, for example, the imposing staircase hall at Wardour Castle, Wiltshire, c. 1775.

At Wentworth Woodhouse, Yorkshire, the saloon floor (c. 1758) is of inlaid marble and not scagliola, as is often claimed. With dimensions of 60 ft square by 40 ft high, the space is well able to take the intricate radiating pattern, which was based (as was the room itself) on the hall in the Queen's House at Greenwich. The central pattern was given a border with a diamond pattern around the edges. But a year or two before this, in 1756, Isaac Ware had written in his *A Complete Body of Architecture*, 'The use of carpeting at this time has set aside the ornamenting of floors in a great measure'. Timber floors, never out of favour, were originally laid with the intention of being seen, until many were covered, from about the middle of the eighteenth century, with Exeter, Axminster or Wilton carpets.

The class of timber imports for flooring, known as 'deals', was defined in customs regulations as sawn boards up to $\frac{3}{4}$ in thick, from 7 to 11 in wide and 8 to 20 ft in length. A width above 11 in placed the timber in the category of 'planks', on which the highest rate of duty was paid. Norway deals were generally 10 to 12 ft long and Baltic and White Sea deals 14 to 20 ft. They were reckoned by the 'long hundred' or six score: thus a 'standard' of deals consisted of 120 lengths of 12 ft by $1\frac{1}{2}$ in by 11 in timber.

More exotic timbers, particularly cedar and mahogany, could be obtained at ports such as Bristol and at Antwerp, where there was an international Exchange: in 1700 over 240 ships arrived in Bristol, some carrying cedar planking from South Carolina, whilst Hull in East Yorkshire dealt with the Scandinavian trade.[10] In 1702, when Castle Howard, Yorkshire, was being built, the joiner Sabyn was paid for two days spent selecting deals for flooring which had come to York from Hull. These would often be of varying width, with a tendency in the early years for boards to be comparatively wide. The boards were rough-planed and then set on one side to season. There is no evidence that the seventeenth-century practice advocated by John Evelyn in his discourse on forest trees (*Sylva*, 1662) was still followed: that is, to immerse the timber in water (preferably running water) for a fortnight and then rear it and turn it daily so that the sun and wind could freely play on all surfaces. If this method were followed and the boards were only nailed firmly the second year after laying, Evelyn asserted that the planks would 'lie staunch, close, and without shrinking in the least, as if they were all in one piece ...'.

Oak boards were used in the 1740s in the best rooms at Temple Newsam House, Leeds, and throughout the new wing at Claydon House,

Buckinghamshire, in the 1750s, while deal was used in the upstairs rooms. An exception to the norm was the flooring to the best rooms at Claydon, where mahogany was used in the late 1760s, not long after its wide acceptance in England as the best wood for furniture. A half-landing on the inlaid staircase at Claydon contains a board almost 20 in wide, with those in the Great Room ranging from $5\frac{3}{4}$–$9\frac{3}{4}$ in wide. The intention was always to lay the boards so well that the end joints resting on the joists were almost invisible.

In the late seventeenth century Celia Fiennes had noted many inlaid floors on her travels and there are several early-eighteenth-century houses in which the practice was continued. On one of the landings of the main staircase at Beningbrough Hall, Yorkshire, the initials and coat of arms of John and Mary Bourchier and the date '1716' are inlaid, and a design survives for the parquet, 1719, on the staircase of King's Weston, the Vanbrugh house on the edge of Bristol.[11] Pride of achievement must, however, go to the craftsmen working in the 1720s and 1730s under Francis Smith's direction at two Shropshire houses, Davenport House and Mawley Hall.

Davenport House is dated '1726' on the rainwater heads, and its saloon is a masterpiece of applied cabinet-work in mahogany. This is at its most lavish on the walls but the floor has a diamond trellis pattern in a lighter wood to the ground. The same elaborate inlaid wainscoting is found at Mawley Hall (dated '1730' on the rainwater heads), again with a trellis pattern on the floor. It has been suggested that a decline in the popularity of inlaid furniture in the Palladian period induced 'some unemployment expert to develop this fresh field'.[12] Whatever the truth, the inlaid rooms at Davenport and Mawley are of a very high standard of technical accomplishment and aesthetic refinement.

I shall conclude this section with a brief account of painted and stencilled floors. Controversy over date has surrounded the best surviving example of an early painted floor, in the Tyrconnel Room at Belton House, Lincolnshire. Whilst no bill survives for its painting and no reference is made to it in the early literature relating to the house, it is reasonable to assume that it is of the late eighteenth century because of its neo-Classical motifs, although nineteenth-century dates have also been advanced. Anthony Wells-Cole, who has made a special study of the role Continental engravings played in English decoration, has also noted a similarity between the Belton floor and the earlier stylized acanthus, dot and line compartments and anthemion-like motifs in a suite of designs for garden parterres by Jean Le Blond (c. 1635–1709) issued towards the end of the seventeenth century.[13] One other good painted mid-eighteenth-century floor to survive is in the dining-room at Crowcombe Court, Somerset (*c.* 1760), which has simplified foliate motifs painted on the oak boards. The painted designs gave refinement to a structural feature, and this was further enhanced on many occasions by laying painted floorcloths, a type of hard-wearing painted canvas, introduced into English country houses during the early eighteenth century. They were available in plain colours or various decorative patterns.

WAINSCOTED WALLS

In the early years of the reign of George I (1714–27) natural wood panelling almost completely disappeared from English houses. When deal or pine wainscot was used, its surface and yellowish colour were disguised by painting or graining, a legacy from a fashion current in the first few years of the eighteenth century. The popular conception of the interior of a Queen Anne house *c.* 1710 is still of one with pine-panelling, painted in 'Georgian green' (which represents a different hue to almost every eye). The truth is always somewhere between the extremes, and may be represented by the panelling in the gallery of Nicholas Hawksmoor's fine house of Easton Neston, Northamptonshire, built for William Fermor, 1st Lord Lempster, 1699–1702, and in the hall at Hanbury Hall, Hereford and Worcester, *c.* 1705. The date 'MDCCII' (1702) appears on the east front of Easton Neston and '1701' appears above the stone centrepiece of the east front at Hanbury Hall. However, in both houses the painted decoration by Sir James Thornhill dates to a few years later – 1702 to 1713 at Easton Neston, and *c.* 1710–12 at Hanbury Hall.

Wainscoting in various forms, formed in a slightly old-fashioned way, is found in most of the houses designed by Francis Smith (1672–1738), the Warwick architect, and in interiors by the elder John Wood of Bath (1704–54). This is not surprising in Smith's case, as his family had been active as builders in the Midland counties for a long time. He was out of his own training as a mason by the early 1690s and, with the family's help, had completed a number of houses by 1710. As the Smiths had control of a stone and marble yard in Warwick and also dealt in timber, it was easy to offer to patrons a complete service of carpenter's, bricklayer's, mason's, joiner's and plasterer's work. They did this for the 1st Earl of Cholmondeley (Cholmondeley Hall, Cheshire, dem. 1805) and for Sir Roger Cave at Stanford Hall, Leicestershire, 1697–1700. Whilst some of the tasks were sub-contracted, it was all done within their overall control: the Smith 'team'

67. *The first oak room, c. 1724, at Sutton Scarsdale, Derbyshire;*
the joiner was Thomas Eboral, the carver Edward Poynton.
The room was re-erected at the Philadelphia Museum of Art in 1928.

rose to exceptional heights of accomplishment by the 1720s, and this is evident in their work, 1725–30, at Ditchley, Oxfordshire and, as noted earlier, at Davenport Hall and Mawley Hall, both in Shropshire.

At Ditchley, Smith was working to the designs of James Gibbs but at Davenport and Mawley he acted as architect, although there is no surviving documentation to confirm this. These houses are reliably attributed to Smith; some of his team of craftsmen, who were noted on a lead rising-plate at Sutton Scarsdale, Derbyshire,[14] including joiners, carpenters and stuccoists, are assumed to have travelled from one house to the other. At Davenport (1726) and at Mawley (1730) the splendid inlaid rooms, done to a high standard of decorative woodworking, were in an outmoded style for their dates. Furthermore, the entrance hall at Davenport is decorated in painted wood to represent channelled ashlar, with the imposing rusticated doorways having dominant keystones and bearing a similarity to those on the west front of James Gibbs's London Church of St Martin-in-the-Fields (1726). Some of the same wood channelling is present on the arches of the staircase hall at Mawley Hall, and the wainscoted Large Drawing Room there has rather old-fashioned swags and other carvings in oak above the overmantel. The same sort of 'Wren tradition' in woodwork is apparent in the oak panelling at Smith's Ombersley Hall, Hereford and Worcester (1723–30). Until the discovery of the bills[15] it was thought to have been decoration of the 1690s.

In March 1729 the elder John Wood wrote to William Brydges of Tibberton, Herefordshire (a cousin of the imperious James Brydges, 1st Duke of Chandos), to give full details of fitting up the saloon there with woodwork.[16] He wrote:

If the Salon is executed after this new design the Pannels must be one Inch thick at least & Canvass shou'd be Glewed at the back of the Joynts, the Pannels ought to be glewed up [for]th with & planed over, and if they were planed over the Backside primed with Oyle & Coulour it would not be money ill layed out ... the Architrave Base & Sur Base & the Ornaments round the Pannels ought not to be put up untill the wood has done shrink[ing] (which will be in one years time) the work must be painted twice in Oyle as soon as it is fastend up against the walls. . . .

A feature of many early-eighteenth-century interiors was a shelved recess or cupboard framed in as part of the wainscot. Such recesses were often given a semi-hemispherical head, fluted or carved as a shell and framed by pilasters. They tended to disappear as the fashion grew for papered or fabric-hung walls from the middle years of the eighteenth century.

When the provision of elaborately carved and pierced additions to overmantels and cornices died away in the early years of the eighteenth century, the carver rose again as a specialist joiner who enriched fixtures with a variety of mouldings. Working to a high standard were those who embellished interiors, particularly James Richards (d. 1759), the 'Master Carver and Sculptor in Wood' of the Board of Works.[17] He had succeeded to this post in 1721 at the death of Grinling Gibbons and became one of the most accomplished carvers of the Palladian years, working in particular for the architects Colen Campbell and William Kent. Campbell used him from 1718 and Kent was ready to give him work more or less as soon as Campbell died, in 1729. The carving Richards did on the Royal State Barge, which Kent had designed for Frederick, Prince of Wales, 1731–2, is of a consummate quality, with riotous sea-creature motifs. On some of the

68. *Detail of painted and gilded carving above the chimneypiece in the Circular Room at Chiswick House, Middlesex, probably by James Richards c. 1728.*

overdoors at Lord Burlington's Chiswick villa a few years previously Richards had again demonstrated his considerable skill in his carved swags, masked faces and precise scrolls.

The richest woodcarving belongs, however, to the late 1750s; some of the most accomplished was done for the 9th Duke of Norfolk at Norfolk House in London. Norfolk House was demolished in 1938 and the collections dispersed but, fortunately, the Music Room was saved and re-erected at the Victoria and Albert Museum, London. The richly gilded woodcarving was started in 1752 by the French carver, John Cuneot, who received over £2,643 for carving and gilding, 1752–56.[18]

For Ralph, 2nd Earl Verney at Claydon House, Buckinghamshire, the erratic joiner and carver, Luke Lightfoot (c. 1722–89), took charge in 1759, acting as master builder, surveyor, mason and carver. Soon he was charging the earl for work done on materials he had sold elsewhere – over £30,000 for some £7,000 worth of goods – and he was finally taken into the Chancery Court in 1771 to redress the matter.[19] However, Lightfoot's carved woodwork in the Rococo and Chinese styles at Claydon is of such

69 (right). Detail of Rococo carving in the North Hall at Claydon House, Buckinghamshire, by Luke Lightfoot c. 1760.

70 (below). Detail of the carved recess in the Chinese Room, c. 1760, at Claydon House, Buckinghamshire.

71. *Part of the wooden ceiling of the North Hall, at Claydon House,*
Buckinghamshire, carved by Luke Lightfoot c. 1760.

a high quality, including the wood ceiling of the North Hall, that much
might be forgiven him by the present-day viewer. Claydon is the only
known setting for his mercurial talents and he ended his days keeping an
ale-house in Southwark.

PAINTED WALLS
AND CEILINGS

We are fortunate that the eighteenth-century chronicler, George Vertue
(1683–1756), kept a record of artistic activity over some forty years (1713–
54) and was interested in all forms of painting.[20] In history painting he
traces the rise of Sir James Thornhill and the domination of Venetians such
as Giovanni Antonio Pellegrini and Sebastiano and Marco Ricci. In the
early years of the century commissions were still given to Antonio Verrio
(d. 1707) and to Louis Laguerre (d. 1721). At Petworth House, Sussex,
Laguerre's men took measurements, *c.* 1719, and then the French artist
painted the staircase walls with 'The Triumph of Elizabeth, Duchess of
Somerset, surrounded by her family' and the ceiling with 'An Assembly of
the Gods'. At Blenheim Palace, Oxfordshire, Laguerre supplanted Thornhill,
whom the Duchess of Marlborough thought too expensive. In the saloon

he stayed in style true to the fresco technique, depicting a feigned colonnade resting on Grinling Gibbons's marble dado and assembling people from the four continents to pay homage to the duke, a theme he borrowed unashamedly from Charles Le Brun's 'Escalier des Ambassadeurs' at Versailles. It was to be his last work, for he died on a visit to the Lincoln's Inn Fields Theatre on 20 April 1721.

It is not known how James Thornhill (*c.* 1676–1734) came to take up painting as a profession. He was not knighted until 1720 when his best work was done, and within a year or two of that he was rejected for the painting at Kensington Palace (1722) in favour of William Kent. His

72. *Louis Laguerre's oil-on-plaster painting on the walls of the staircase, c. 1719, at Petworth House, Sussex. The staircase balustrade itself was designed in Sir Charles Barry's office in the early nineteenth century.*

apprenticeship to the Sergeant Painter, Thomas Highmore, had ended in 1696 and his first work seems to have been under Verrio at Hampton Court (1702–4). Thornhill emerged as a major painter in 1705 with the commission for the hall and staircase of Stoke Edith, Hereford and Worcester. This was destroyed by fire in 1927 and the work can only be judged from photographs.[21] However, many other commissions give ample testimony to Thornhill's skills, notably his masterpiece, the Painted Hall at Greenwich Hospital (1708–27), and in domestic settings at, for example, Blenheim Palace (the hall ceiling, 1716); Chatsworth (1702–8); Hanbury Hall, Hereford and Worcester (c. 1710); and in the chapel at Wimpole Hall, Cambridgeshire (1724). The staircase walls at Hanbury are filled with many figures engaged in the arcane complexities of mythology: Thetis visiting Vulcan's forge, Achilles choosing the spear and Ajax and Ulysses contending for the arms of Achilles. On the ceiling overhead a figure of Mercury holds a small likeness of Dr Henry Sacheverell that has been set alight by the Furies, dating the work to about 1710, the year of Sacheverell's trial. His arrest had been occasioned by his outspoken preaching against the government in November 1709. The chapel at Wimpole Hall rises to the full height of the house and has a family gallery. Thornhill painted the walls and ceiling, and proudly signed the work over the door. Whilst the colouring is less exuberant than at Greenwich, the altar-wall has a large 'Adoration of the Magi' and there are painted niches with simulated statues and painted coffering on the ceiling. It is in the grand manner of Verrio and Laguerre, but lacks their *bravura*.

In the early years of the eighteenth century the most important centre of painting in Italy was Venice. Its greatest figure, Gianbattista Tiepolo, never visited England but many of his predecessors and contemporaries did, bringing with them a colourful palette allied to lightness of touch, qualities hitherto almost unknown in England. On the Duke of Manchester's return to England from his diplomatic missions on behalf of Queen Anne in 1708, he was accompanied by two Venetian painters, Giovanni Antonio Pellegrini (1675–1741) and Marco Ricci (1676–1730). Pellegrini's brightly painted turbaned figures on the staircase walls of the Duke of Manchester's seat, Kimbolton Castle, Cambridgeshire (remodelled by Sir John Vanbrugh, 1708–20), are typical of his late-Venetian style. This is still seen to great advantage in what survived of his work after the fire of November 1940 at Castle Howard, Yorkshire, Vanbrugh's first 'great fine house', and indeed, in photographs of the destroyed dome painting.

Marco Ricci, who specialized in architectural and landscape fantasies, also worked at Castle Howard but, according to Vertue, eventually took himself

73. *Sir James Thornhill's oil-on-plaster painting on the walls of the staircase,*
c. 1710, at Hanbury Hall, Hereford and Worcester,
with scenes of Thetis, Vulcan, Achilles, Ajax and Ulysses.

back to Venice 'upon some disgust with Pellegrini'. He returned to England later with his uncle, Sebastiano Ricci (1659–1734), the leader of the Venetian school. Of the elder Ricci's mural works now remaining in England the most important are two splendid canvases on the staircase of Burlington House, Piccadilly, *c.* 1715, and the masterly 'Resurrection', in oil on plaster, on the dome of the apse of the Chelsea Hospital chapel.

Two other active Venetian painters in England were the mediocre Antonio Bellucci (1624–1726) and the mysterious Francesco Sleter (1685–1775). Bellucci's best-known paintings were those he did in about 1720 for the Duke of Chandos's chapel at Cannons, Middlesex. These were acquired at the demolition sale at Cannons in 1747 by Thomas, 2nd Lord Foley, and re-instated with gilded papier-mâché embellishments, in the ceiling of the church at Great Witley, Hereford and Worcester. The canvases depict the 'Nativity', the 'Deposition' and the 'Ascension', with ovals of cherubs holding the symbols of the Passion. Sleter, who Anglicized his name to Slater (and may have come from the northern Veneto) is also best known for work he did for the Duke of Chandos's chapel at Cannons (he designed the windows, which were painted by Joshua Price, now in Great Witley Church), and for his lively mythological paintings at Mereworth Castle, Kent, and Moor Park, Hertfordshire. He died in his ninetieth year at Mereworth in 1775 and his burial in the churchyard there is commemorated by a tablet on the south wall of the church.

Bellucci's pupil, and much his superior in ability, was Jacopo Amigoni or Amiconi (1682–1752) who followed his master to England in 1727 or 1730. The four elegant canvases *c.* 1732 depicting the story of Jupiter and Io, set into Giuseppe Artari and Giovanni Bagutti's gilded stucco frames at Moor Park, Hertfordshire, show him at his best; they are colourful, well-composed canvases of appealing subject-matter.

In spite of this bright work by the Venetian decorators, many English patrons still looked to the riches of the Imperial City of Rome, which they had seen on their Grand Tours, with Raphael and the Seicento as their artistic inspiration. Thus, in July 1709 three patrons, Sir William Wentworth, Burrell Massingberd and Sir John Chester, imbued with these ideals, sent the young Yorkshire-born painter William Kent (1685–1748) to study in Italy. Kent became the pupil of Benedetto Luti (whose portrait of Kent in 1719 is at Chatsworth) and in 1717 he was ready to fresco the ceiling of the little church of S. Giuliano dei Fiamminghi with a glorification of the eponymous saint. Kent, despite all his efforts, never made a good painter but, on his return to England, he exploited to some effect the convention of an assembly of figures under a colonnade, as well as producing brightly

74. *Painted panels of the gallery ceiling*
at Mereworth Castle, Kent, by Francesco Sleter c. 1735,
incorporating medallions of mythological subjects and the seasons.

coloured versions of antique Roman grotesques for the staircase at Kensington Palace (*c.* 1725–7). He also incorporated these into his work (*c.* 1739) for Lt-General James Dormer, at Rousham, Oxfordshire. Another type of decoration favoured by Kent was in the 'mosaic taste', which he used in ceilings painted for his mentor, Richard Boyle, 3rd Earl of Burlington, at Chiswick House, Middlesex (*c.* 1727–35), and at Houghton Hall, Norfolk. Here, Sir Robert Walpole confined Kent as much as he could to a monochrome scheme, fearing the painter's unhappy use of colour. However, marine deities amid foliated scroll work in green, pink and white on a gold mosaic ground are depicted on the ceiling of the White Drawing Room, and the monochrome, where it was in use, was often in richly laid gold.

75. *The King's Staircase c. 1725–7, at Kensington Palace, London,*
painted in trompe l'œil *style by William Kent, with a representation of George I's court.*

More skilful than Kent in his imitation of the approved Roman manner was the Piedmontese painter, Giuseppe Mattia Borgnis (1701–61). He was invited to England in about 1736 by Sir Francis Dashwood, and set to work in his patron's Italianate villa in Buckinghamshire, West Wycombe Park. His frescoes there give an excellent idea of the taste of an English virtuoso with Bacchus, Aurora, biblical subjects after Raphael in the Vatican *logge*, banquets of the gods, nymphs bathing and even the Aldobrandini marriage adapted to the staircase and ceilings of the principal rooms.

The lively forms of North Italian Rococo practised by the Venetians soon gave way to the greater elegance of the French Rococo. It has been demonstrated by Mark Girouard[22] that the group of artists who frequented the St Martin's Lane Academy and the neighbouring Slaughter's coffee house were mainly responsible for promoting this new taste for the Rococo in England. The group's leading personalities were Sir James Thornhill's son-in-law, William Hogarth (who never forgave William Kent for taking the Kensington Palace commission from his father-in-law), the painter Francis Hayman, the engraver Hubert-François Gravelot and the sculptor

Louis-François Roubiliac. Another member was the specialist in exotic forms of the grotesque – chinoiserie, turquerie and singerie – Andien de Clermont (fl. 1716–1783). One of the liveliest of Clermont's monkey decorations is the cove of the parlour ceiling at Kirtlington Park, Oxfordshire (1744). In one scene 'a monkey-man mounted on a greyhound and clad in doublet and plumed cap struggles with a fowling-piece . . . and in another an elegant monkey-lady in yellow satin follows the chase on a lively foxhound-steed'.[23] It allowed a patron to feel he had entered at least a fabled world of the chase without stirring a single gout-laid limb.

Apart from decorative painting, there was steady employment for house painters. The painting of items several times over was occasioned partly by the need for a durable finish but as much by the difficulty of achieving an even colour from the pigment suspended in the oil. Whilst ready-mixed paint was available, ground into oil by laborious manual work, or by the use of a horse-mill, it was still difficult to render paint fluid. A wide variety of manuals set out extensive directions but when the Earl of Leicester's great new house of Holkham, Norfolk, was ready for painting in the late 1750s John Neale had to be paid for 61 days' work in mixing and grinding colours at 2s 6d a day.

The use of distemper predated that of oil and varnish. Spanish white, which is mentioned frequently in eighteenth-century archives, or whiting was the common distemper colour, broken into water mixed with strong size. It was used by plasterers to whiten ceilings. The house painter was also adept at graining and marbling in imitation of wood and marble. He was also associated with the practice of paper-hanging.

Wallpaper was fastened to a wooden framework set over the surface of the wall. The worker stretched fine canvas on the frames, and then the wallpaper was applied to the canvas. Chinese papers (often called 'India papers' in accounts), brought to England by the East India Company, had established the fashion for wallpaper from the late seventeenth century. They were fixed in this way, and it has been possible in several cases of impending destruction of the setting to remove the lengths to other rooms or to museums and country-house settings.[24] Saltram in Devon has four Chinese papers which may well be among the earliest extant in the British Isles, dating from the reign of K'ang Hsi (1662–1722). Sophisticated touches could be given by picking out the gilding with a colour to match the colours in the room. The State Bedchamber at Nostell Priory, Yorkshire, has eighteen sheets of Chinese paper with every sort of bird in brilliant blues, pinks and greens on an originally white ground, bought in April 1771. The Chippendale furniture matches, in green and gold lacquer with chinoiserie

76. *The Chinese Bedroom at Belton House, Lincolnshire. This room, which was often used by the Prince of Wales (Edward VIII), is hung with a well-preserved, eighteenth-century Chinese wallpaper. The bed, cornice and dado are painted to imitate bamboo. The bed, with its glazed chintz curtains, is of c. 1840.*

patterns. Sixteen rolls of paper, each about 4 ft wide, were obtained by William Windham for Felbrigg Hall, Norfolk. The paper was supplied (as an inscription found on the back during restoration by John Sutcliffe in 1974–5 established) by his architect, James Paine (1717–89), in 1751. Ducks, pheasants and birds of paradise can be seen among lotuses and peonies on a white ground.

PLASTERED AND STUCCOED SURFACES

Stucco in England, as distinct from plasterwork, enjoyed only brief popularity on two occasions: it was used for a short time in the reign of Henry VIII, when Italians worked at Nonsuch Palace, and again in the first half of the eighteenth century, from 1709 to the last recorded use at Shugborough, Staffordshire, in 1763. Throughout both periods and in the intervening years, British plasterers, working to long-established methods – that is, adding animal hair for strength, rather than stucco's requirement of marble-dust and supporting armatures – were active alongside their foreign competitors, and some learned new tricks to add to their cherished repertoire.

Stuccoists generally employed a wider range of engraved sources of classical ornament and a richer range of mythological stories than plasterers, who relied more on themes culled from the Bible and from emblem books. They worked harmoniously alongside one another, and on occasion a plasterer such as Thomas Perritt of York (1710–59) or Thomas Clayton (fl. 1710–72), who was active in Scotland, mastered enough of the different technique to style himself, additionally, a 'Stukoe man'. This was an asset in pleasing patrons who had seen the *bravura* of stucco in foreign settings, but they were not as precise as we are in observing the distinction between plasterers and stuccoists.

The *stuccatori* who worked in England in the eighteenth century came, almost without exception, from the canton of Ticino in Italian Switzerland. Two of the best known were Giovanni Bagutti of Rovio, near Lugano, and Giuseppe Artari of nearby Arogno. They worked together in England as partners until a little after 1730 with the older man, Bagutti, taking the main responsibility. They did their most important work for the architects John Vanbrugh, James Gibbs, Colen Campbell, Giacomo Leoni and Francis Smith, with Bagutti, at Vanbrugh's Castle Howard, Yorkshire, as early as 1709, accepting the first recorded eighteenth-century stucco commission in England.

Giuseppe Artari and his 'partners' were at Ditchley, Oxfordshire, in 1725. There Artari was joined by his brother and a distant relative, Francesco Serena and Francesco Vassalli. The record of 'The Italian Plaisterers' Account for worke done by them in severall rooms att Ditchley'[25] listed a number of items with their respective costs. The account details nine heads, eagles, roses, festoons and the costs for various rooms. Some of the detail of this work has disappeared: for example, the nine heads include some of later date and the four eagles have left their outline on the wall but have been replaced by lion-mask lights of an early-nineteenth-century date; however, enough survives to demonstrate its spirited quality and the technical accomplishment of the craftsmen. This is also true of Francesco Vassalli's work, particularly in the north of England at Towneley Hall, Burnley (1729–31), and Castle Howard (Temple of the Four Winds, 1736), and of the work of the stuccoist Giuseppe Cortese, who spent most of his adult years working in Yorkshire, dying there in 1778. He was particularly active in houses designed by the competent John Carr of York, working alongside

77. The stucco chimneypiece overmantel at Castle Howard, Yorkshire,
by Giovanni Bagutti 1709–12. This is the first record of his employment in England
working for Sir John Vanbrugh and the 3rd Earl of Carlisle.

78. *The ceiling of the King's Bedroom, c. 1729, at Compton Place, Sussex,*
plastered by Charles Stanley and others under the supervision of Colen Campbell.

Carr's favourite English plasterer, James Henderson, who acted as one of
Cortese's executors.[26]

A foreign stuccoist working in England at this period who was exceptional in not coming from the Swiss Ticino was Simon Carl (Charles)
Stanley. He was born in Copenhagen in 1703 of an English father and a
Danish mother. After an apprenticeship which gave him work in the
company of several talented stuccoists, and a period of further study in
Amsterdam, he was in England by 1727, and was soon in the company of
the sculptors Peter Scheemakers and Laurent Delvaux. However, when they
left for Italy he stayed on in England to work on sculptural monuments,
and on plasterwork in the south of England at Compton Place, Sussex.

Few English houses surpass Compton Place in plaster decoration. It was
built for Spencer Compton, Lord Wilmington, by Colen Campbell in the
late 1720s. The King's Bedroom ceiling commemorates in bold relief the
amours of Venus and Adonis. The border is rich, with its sphinx-like figures,
moulded *putti* and elaborate shells and foliage, akin to much in the Danish
Baroque castles where Stanley had mastered his art. For a short period in
the early 1740s Stanley seems to have joined up with the successful Oxford

plasterer, Thomas Roberts (1711–71). The evidence for this is an estimate they submitted in 1744 for work at James Gibbs's Radcliffe Camera in Oxford, but Gibbs chose Giuseppe Artari to provide the restrained coffering. He had, after all, known of Artari's work for over twenty years.

This connection between Stanley and Roberts may suggest again a means whereby the Englishman learned the techniques of working stucco, and there is some slight evidence to suggest that Vassalli was for a time in

79. The Cabinet at Felbrigg Hall, Norfolk, remodelled in 1750–52.
The late-seventeenth-century ceiling had further ornament added.
The crimson worsted damask on the walls, and the chimneypiece were installed c. 1824.

80. The hall ceiling, c. 1760, at Holkham, Norfolk, plastered by
Thomas Clark of Westminster. The cove is based on the Pantheon of Agrippa
and the ceiling on an Inigo Jones design.

Thomas Clayton's Scottish team of plasterers. When Clayton's son was
born at Hamilton on 8 March 1743, he was christened 'Thomas Varsallis
Clayton', an unlikely second Christian name for the young baby. Moreover,
the excellence of the overdoor stucco figures that appear amid Clayton's
work in the dining-room at Blair Castle, near Perth, suggest the hand of a
Ticino stuccoist; Vassalli perhaps went on to act as godfather to the new
young Thomas Clayton.

When the architect James Paine finished the Doncaster Mansion House
in 1748 he spent some time drawing up a description of his work there,
which was published in 1751. In the note to Plate XXI in his book, he first
observed that the ornaments of the banqueting room 'are of stucco (executed

by Mr Rose and Mr Thomas Perritt) inferior to none of the Performances of the best *Italians* that ever work'd in this Kingdom'. Joseph Rose, senior (*c.* 1723–80), who had trained under Thomas Perritt (1710–59) in the 1730s, coming out of his apprenticeship at York in 1738, became head of a family firm which, under the leadership of his nephew, also Joseph Rose (*c.* 1745– 99), did most of the neo-Classical plasterwork in houses designed by Robert Adam and James Wyatt. Perritt and Rose's work at Nostell Priory and at Temple Newsam House, both in Yorkshire, in the 1740s, certainly support Paine's later assertion as to their quality. It was exuberant and well fashioned and representative of what good English firms could do. Rose in his own capacity was no less successful in, for example, his Rococo plasterwork (*c.* 1752) at Felbrigg, Norfolk, for William Windham,[27] again under James Paine's supervision, and with the help of his 'man', George Green.

Finally, in the last years of the 1750s work started on the Marble Hall at Holkham Hall, Norfolk, based on a design first published by Palladio and modified in the eighteenth century by Kent and Brettingham. Thomas Clark's great coffered ceiling was completed in about 1760; and a bust, of the builder Thomas Coke, 1st Earl of Leicester, was placed over the door to the saloon.

WINDOWS

One of the forms of window popularly associated with the Palladian revival years of the eighteenth century was the 'Venetian window', which we have referred to in its introduction to English architecture by Inigo Jones. He had looked back in particular to Scamozzi, whose *Idea della Architettura universale* (1615) contains a group of *palazzi* with this central motif, derived from an earlier prototype by Serlio. Isaac Ware, in his comprehensive treatise *A Complete Body of Architecture* (1756), wrote that Venetian windows were of 'a kind calculated for shew, and very pompous in their nature; and, when executed with judgment, of extreme elegance'.[28] Although there was no example of a Venetian window in the first volume of Colen Campbell's *Vitruvius Britannicus* (1715), it was soon in use in the Vanbrugh– Hawksmoor group and in the Burlington circle, and by about 1717–8 several examples can be cited.[29] In particular, its use on the south front of Campbell's Houghton Hall, Norfolk (1722), led to its repeat, with modifications, at William Kent's Holkham Hall, Norfolk (1734), Henry Flitcroft's Woburn Abbey, Bedfordshire (1747), and at Croome Court, Worcestershire, *c.* 1751–2, designed by Lancelot 'Capability' Brown. The appeal of the Venetian window continued and influenced designs by the strictly Palladian Isaac Ware at Wrotham Park, Middlesex (*c.* 1754), and

81. Detail of the chapel, c. 1723–6, at Grimsthorpe Castle, Lincolnshire, with its 'Venetian' window.

even by Robert Adam on the south front of the Register House at Edinburgh (1789).

The symmetry which this principal feature imposed on a room or staircase-hall meant that other windows were arranged with the Venetian one at the centre of the range. Glazing bar thicknesses were also important. Letters written to the Earl of Strafford in 1713–14 by the York joiner William Thornton (1670–1721)[30] are filled with such details: '& that it is ye same thickness I have done for Mr Bourchier and others wch hath proved to turn well better than those of thinner stuff'. This is valuable confirmation in an otherwise humdrum note of Thornton's involvement in the joinery and carving for John Bourchier at Beningbrough Hall, north Yorkshire. He is listed as the architect of Beningbrough in a copy of the *Builder's Dictionary* for 1734,[31] albeit with some dependence on engravings of the façades of Bernini's Palazzo Chigi in Rome, as given by Domenico de'Rossi in his *Studio d'Architettura Civile* (1702–21), and on plates later published in Borromini's own *Opus Architectonicum* (1725). Much of the internal decorative work took its inspiration from engravings by Daniel Marot and provides an excellent example of a York craftsman transcribing the current pattern-books with subtle variations. Nevertheless when he came to deal with the three window-openings in the upper stage of the entrance hall his system of vaulting – similar to that in Borromini's church of the Propaganda Fide – caused simple arcs to cut across the corners of the square-headed window-openings.

82. *Detail of wood carving by William Thornton of York,*
c. 1716, at Beningbrough Hall, Yorkshire.

On the west side of the saloon at Houghton Hall, Norfolk, the sash-windows with fifteen glass panes in the two stages are set into a lavish broken-pedimented windowcase, carved by James Richards in 1728. This matches the lofty pedimented doorcase, which has Corinthian columns flanking double eight-panelled mahogany doors on the east wall and rises almost to the cornice. Something of this giant order carried through to window and doorcases in other grand state rooms, such as the saloon at Woburn Abbey, Bedfordshire. Here James Whittle (d.1759) and his partner Samuel Norman (fl. 1746–67) worked for the architect Henry Flitcroft and provided most of the carved woodwork, *c.* 1755–6.[32] Their bill lists for the saloon: '3 Setts of window Architrives, with Scrole bottoms of Large OG shell knotchd, bead Strung and raffled Tong, window Staffs with rich raking leaf as before ... £17. 1s. 0d.' Further enrichment was given to the window shutters: 'Carving the rich ornaments in the suffits with rich raffld flowrs, Apollo's head & Glory, very rich foliage leaves. 2 ft Long 11 in wide. Six of the Above Ornaments ... £20. 14s. 0d.' The 4th Duke of Bedford must have thought it money well spent.

DOORS

The architects working in the Palladian years of the 1720–40 period re-introduced doorcases to important state rooms, giving them a more solid and imposing appearance by the use of large enriched mouldings. Between the architrave of the door and its pediment there was a frieze which was usually pulvinated (that is, with a bold convex moulding) and ornamented across its width with ribboned bay or oak leaves. It was also common to flank the doors with a case against which Corinthian or Ionic columns or

83. 'A Corinthian Door for a Room of State' from
Batty Langley, A Sure Guide to Builders (1729), Plate 48.

84. *Carved, painted and gilded doorcase by James Richards, c. 1723,
leading from the saloon to the Rotunda, at Mereworth Castle, Kent.*

pilasters were set, with a shell, lion's head or Classical mask incorporated in the frieze. The pediment, if broken, was often filled by a plaster bust as in the double doorcase of the saloon at Holkham Hall, Norfolk.

85. *The door and alcove in the Chinese Room, at Claydon House, Buckinghamshire, carved by Luke Lightfoot c. 1760.*

Doors were usually made in mahogany with six or eight fielded panels of varying size, edged with carved mouldings. One of these mouldings was often set vertically down the centre of the doors to give an added enrichment, especially when gilded. A variation was a deal door, painted white, with gilded mouldings that contrasted well with walls covered in crimson fabric or Chinese paper. These doorcases invariably had a pedimented top set on brackets above a frieze with carved swags centring on a mask-face.

Some of the most elaborate doorcases of the 1720s, as at Ditchley Park, Oxfordshire, and the Octagon Room, Orleans House, Middlesex, both designed by James Gibbs, have reclining stucco figures set nonchalantly above the pediments, an imperious touch to an already dominant feature of the room. A variation, common to the 1740–50 period in particular, was for the head of the door architrave to include a moulded central tablet bearing carved foliage and a carved head. 'No ornament', according to Isaac Ware in his *A Complete Body of Architecture* (1756), 'was so fit as a head' and when this, or similar ornament, was coupled, as at Claydon House, Buckinghamshire, with the wild carved extravagances of the Chinese taste, done in the middle years of the century, the effect was very striking. The literary critics railed that all the world was running mad after Chinese ornaments – of pagodas, tinkling bells, obsequious mandarins and decorated parasols.

CHIMNEYPIECES

Architects of the early Georgian period, such as William Kent (in the 1720s and 1730s), often turned back to the designs of Inigo Jones. Indeed, Kent had been given the task by Lord Burlington of editing the *Designs of Inigo Jones, with some Additional Designs* (by Lord Burlington and himself). These were published in two volumes in 1727 and reference to them and to Isaac Ware's *Designs of Inigo Jones and others* (*c*. 1733) show how the chimneypiece designs by Jones and Webb were designed or freshly adapted. A good example is provided by the two 'continued' chimneypieces in the long gallery at Temple Newsam House, Leeds. Erected there in 1739 by the mason Robert Doe, they were a direct copy of John Vardy's Plate 36 in his book of Kent's designs issued in 1735, and based on Sir Matthew Decker's chimneypiece at his house on Richmond Green, Surrey. With canvases of classical ruins by Antonio Joli set within them, they were the perfect decoration for the 7th Viscount Irwin's new gallery, one of the finest mid-Georgian spaces in England.

The architectural forms that made up the majority of chimneypieces often gave them their name; John Crunden's *The Chimneypiece Makers' Daily Assistant* of 1766 showed the varieties common in the first half of the eighteenth century: (1) the architrave type, and those with (2) trussed pilasters or (3) caryatid or terminal supports or columns to bear the mantelpiece. Chimneypieces were made up of one or two storeys, being of 'simple' or 'continued' type. The latter, especially those of *c*.1728–30 at Houghton Hall, Norfolk, or Clandon Park, Surrey, sculpted by John Michael

86. Continued chimneypiece, one of a pair,
in the hall at Clandon House, Surrey.
Carved in marble by John Michael Rysbrack c. 1728.

Rysbrack were among the most important and were related, for maximum effect, to the overdoor mythological panels of the rooms they were in.

Some of the principles which allegedly governed size were also set out in many manuals of instruction. For example, Robert Morris in his *Lectures on Architecture* (1751) gave his first rule as follows:

To find the height of the opening of the chimney from any given magnitude of a room, add the length and height of the room together, and extract the square root of that sum, and half that root will be the height of the chimney.

The breadth was established by adding the length, breadth and height of the room and extracting half the square root of the sum; the depth was one quarter of the combined height and breadth of the chimney. Sir William Chambers was more general in his dimensions and preferred two chimneypieces in large rooms, 'regularly placed, at equal distances from the centre of the wall in which they are both placed'. The farther the chimney-pieces were from a door the better, and they were rarely placed on front window walls owing to the weakening of the walls by carrying shafts as well as window openings, and the consequent appearance of the chimney on a principal elevation.

87. *Drawing for a chimneypiece, by Sir Henry Cheere (1703–81).*
Pen, ink, wash and watercolour, c. 1750.
(Victoria and Albert Museum, London, No. D715(3)–1887)

Two sculptors, among many, responsible for fine statuary marble chimneypieces were Sir Henry Cheere (1703–81) and his younger brother, John Cheere (1709–87), who was also a figure-maker and a painter. Henry Cheere's yard at Hyde Park Corner[33] produced much that made a major contribution to English Rococo. His manuscript 'Book of Chimneypiece Designs'[34] shows his ability to incorporate rich varied-coloured marbles in his designs, and his skills in adapting both the Classical and Gothic styles and in depicting flowers, animals and figures. Among the many examples of his work the chimneypieces at Ditchley Hall, Oxfordshire, and Wallington Hall, Northumberland, are particularly fine. Naturally Cheere had his competitors, for example, Thomas Carter, his son, Thomas junior, and John Devall. Devall's work is seen to advantage at Woburn Abbey, Bedfordshire.

The younger Carter is credited with providing two massive chimneypieces with Siena marble friezes for the saloon at Uppark, Sussex, c. 1754, although there is no documentation to support this; these survived the tragic fire in August 1989 almost undamaged. Their friezes have finely modelled plaques depicting 'Romulus and Remus' and 'Androcles and the Lion'. This work for Sir Matthew Fetherstonhaugh was probably under the architectural supervision of James Paine, who had worked at Sir Matthew's London House, 1752–6. Paine was a consummate designer of chimneypieces, which often have slender tapered pilasters with pedimented centrepieces, as at Uppark.[35]

Isaac Ware in his oft-quoted book of 1756, *A Complete Body of Architecture*, gives a long list of the plain and variegated marbles available from Italy, Spain, Egypt and from several places in England, such as Derbyshire and Devon. Festoons of flowers, trophies, foliage and key-frets were usually cut in white statuary marble and set against a coloured or variegated marble ground. Attention was, of course, paid to fitting the decoration to the purpose of a given room: a vine-wreathed head or Bacchic motifs were found on chimneypieces in dining-rooms, and also many subjects drawn from Aesop's *Fables*.[36] Throughout, the use of marble for chimneypieces indicated an underlying loyalty in the choice of subjects to a continuous Classical tradition. Departures from this were usually expressed in other materials – the French Rococo style in carved limewood and the revived Gothic in stone. Finally, Ware condemned any architect whose chimneypiece did not correspond to his overdoors: simple, direct advice and, alas, often ignored.

STAIRCASES

Changes in the plan of houses accounted for the variations in size and treatment of the staircase. Elizabethan and Jacobean staircases led from the ground to the high upper floors where the great chamber and long gallery were situated. But the Palladian revival of the early eighteenth century determined that the ground floor should be treated as the basement and that the first floor should be the Italian *piano nobile* or principal floor, on which the state rooms were grouped. These were reached by an external flight of steps and a grand staircase was usually sacrificed, although a restricted site or other constraints on planning prevented its entire disappearance. The Palladian staircase did not run up beyond the first floor as the course to the floor above rendered the height of the well disproportionate to the walls. In Palladio's own villas the staircase was made

88 (left). The staircase c. 1729, at Compton Place, Sussex, carved by James Richards. Compton Place was built from a late design by Colen Campbell (1676–1729).

89 (right). The staircase at Mawley Hall, Shropshire, with its undulating mahogany hand-rail and carved string, c. 1730.

small and placed so that it did not affect the 'geometrical harmony of the parts'. Colen Campbell, with this in mind, often used identically paired staircases and James Paine followed this idea at Heath House, Wakefield, 1744–5. The staircase was encircled by the principal rooms.[37]

At Nostell Priory, Yorkshire, c. 1745, Paine erected the north and south staircases, on the walls of which are plaster panels bordered by Greek-fret ornament, with shells and swags of flowers disposed about them. Bas-relief heads are set over the doors, and the stair balusters under a mahogany rail were fashioned in wrought-iron (probably by Thomas Wagg), elaborately scrolled and running to open-work iron newels. Staircase ironwork soon made its appearance in the practical manuals, such as William and John Welldon's *The Smith's Right Hand*, 1765. However, it needed to be interpreted in the correct way: James Paine's work demonstrated an integrity in the harmony of one part of the staircase scheme to another that was rarely excelled by other contemporary architects.

The finest mid-eighteenth-century staircase is, perhaps, that created by William Kent for Lady Isabella Finch at 44 Berkeley Square, London. A single flight leads to a half-landing where the stairway divides into two to swing up to the first floor, reverting to a single flight to the second floor. The balustrade is of wrought-iron S-shaped scroll-work, identical to that at Holkham Hall, Norfolk, and at 22 Arlington Street, London. It was a theatrical composition, which in 1764 Horace Walpole declared to be 'as beautiful a piece of scenery, and considering the space, of art, as can be imagined'. The smith Kent employed was Benjamin Holmes (fl. 1742–60). When compared with the splendid joiners' staircases by the Eboral family in a Francis Smith house, such as Mawley Hall, Shropshire, c. 1730, the advance in technique within a few years can be seen. The Mawley staircase has a mahogany rail, rippling as a simulated serpent from its curved tail on the upper landing to a fearsome head at the ground-floor newel. The string boards (that is, those next to the well-hole which receive the end of the steps) are deeply carved with ornaments of the chase. But there is an archaic

90. 'The Geometrical Construction of Banisters and Ballustrades'
from Batty Langley, The Builders' Chest Book *(1738), Plate 68.*

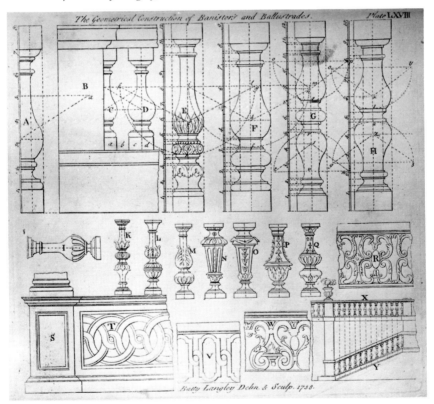

feel to it all, with the inlaid treads done in a parquetry technique: Kent and Paine could progress from this by using stone cantilevered steps, wrought-iron balusters and a good handrail that was continuous to the top. Perhaps the best example of Paine's skill in designing staircases is that at Stockeld Park, Yorkshire, *c.* 1760, which uses iron balusters of bow shape and rises in an apsidal-ended form to create an exciting series of interlocking voids and openings. Two great niches are angled on the landings to provide access to rooms without the use of corridors.

Neither Kent nor Paine needed any help from Abraham Swan's *The British Architect or ... The Builder's Treasury of Staircases* (1745, with later editions, e.g. 1750, 1758) or the precise geometrical setting out of banisters and balustrades that Batty Langley had given in Plate 68 of his *Builder's Chest Book* (1738). However, when the staircase at Blair Castle, Perthshire, was installed in 1757 it was still old-fashioned enough in appearance, with acanthus balusters and panelled newels, to be inspired by Swan's first edition. Indeed, it appears as his design in his *Collection of Designs in Architecture* (Vol. 1 Plate 31), although this was published in 1757. In fact, Swan's designs were particularly popular abroad and were used in many eighteenth-century colonial houses.

SERVICES

What Mark Girouard has called 'The Social House'[38] was one of the inexorable pressures that urged architects, surveyors and 'ingenious gentlemen' and their craftsmen to provide more facilities for many visitors. A water-tower was erected at Carshalton House, Surrey, in 1719–20, containing a water-wheel powered by a mill-stream. This turned a pump to send water to a lead cistern, which was then connected both to the house and to a bathroom at the base of the tower. It was a long step forward from Sir Francis Willoughby's plunge bath of the 1580s deep in the sandstone beneath Wollaton Hall, Nottingham, but comparable in the convenience of a hot-and-cold water service to the early-eighteenth-century 'bagnio' at Blenheim Palace. This was under the Duchess of Marlborough's bedroom and she could descend to it by a back staircase. The 1st Duke of Chandos could also boast the provision of four water-closets at Cannons with 'a wainscot bath lined with ledd' as well as a bathing room with 'marble cistren and marble lineings to the room'.[39] However, the technological capacity to raise water – so well understood by the hydraulics experts of French formal gardening – was little used in the English country house and 'running' water above ground level remained rare. Cheap labour

91. William Hogarth, 'The Assembly at Wanstead House', Essex, 1729.
Oil on canvas, 25 × 29¼ in, (Philadelphia Museum of Art).

was available to carry water to all parts of the house, with cold baths popularly regarded as efficacious to good health. There was little improvement to the system for another thirty years – Joseph Bramah did not patent a water-closet until 1778 – and families clung to the environs of the fireplace for warmth or stood near the various stoves popularized by smiths such as the Welldons. Hogarth's painting of 'The Assembly at Wanstead House' (Philadelphia Museum, 1729) shows the company taking tea or playing cards near the fireplace. The recently married couple in his 'Marriage a la Mode' (National Gallery, London, *c.* 1743) sprawl at the breakfast table drawn up close to the lighted fire. The kitchens were far away and perhaps Alexander Pope's 'Epistle IV to Richard Boyle, Earl of Burlington'[40] summarizes best the place of servant, served and services:

> But hark! the chiming Clocks to dinner call;
> A hundred footsteps scrape the marble Hall:
> The rich Buffet well-colour'd Serpents grace,
> And gaping Tritons spew to wash your face.

...
Tis Use alone that sanctifies Expence,
And Splendor borrows all her rays from Sense.

The plan of the ground floor at the Duke of Chandos's house of Cannons, *c*. 1720, shows a pantry, confectionery room, still room, store-room, a servants' hall, 31 ft long, and rooms for many grades of staff including the Gentlemen of the Horse and the chaplain. A detailed study of the economy of the house[41] shows the space that needed to be provided not only for food preparation, cooking, laundry and wine and beer storage, but for the many visitors who were shown over the house and grounds. The house 'fed itself from its fields and farms, kitchen garden and dairy'. It was the successful exemplar to which many aspired but the 2nd Duke could not deal with it all and demolition and sales of contents of Cannons started in 1747, with one of the duke's former cabinet-makers, William Hallett (1707–81), eventually building his own house on the central foundations. It was a sign that he needed little more than a butler, cook and a few house staff to deal with a small building of convenient plan, a forerunner of the 'villa with wings', so popular from the 1750s onwards for the incorporation of the necessary service areas and guest apartments.

Five

VISIONS AND REVIVALS,
1760–1830

King George III was stigmatized in the Declaration of Independence as 'unfit to be the ruler of a free people' – the king who 'lost' the American colonies. Despite his lack of political acumen, he was a considerable patron of the arts and of science and was accomplished both in playing music and in architectural drawing, which he had been taught by William Chambers, who later built him an observatory at Kew. He was also one of the great book-collectors of the eighteenth century, and his library is one of the richest collections in the British Library.[1]

The king's mature years were beset by tragic bouts of the hereditary disease of porphyria which, during their passage, gave him many of the outward signs of insanity. In 1811 he finally lost contact with reality and his eldest son, George, born to him in 1762 by Charlotte of Mecklenburg Strelitz, became the Prince Regent. With his brothers the Prince Regent was held in some contempt, was caricatured cruelly by Gillray and others, and remains best known for his Francophile interests, manifested at Carlton House, and for his rebuilding of the small farm at Brighton which became 'The Royal Pavilion'. He succeeded at his father's death in 1820 as King George IV, having acted for nine years as the Prince Regent. This gives to the period its appellation of 'Regency', a term often misapplied but useful in denoting decoration in the last years of the eighteenth and the early years of the nineteenth century. George IV, corpulent and subject to dropsy, died at Windsor Castle on 26 June 1830, oblivious at last of the regal self-indulgence which gave him his lasting, visible, memorial. Rising from the green lawns and within view of the sea at Brighton, it is, with all its coiled dragons and leering mandarins, a wonder to behold: an English 'house' interior almost impossible to understand fully.

In Rome in the 1740s and 1750s doctrines were being expounded that imparted an urgency to the development of Classicism. An active group of young French artists studied at the king's expense at the French Academy which was housed in the Palazzo Mancini. They were instructed in a detailed study of the famous monuments of Classical antiquity and of buildings, paintings and sculpture of more recent times.[2] The Classical remains lay almost undiscovered or in weed-covered splendour; they excited all impressionable minds by their scale and precise decoration. In addition, a considerable amount of new building was in progress – the Spanish Steps, the façade of San Giovanni in Laterano, the Fontana di Trevi. They vied with the established masterpieces by the Renaissance architects, and all had been finely engraved by the skilled members of the Bibiena family and by Giovanni Battista Piranesi. Neo-Classicism soon replaced the spirited

92. *Detail of Piranesi's dedicatory plate in his* Campus Martius
with the head of Robert Adam and his own; engraved 1756, published 1762.

delights of the Rococo, and every patron in England who wished to be up-to-date in stylistic matters wanted to be rid of a style which lacked symmetry and was seemingly uncontrollable in format; soon patrons and their architects were to be involved in promoting the new Classical revival. The *goût grec*, or the *style antique*, were terms which set out meaning one thing and ended as labelling antique exaggerations. The rivalry for patronage was to focus on the careers of William Chambers (who had studied at the French Academy) and Robert Adam. The measure of the first stage of this competition was given in a letter from Robert Adam to his brother James, written at Naples on 18 April 1755. Concerned with the considerable abilities of William Chambers he concluded: 'Time alone can determine whether I am meet to cope with such a rival ... as it will require a very considerable interest to succeed Chambers who has tolerable friends and real merit.'[3]

There was also a need to overcome the inability of English craftsmen to translate a new style into English architecture. The Abbé Le Blanc in his

Letters on the English and French Nations (1747) had mentioned the great skill of English workmen: 'but notwithstanding all their endeavours they have not been able to attain it [gracefulness in the shape of things]. As much as I admire their invention in mechanical arts, I am equally offended at all their productions in the arts of taste.'

He judged the English harshly because they had not adhered to the 'simplicity' of the ancients. The Rococo, and the exotic Gothic and Chinese derivatives, had affected the appearance of almost everything and had violated simplicity. There was a reluctance to design anything to be contained within a regular pattern: Hogarth's 'line of beauty', which he had expounded in his *The Analysis of Beauty* (1753), was the S-curve, and it dominated all Rococo ornamentation. In seeking to establish principles by which taste could be defined, the very nature of taste itself was neglected and overlooked. It was this situation that Chambers and Adam sought to correct; both realized that part of the solution lay in the education of their craftsmen, for the opportunities were considerable, with patrons amenable to change, even if they continued to pay for the privilege as tardily as ever.

THE HOUSE PLAN

One of the significant developments in eighteenth-century architecture was to provide additional accommodation for services by adding wings to a central block. The origins of this were not new, with the basic idea common to several villas by Palladio. The design was developed in drawings of the 1720s by Colen Campbell and was effectively used by James Paine at Kirkstall Grange, Leeds, in 1752. This house antedates by two years Isaac Ware's Wrotham Park, Middlesex, hitherto considered the prime example of a fully developed 'villa-with-wings'.[4]

The great-house-plan had been set down early in the eighteenth century with the building of Colen Campbell's Wanstead House, Essex, and Houghton Hall, Norfolk. A struggle then ensued between 'the greater house and the villa' and many large and small houses were built on the villa plan.[5] Service wings were linked to the central block by quadrant passages, a pattern well illustrated by Holkham Hall, Norfolk, and by James Paine's plan of the north front of Kedleston, Derbyshire. Paine had taken over there from Matthew Brettingham, 'being employed to make the plans for this magnificent mansion in the year 1761 ... [but] the noble owner [Nathaniel Curzon, 1st Lord Scarsdale] placed this great work in the hands of those able and ingenious artists, Messrs Robert and James Adam; who made

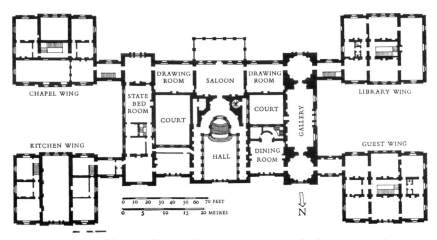

Fig. 12. *Holkham Hall, Norfolk, 1734–65, showing the dominance of the central hall and saloon, and the service wings connected to the main pile by corridors, from* Vitruvius Britannicus, V, 1771.

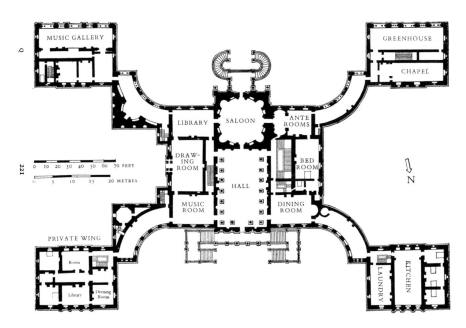

Fig. 13. *Kedleston Hall, Derbyshire, plan of the first floor, c. 1760–70, by Robert Adam; the two south pavilions and colonnades (top of plan) were not built. From* Vitruvius Britannicus, IV, 1767.

93. *The hall at Kedleston, Derbyshire, with alabaster columns, largely complete by 1765.*
George Richardson designed the ceiling and the Classical casts in the niches,
acquired in 1758, were moved there in 1788.

several alterations in the Author's plans ... and the whole was carried on under their direction'. The involved story of Brettingham, Paine and the Adam brothers' part in the design of Kedleston has been told elsewhere and changes the previously accepted view. Adam was in complete charge of the central block by April 1760 and 'also had considerable influence on the interiors of the pavilions'.[6] The plan, with its four pavilions – those to the south-west and south-east were never built – came from Palladio's Villa Mocenigo, which he had illustrated on Plate 58 of the second book of his *Quattro Libri* (1570). Nevertheless, the Kedleston façades clearly express that almost indefinable phase of 'movement' in architecture which Adam describes as 'the rise and fall, the advance and recess with other diversity of form, in the different parts of a building, so as to add greatly to the picturesque of the composition'.[7] The plan of all Adam houses was, in the further words of the two brothers, to contain 'variety in the outside composition, and in the decoration of the inside, an almost total change'.

At the centre of many eighteenth century house plans was a great hall and saloon on the central axis. They are so placed at Kedleston, with Lord Scarsdale describing them in 1769 as 'the Greek Hall and Dome of the Ancients, proportioned chiefly from the Pantheon at Rome and from Spalatra'. To the east, the music room, drawing-room and library represented, respectively, the arts of music, painting and literature. The balancing rooms to the west contained guest-rooms and the dining-room, connected to the kitchen pavilion. The family apartments were in the north-east pavilion linked by a quadrant corridor to the music room.

It is hardly surprising that Adam's considerable achievement in influencing, for a time, the interior decoration of many English houses should tend to push his work on exteriors into shadow. Often, as at Kedleston, he took over from other architects, or worked, as at Syon and Osterley, at amending earlier houses. At Osterley he emulated William Talman's work in the early eighteenth century at Witham Park, Somerset, and gave the house a double portico, which, in Horace Walpole's words, of June 1773, filled 'the space between the towers of the front and is as noble as the Propyleum of Athens'.

The smaller country houses designed by Sir William Chambers after 1765 did not follow Palladian prototypes, although his villa designs of a few years earlier had been refined and successful in their reliance on the exemplars in the Veneto. In 1762 Chambers designed Duddingstone, near Edinburgh, for the 8th Earl of Abercorn as the 'ultimate villa', with the attachment of a splendid temple-like portico, reared on four Corinthian columns from a single step. The most important room within was the hall, with a simple restrained plaster ceiling by Thomas Collins (1735–1830) and a staircase of iron S-balusters, which divided into two flights after a single flight of ten steps. The plans have been described as 'stereotyped' but with an interesting variety of staircases. It was the founding of the Royal Academy in 1768, and Chambers's appointment as Comptroller of the Works in 1769, which led to an easing of his country-house practice. Nevertheless, his many London town houses (with others in Edinburgh and Dublin) allowed him to show his flair both in their placement on difficult sites – a problem Wren had earlier encountered with the City churches – and in his use of elaborate staircases, many, alas, destroyed, as at Gower House, Whitehall (1765–70, dem. 1886), and at Melbourne House, Piccadilly (1771–6, dem. 1803–10). Both these were exceeded by the surviving

94. *The entrance hall, c. 1761, at Syon House, Middlesex.*
A room in the grand Roman manner executed to the design of Robert Adam.
The plasterwork, by Joseph Rose & Company, is in the heavy, early Adam style.
In the foreground is a bronze replica of the Classical sculpture, 'The Dying Gaul'.

staircases at Somerset House in the Strand, where an ingenuity with the use of space is matched by the quality of execution. Chambers used many of the same craftsmen as Adam, and his plasterer, Thomas Collins, acted as an executor and trustee to his will in 1796.

Of Adam and Chambers's contemporaries it was Sir Robert Taylor (1714–88) who showed the most ingenuity with his house plans. He broke away from the grouping of rooms in relationship to each other – ante-room, bedroom, cabinet and closet – and provided living-rooms on the first floor and bedrooms on the upper floor. These were often octagonal or oval. He also lit his dramatic cantilevered staircases from the top, as at Chute Lodge, Wiltshire (1768), and Danson Hill, Bexleyheath, Kent (1762–7). The top lighting at Sharpham House, Devon (c. 1770), is in the form of a 'huge oval cylinder with the dome springing directly from the walls' while the stairs and landings are cantilevered without any support from below.[8] The arrangement at Sharpham allowed 'for a hall opening into an atrium and the atrium into the staircase, with no intervening walls or doors' – something new in English architecture.

This concern to site the staircase at the centre of things and to place the main rooms round it applied to the work of James Wyatt (1746–1813). All his skill was lavished on the house interior: C. F. Cockerell wrote to Joseph Farington in 1798 that 'the finishing and decorations of Wyatt are generally beautiful, but his outside designs are blocks of stone'. There was also a move to give the hall a major space. At Heveningham Hall, Suffolk (where Wyatt replaced Sir Robert Taylor after the shell of the building was finished), the hall rises to the height of two storeys, and is comparable to Adam's fine Classical hall at Syon House. It was, in the words of François de la Rochefoucauld, who noted it in his *A Frenchman in England* (1784), 'extremely dignified and magnificent' and he thought the dining-room had 'perfect proportions' and decoration more elegant than he had ever seen. Wyatt had an extensive practice and was full of ideas but would often lose his first ardour in the execution of schemes. Many clients grumbled at his dilatory and unbusinesslike ways, and his career has always been tangled with the large and complex family from which he sprang.[9]

James Wyatt's nephew, Jeffry Wyatt (1766–1840), stated a determination 'to distinguish himself from the numerous branches of his family of the same profession' and thus took the surname of Wyatville when he was knighted by George IV (although he doubtless also wanted to highlight this mark of royal favour). Of almost 150 major commissions executed by Sir Jeffry, most of them were started in the first twenty years of the nineteenth century. He specialized in medieval and Elizabethan styles, carrying out many alterations to great houses, such as Longleat and Wollaton. His career was, however, directed towards his main commission of remodelling Windsor Castle. He started work there in 1824 and was employed until his death. He was especially competent at introducing modern comforts to his house plans – central heating, efficient water supplies, conservatories, orangeries and sculpture galleries, as at Chatsworth, Derbyshire.

In terms of house plan the last of the innovative architects I shall briefly deal with is Sir John Soane (1783–1837). One of the most distinguished of Henry Holland's pupils, Soane trained in the Royal Academy Schools. Through the intervention of Sir William Chambers, he received the 'King George III Travelling Scholarship' in 1778, and spent two years studying in Italy. On his return, in 1780, he tried to build up a modest country-house building practice and, being skilful in integrating Gothic and Greek elements, he created at least fifteen fine houses before 1800. His office grew large, and over Soane's lifetime some thirty pupils worked in it, twelve hours a day, for an average of five years.[10]

Soane showed great care in relating the plan of a house to a site and had a fondness for creating complex internal arrangements of a highly idiosyncratic nature: shallow domes, consoles on their sides and columns with strange unordered capitals. He also introduced light through lanterns and clerestories and was constantly 'controlling' the light and shade by an ingenious and extensive use of segmental arches. This is seen to great advantage in the drawing-room at Wimpole Hall, Cambridgeshire (an early work of c. 1791). Soane developed Classical forms suitable to the architecture of his day without rigorously following Vitruvian or Palladian precepts. He was an ardent user of wooden models[11] to demonstrate his plans and to enable discussion with his patrons on, for example, the best ways of lighting staircases and reception rooms to avoid dark corridors and corners.

In his *Plans, Elevations and Sections of Buildings erected in the Counties of Norfolk, Suffolk* ... (1788), dedicated to George III, Soane stated that the main object of his plans was to 'unite convenience and comfort in the interior distributions, and simplicity and uniformity in the exterior ...'[12] With a fortune left to him in 1788 by his wife's uncle, George Wyatt, Soane need have done little more thereafter but dream visions – of triumphal bridges and Piranesian spaces. Instead, he designed or altered almost a hundred country houses, some sixty London and other town-houses and near thirty public buildings. To most of them he brought what he later called 'the poetry of architecture', an elusive effect created by an original touch with composition. Using the Vanbrughian advance and recession of planes and ingenious lighting, Soane invested his interiors with fascinating

95. *The Yellow Drawing Room, c. 1791, at Wimpole Hall, Cambridgeshire.*
Designed by Sir John Soane with a skylight dome over the 'crossing'
and 'transepts' in the form of semi-circular 'apses' either side.
This gives a superb spatial effect and a 'concealed' light source.

spatial complexities. This was intellectually ahead of all the competition
and, as G. Wightwick put it: 'If any one shall ask – in what style is such,
or such, of his buildings? – the answer would be, It is ... Soanean.'[13]

At this stage of a short narrative it is obvious that my normal chapter-
by-chapter consideration of 'floors' is less necessary. They were of wood,
marble, stone or scagliola (as in the Syon ante-room), with little variation

96 (opposite). The ante-room, c. 1761–5, at Syon House, Middlesex.
This richly coloured room with scagliola floor, gilded statues and trophies has columns,
two of which were shipped to Robert Adam from Italy.

from what had gone before. In addition, Isaac Ware, commenting in his *A Complete Body of Architecture* (1756) on the decline in the use of inlay, noted that it was the custom to cover a room entirely with carpet, and near-contemporary inventories confirm this.[14] I have therefore given the space over to a short discussion of the uses to which various rooms were put, as their occupants, scattered informally through them, escaped from the restrictions represented by the mute starched poses of many a resplendent 'conversation-piece' canvas.

ROOMS AND THEIR USES

In the description in their *Works in Architecture* (1773–8) of the principal floor of Syon House, Middlesex, the Adam brothers chose to enter minutely into the description of its plan because they imagined it was: 'one of those branches of our art, which has not hitherto been treated of with any accuracy, or studied with any care; though of all others the most essential, both to the splendor and convenience of life.'

The hall was devised as a spacious apartment, intended as the room of access, where servants in livery attended. It was finished with stucco, 'as halls always are', and was given a noble effect by recesses at each end and by the siting of classical statues. The ante-rooms to each side were for the attendance of servants out of livery, and also for tradesmen. Next to the ante-rooms were the public and private eating rooms, the public one finished with stucco and adorned with niches, marble statues and a great circular recess at each end. The private one also had its recesses and stucco finishing, which did not allow cooking smells to linger, as they would on fabrics, and was equipped with backstairs for the use of servants. Next to the great 'eating room' was a splendid withdrawing-room for the ladies, or *salle de compagnie*, 'as it is called by the French'. This had a coved and painted ceiling. The room was so situated that it prevented the noise of the men remaining in the eating room from being troublesome to the ladies when they had retired to the adjacent gallery. The gallery had a small closet at each end, one for china and the other for miniatures, and there was access by stairs to the ranges of apartments on both sides. These private apartments consisted of a bedchamber for the Duchess of Northumberland, an ante-room for attendance by her maids, her toilet or dressing-room, her powdering-room, water-closet and outer ante-room, with backstairs leading to wardrobes and the maid's bedroom. On the other side was a dressing-room for the duke, a powdering-room, writing-room, water-closet and stairs for His Grace's *valet de chambre* and for access to his wardrobes.

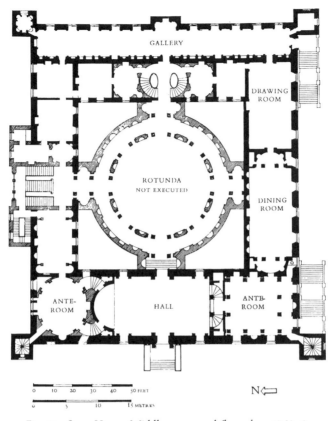

Fig. 14. Syon House, Middlesex, ground-floor plan, 1762–9,
by Robert Adam, from his Works in Architecture, *1773–8.*

Syon was a house devised internally for the reception of a large number
of people. This was also true of the Scarsdales' great Derbyshire house of
Kedleston Hall. Dr Johnson found the large hall 'too massy', but a sequence
of ten rooms was given over to reception, entertainment, hospitality and
rest. When Mrs Fanny Boscawen, wife of Admiral Edward Boscawen, visited
Holkham Hall, Norfolk, in 1774 she found 'all the rooms in the house are
every day and all day open, not one uninhabited chamber or closet shut
up'.[15] In 1786 the state apartments at Audley End, Essex, were similar to
those at Syon, being described as comprising 'a bed-chamber, two dressing-
rooms, two powdering closets, an ante-chamber and servants' room. The
bedchamber, gentleman's dressing room and ante-chamber are hung with
grey water tabby, ornamented with crimson and gold ...'[16]

Inventories are invaluable for indicating the purpose of rooms, in addition
to their exact contents at a given date. That of 1770 for Chiswick House,

Middlesex,[17] still seems to represent the contents of the house in the 1750s when the 3rd Earl of Burlington and his wife lived there. Apart from the grand well-furnished rooms, which one would expect, there was a nursery, a steward's and a housekeeper's room, a still room, butler's pantry, linen room, laundry and wash-house, maids' and coachman's rooms, a garden room, servants' hall, larder, scullery and porter's lodge.

At Osterley Park, Middlesex, the 1782 inventory[18] shows that the butler, cook, steward, housekeeper and footmen were housed in the south wing, together with the kitchen, still room, laundry, dairy, bake- and brew-houses, with additional servants' rooms over the stables. There was a strong beer cellar, an ale cellar and a small beer cellar as well as a mill house, coach house and several greenhouses, hothouses and tea rooms, together with a timber yard and even a menagerie. All these served the needs of the Child family, who gathered in the state rooms on the ground and first floor, whilst the top floor was given over to a private apartment for Mr and Mrs Child, a bedroom and a study for Miss Child, eleven other bedrooms (of which one was for a servant) and three dressing-rooms.

Many eighteenth-century house-plans made provision for sculpture galleries and libraries, for instance, at Petworth, Sussex, and Stourhead, Wiltshire, whilst early nineteenth-century plans had rooms for billiards and even heated conservatories. In addition, there was often a sensible compromise over useful and useless space. Humphry Repton, who designed Sheringham Hall, Norfolk, 1812–9, for Mr and Mrs Abbot Upcher, a young couple 'who might have stepped straight from one of Jane Austen's novels', noted that they required a single large 'living room', an ample eating

97. 'A Section of a Drawing Room' by Thomas Sheraton, from his work, The Cabinet-Maker and Upholsterer's Drawing-Book (1794).

98. *Sir Richard Colt Hoare's library at Stourhead, Wiltshire;*
watercolour by Francis Nicholson, 1808. The painted glass window was by
Francis Eginton, and the library was completed in 1792.

room, and 'no useless drawing-room'.[19] Repton felt that for 'Comfort and Respectability' they needed facilities for 'indoor exercise, howbeit without the waste of a large hall, or ... galleries'. Nevertheless large halls wasting a great deal of space and demanding considerable resources to heat continued to be built, for example, at Ickworth, Suffolk.

The plan for Sheringham also included 'the gentleman's own room, for guns, papers and Justice business' and on the other side of the hall an 'occasional' ground-floor bedroom, 'either for guests, or in case of sickness or infirmity'. This was designed so that the door to the living-room from the corridor 'could be effectually closed and access be only through an anteroom, where a fire betwixt the two large rooms constantly inhabited will exclude all cold air from the passage'. There was a slow move towards seasonal planning, with arrangements to open up a house to the garden and in winter to a conservatory 'winter garden'. Repton used the analogy that:

We make a difference twixt summer and winter in our clothes; in France the furniture is always changed with the seasons, from Chintz and silks to Cloth or Velvet, carpets substituted for mats. So would the living room, with the heating

of the approaches mentioned above, be as pleasant in winter when its recesses and connecting *agrements* connect it with the flower garden.

The plan of Oakley Park, Shropshire, which C. R. Cockerell remodelled for Robert Henry Clive (grandson of the great Clive) from 1819, shows a 'breakfast room' connecting to a study, near to the kitchen and flanked on the east by a conservatory, which was to have cast-iron pillars. In many early-nineteenth-century houses light came from oil lamps (although Colza oil was not introduced until 1834). There was work enough for maids, tending fires and polishing the bright cut-steel grates, with their apertures for inducted hot air, decorated with Greek and Gothic motifs, and the radiating steel bars designed for the same purpose in the hearth. With heavy fringed curtains drawn, winter could be banished for a few brief hours from at least one room.

PLASTERED WALLS
AND CEILINGS

In their *Works in Architecture* (1773–8) Robert and James Adam stated that they had introduced 'a great diversity of ceilings, freezes and decorated pilasters' and that they had 'added grace and beauty to the whole, by a mixture of grotesque, stucco and painted ornaments ...' The plaster ceilings in Adam schemes of decoration have been placed in five main categories.[20]

1. Simple concentric oval and circular rings, of which the entrance-hall ceiling at Osterley Park, Middlesex, is an example of the basic form.
2. An arrangement and division of the concentric rings or ovals by enrichments in plaster or composition (for example, the drawing-room ceiling at Mersham Le Hatch, Kent, 1766).
3. Ceilings in which a central motif in plaster or paint is emphasized (for example the library at Newby Hall, Yorkshire).
4. Tripartite patterns in which two or more end sections flank a large central square, circle or rectangle (for example, the library ceiling at Kenwood, Middlesex).
5. Overall patterns, of which many versions abound (for example, the Second Drawing Room at 20 St James's Square, London.

A sixth version may be allowed where enrichment of a cove or apse is involved.

The variety of Adam ceilings can be traced in the many surviving drawings at Sir John Soane's Museum, London, in house archives at Kedleston and elsewhere, and in well-illustrated surveys.[21] Even the provincial

99 (opposite). The hall, c. 1827–32, at Ickworth House, Suffolk, built for Frederick, 4th Earl of Bristol and Bishop of Derry. The scagliola 'porphyry' columns frame a mighty space housing Flaxman's 'Fury of Athamas', 1790.

100. The entrance hall, 1767–8, at Osterley Park, Middlesex, by Robert Adam.
The decoration of this room was a successful synthesis of flat and linear motifs,
plastered by Joseph Rose & Company.

plasterer found himself able to imitate much that was in the Adam style when George Richardson (*c.* 1736–1813), principal draughtsman to the brothers for over eighteen years, issued his *A Book of Ornamental Ceilings in the style of the Antique Grotesque* in 1776.

In the *Works* the brothers addressed the problems of colour, although they had been active in its use for almost twenty years:

We have thought it proper to colour with the tints, used in the execution a few copies of each number, not only that posterity might be enabled to judge with more accuracy concerning the taste of the present age, and that foreign connoisseurs might have it in their power to indulge their curiosity with respect to our national style of ornament; but that the public in general might have an opportunity of cultivating the beautiful art of decoration, hitherto so little understood in most of the countries of Europe.

The earliest Adam drawing in the Kedleston archives is that for the State Drawing Room ceiling, dated 1759, although cautionary words have been written suggesting that this date represents only the conception of the idea. The execution of the design probably occurred in the mid-1760s.[22] The drawing shows a loose arrangement of acanthus scrolls in the cove and is representative of the Rococo-influenced style that Adam practised for a short time after his return from Rome in 1758. Such early ceilings he normally left white — there is an example of one from 1759 at Hatchlands, Surrey — and it is interesting that five designs in grisaille for the library (1760) at Kedleston imply (as with the Music Room ceiling) they should be left without colour. The earliest coloured Adam design to survive in the Soane Museum, also dated 1760, is for Lady Scarsdale's dressing-room at Kedleston. The ground of the frame is deep blue, and outside and within this, the ornament is coloured yellow (an indication of gilding) on a white ground. It was intended that the ceiling should contain inset painted panels. They were drawings (and a number are so labelled) 'in the style of the Ancients' with the palaces of Augustus and of Titus in Rome serving as ready sources.[23] The design for the ceiling of the great staircase, preserved

101. Ceiling of the drawing-room at Mersham Le Hatch, Kent, showing the central panel, 1766. Executed to Robert Adam's design by Joseph Rose & Company.

at Kedleston, is dated 1764 and shows six alternative colour schemes, but the three designs for the Painted Breakfast Room (dem. 1807) there, of 1760, show a more lavish use of deep-blue panels on dado, doors and in the ceiling centre, overlaid with gilded ornament. It was in fact a 'Painted Room' with subjects after the 'Baths of Diocletian' painted in London on rolls of paper by Agostino Brunias (who had come back to England with Adam) and then cut out and pasted up *in situ*.

While Adam was thus a principal user of colour on walls and ceilings, a fine blue had already been used in the French-style interiors at Chesterfield House, London, in 1748 and the ceilings of the dressing-room and state bedroom at Norfolk House, 1756, had 'party colour'd' paintwork on them.[24] Sir William Chambers had also noted in his *Treatise on Civil Architecture* (1759) that the usual method was to gild all the ornaments, 'and to leave the grounds white, pearl colour, light blew, or of any other tint proper to set off the gilding to advantage'. His fine design for the ceiling of the gallery at Pembroke House, Whitehall (1760), shows a pale blue-grey ground acting as a foil for the gilding, with that for the saloon having a pink ground.

It says much for the business acumen of Adam's principal plasterers, Joseph Rose & Company, that they adapted their business to suit the architect. The early ceilings were by Joseph Rose, senior (*c.* 1723–80), whom I have noted working for James Paine in various Yorkshire houses such as Nostell Priory and Cusworth Hall. He settled in London in about 1752, with his first job under Paine being at Sir Matthew Fetherstonhaugh's London town house (1752–4). He was joined in 1766 by his nephew Joseph (1745–99) who had returned from a trip to Italy, and they had assistance from the elder Joseph's son and nephew, both named Jonathan. The younger Joseph saw the advantages of gearing the firm to the new neo-Classical mood and they never lacked for work, provided mostly by Adam but also by James Wyatt and even occasionally by William Chambers, as at Milton Abbey, Dorset. Chambers thought it best on most occasions, however, to use Thomas Collins, with whom he had long established a connection.

The heavy forms of Greek Doric ornament, which had been portrayed in the first volume of James 'Athenian' Stuart and Nicholas Revett's *Antiquities of Athens* (1762), had attracted bitter criticism from Chambers and Adam, who had both attempted something more delicate and elegant. Greek forms had become more common after 1760, especially in plasterwork, and James Wyatt was an exponent of these. He had spent some years in Italy from 1762, travelling as far east as Venice, but unlike Stuart he did not visit Greece. However, his family had worked under Stuart on the Anson estates

102. *The saloon, c. 1768–76, at Nostell Priory, Yorkshire.*
Adam's first drawings are dated 1768. Joseph Rose did the plastering in 1770
and Antonio Zucchi painted the canvases of ancient ruins in 1776.

103. A design for a ceiling in an unidentified house, c. 1785, by James Wyatt.

at Shugborough, Staffordshire, and in their London town house at 15 St James's Square, London. Wyatt knew of ancient Roman stucco interiors, and of the mid-eighteenth-century arguments and teachings on the respective merits of Greek and Roman ornament. The German philosopher Johann Joachim Winckelmann (1717–68), who lived in Rome, had written many invocations to the 'noble simplicity and quiet grandeur' of Greek art, based on the writings of Pliny and Pausanias. Wyatt had the experience of his Italian architectural teacher, Antonio Visentini, to guide his choice of what was relevant both in Winckelmann's writings, and in the antique styles of Greece and Rome.

When James Wyatt returned from Italy in about 1768, Robert Adam had been in practice in London for some ten years. Wyatt was determined not to copy the older man slavishly, but to invest his own ceiling designs with an even greater delicacy, derived more from Greece than from Rome. In 1772 at Heaton Hall, near Manchester, built for the Egerton family, his billiard-room ceiling has a central panel with thinly stringed husks in an oval, surrounding a fan-motif. A second surrounding oval has eight compartments filled with rosettes and anthemion motifs, similar to those in many of the plates in Stuart and Revett's book, and to the engravings of Piranesi. So far the ornament is Roman, but the anthemion frieze in the apse of the dining-room is purely Greek, derived from the inner frieze of the Temple by the Ilissus, and other elements 'are most likely derived from the

Athenian temple of Jupiter Olympus'.[25] In about 1780 James Wyatt, ever restless, turned increasingly to working in the Gothic style, which had also been a lifelong interest of Robert Adam.

The medieval Gothic style was beloved in the mid-eighteenth century. Its propagandists, for example Horace Walpole, realizing that Gothic had survived as a style long after the years of its active use, and drawn to its romantic nature, applied it to temporary structures, such as follies in landscaped parks and garden buildings. Robert Adam and James Wyatt used the Gothic style much more effectively than the Walpolian circle, and many nineteenth-century architects felt themselves to be as good as the medieval masons in applying the Gothic form to churches, town halls and even the Houses of Parliament. From his twenties Robert Adam (1728–92) had interested himself in the romantic and picturesque aspects of landscape and in Gothic buildings. His sketches made in the late 1740s underpinned the later incorporation of Gothic details in his work. In 1778 he used Joseph Rose to Gothicize the interior of Hulne Priory, Northumberland, a former Carmelite House. This lay a short distance from Alnwick Castle, the northern home (with Syon in the south) of his most considerable patron, Hugh Smithson, 1st Duke of Northumberland. Adam's Gothic work at Alnwick Castle was lost in the nineteenth-century remodelling, but the composition overmantels (made of a lightweight form of plaster) of the small rooms of the priory still contain Gothic and heraldic elements.

Wyatt had begun to use Gothic ornament in about 1775, but his early interiors – the hall at Sandleford Priory, Berkshire (1780), for example – merely have simple plaster ceilings edged with Gothic borders and friezes depicting machicolation. Wyatt's most notable building, Fonthill Abbey, Wiltshire, designed for William Beckford (1759–1844), had Gothic stucco, but alas, the abbey has not survived.

Ever since childhood Beckford had disliked his father's Classical mansion, and when the opportunity came in the 1790s to use James Wyatt to replace it, he selected designs for a ruined convent, to which a great wing and an octagon tower were added. The detailing of the plan was poor and even at this stage the structure looked insecure. Nevertheless, Beckford insisted that the building be constructed and at such speed that no foundations were placed under the central tower: one night in 1825 it collapsed, like so much stage scenery. Fonthill Abbey boasted unimpeded perspectives and a great height rivalling a medieval cathedral, whereas Walpole's Strawberry Hill was 'a Gothic mouse-trap', according to Beckford. However, whilst Fonthill has gone, the older house survives, as a dazzling advertisement for the revival of the Gothic style.

104. Ceiling of the Strawberry Room at Lee Priory, Kent,
designed by James Wyatt and probably executed by Joseph Rose & Company, c. 1785;
re-erected at the Victoria & Albert Museum, London.

Most of the plasterwork in Gothic Style done for James Wyatt was by the Bernasconi family, who were probably descended from stuccoists of that name settled at Riva San Vitale, near Lugano. It is not known whether they provided ceilings at Lee Priory, Kent, decorated for Thomas Barrett, under James Wyatt's supervision, between 1782 and 1790. Walpole enthused to his friend Mary Berry that its library was 'the most perfect thing I ever saw'. Lee Priory was demolished in 1955 but the 'Strawberry Room', with its stucco fan-vaulted ceiling of consummate beauty, was re-erected in the Victoria and Albert Museum, London. Wyatt continued using the Bernasconi family throughout his life. The first mention of Bernato Bernasconi is in the 1770–80 period, when he was working at Claydon House, Buckinghamshire: he was described as 'a poor man with a large family'. Francis Bernasconi (1762–1841) was probably Bernato's son; he worked for both James Wyatt and for Sir Robert Smirke (1780–1867) at his Gothic castles of Eastnor, Hereford and Worcester, and Lowther, Cumbria (now a ruin), in the early nineteenth century. The Eastnor plasterwork was entrusted to 'Bernasconi & Son' with Francis Bernasconi in charge. The foundation-stone at Eastnor was laid on 24 April 1812 and Bernasconi's name first appears in the accounts for 1815. His main work was in this year and in 1816 (receiving well over £900 in each) but he was still owed £600 in 1820. The Bernasconi firm's plasterwork recalled perfectly the Perpendicular linearity of medieval Gothic and it was the obvious company to use at Westminster Abbey (1803), York Minster (1803–5), Windsor Castle (1805), and at houses such as Chatsworth, Longleat and at Dodington Park, Gloucestershire, James Wyatt's last house. At Blithfield, Staffordshire, the great hall was plastered in Gothic style in 1822 and the patron, Lord Bagot, said that it was 'as perfect a specimen ... as has ever been executed in modern times'.[26]

A considerable amount of plasterwork in houses designed by Sir John Soane was executed by John and Joseph Baily. John Baily's bust is preserved at Sir John Soane's Museum, together with some of his models of Soane buildings. Soane was an ardent and surprisingly adventurous colourist, as the recent restoration of his schemes at the Dulwich Picture Gallery and Pitzhanger Manor, Ealing, make clear. The breakfast-room at Pitzhanger has marbled decoration and the usual array of shallow arches, which are decorated with thin fret patterns, whilst the gallery at Dulwich (1811) has been restored to a delicate pink, with dark bronzed doors.

The appearance from the 1790s of a number of books detailing Gothic architectural ornament was an important influence on many architects. In 1805, Lord Buckingham employed Soane to design a Gothic library at Stowe, Buckinghamshire, to hold his collection of Saxon manuscripts. The details were taken from Henry VII's Chapel at Westminster Abbey, the plaster ceiling imitating the precise delineations of its prototype, with ribs and quatrefoils in a rich array. It is one of the most satisfying technical accomplishments of the plasterer William Rothwell, who charged over £282 for '509 Pannels large imbost and executed as per Design', on the ceiling.

PAINTED WALLS AND CEILINGS

No Adam interior after the architect's return from Rome was complete without painted decoration. This was done by a number of foreign artists, resident for short periods in England. Notable amongst these are Angelica Kauffmann, her second husband, Antonio Zucchi, Giovanni Battista Cipriani, Biagio Rebecca and Michele Angelo Pergolesi. The painters worked in three main styles: firstly, a widely spaced arrangement of large canvases, mostly landscapes and assemblages of Classical buildings and weed-covered ruins; secondly, a frieze of panels or medallions done in *chiaroscuro* to imitate bas-reliefs; and thirdly, a widespread imitation of Roman grotesque, in which small medallions and panels were inspired directly by study of antique painting.

105. *Drawing of a detail of the Painted Room, Spencer House, London, 1759, showing a serving table with perfume burner, by James 'Athenian' Stuart. (British Library, London, No. 1955. 4.16.13).*

Robert Adam returned to London from Italy in 1758 intent on making his mark. But London society was already able to visit, in 1759, one of the earliest painted interiors in the neo-Classical taste, the Painted Room by James 'Athenian' Stuart (1713–88) at Spencer House, St James's. Whilst it is a little heavy in comparison to later work by Adam (excepting the drawing[27] for the north wall, which shows a lighter and more advanced scheme), Stuart's competent work anticipated the schemes done in the

Adams' office for coloured grotesque work, based on the decorations in the Vatican *Logge*.

The Spencer House room, brilliant, with complex decoration, is of enormous importance in the development of eighteenth-century Classical taste in England. It was, perhaps, fortunate for Adam and Chambers that Stuart's natural indolence prevented him from becoming a considerable threat. Stuart opened everyone's eyes to Greek architecture with the issue of *The Antiquities of Athens* in 1762, produced with Nicholas Revett. This was a first volume of measured drawings of Greek Antiquities and its publication ensured that Stuart was in demand by members of the Society of Dilettanti, who had sponsored his travels to Athens and the Greek archipelago in 1751–3. Since his return, Stuart had been appointed Surveyor of Greenwich Hospital, through the influence of his patron, Lord Anson, for whom he later worked at Shugborough, Staffordshire, and 15 St James's Square, London.

In 1759 Sir William Chambers, in his *Treatise on Civil Architecture* (1759), had also described and illustrated the different types of ornamental ceilings he felt were appropriate for the period – coved, circular and in compartments. The compartments, 'when the utmost degree of richness in decoration is aimed at', could be adorned with paintings, or with bas-reliefs representing grotesque figures, after engravings of subjects by Raphael, Peruzzi, Michelangelo, Ammanati and Algardi. Chambers has been described by Edward Croft-Murray as contributing considerably to 'the transition from neo-Palladian to neo-Classic', and he was closely associated with the first Italian to practise neo-Classical painting in England, Giovanni Battista Cipriani (1727–85). Whilst it is beyond the scope of this study, Cipriani's best-known work under Sir William Chambers's supervision was the painting (1760–2) of panels on the State Coach designed by the architect for George III, and used at coronations of successive sovereigns.[28] Cipriani embellished some thirty-five buildings with his paintings, those in the dining-room and library at Osterley Park, Middlesex, *c.* 1775, being his last known commission. The roundels on the drawing-room ceiling at Syon House, Middlesex, 1765, were first painted by Cipriani in his studio in oil on paper and charged at two guineas each. They were then sent down to the house to be fitted into the spaces left in the gilded and coloured ceiling.

In 1770 Chambers was retained by the 4th Duke of Bedford to fit up the library and dining-room at Woburn Abbey, Bedfordshire. Biagio Rebecca (1735–1808), who had come to England in 1761, assisted Cipriani with the library ceiling there. Three extracts from Chambers's letters[29] speak for themselves of the techniques used and the progress made.

19 May, 1770 ... I believe one of the painters that is about the Library Ceiling will go downe next week to make his remarks upon the light & verify some measures & as he cannot speak a Word of English I should be obliged to you if you would desire anyone in the family that understand Italian to ask for any thing he may Want of the workmen ...

1 June, 1770 ... as I shal want to fix up some paper Patterns in the Library Ceiling at Wooburn Abbey be pleased to have 2 or 3 Plaisterers trusses in the room to form a Moving Scaffold high enough to reach to the top of the Cove.

22 November, 1770 ... the painters have nearly finished the Ceiling for the Library at Wooburn Abbey & will be down soon to put it up. I hope therefore that all your things in the room are nearly done, as when they come the room must be cleared for them & they must have moving Trussels to stand upon.

By 1771, Cipriani had finished his part of the library ceiling at Woburn, and Chambers wrote to ask for the remainder of the money due from his bill of 350 guineas. Rebecca was to be paid £220 1s for painting the ornaments and £10 travelling expenses.

It is regrettable that so well documented a work was swept away when Henry Holland remodelled parts of Woburn in the 1780s. There is, however, a very fine drawing by Chambers[30] of the library ceiling, unparalleled in excellence even in his own work, and blending English, French and Italian elements. It shows the twelve signs of the zodiac around a fan-shaped centre, with the scalloped edge of the fan repeated at the edge of the enclosing square in the form of festoons of flowers. The borders, Rebecca's work, are of griffins and acanthus scrolling with small paintings of Classical figures in joyous stances.

Rebecca's chief skill lay in the imitation of antique bas-reliefs, and his monochrome *trompe l'œil* style was much in evidence in late-Georgian interiors. His best-known work for James Wyatt was at Heveningham, Suffolk, where, as at Adam's Osterley Park, Wyatt's Heaton Hall, Manchester, and Thomas Leverton's Woodhall Park, Hertfordshire, there is an Etruscan ante-room (*c.* 1797–9) with grotesque ornament in terracotta and black, seemingly inspired by antique vase-painting and by the plates found in Piranesi's *Diverse maniere d'adornare i cammini* (1769). In 1774, at Audley End, Essex, Rebecca used engravings by George Vertue to create an interesting series of portraits after the sixteenth-century picture 'The Visit of Queen Elizabeth to Blackfriars', attributed to Marcus Gheeraerts the Younger and now at Sherborne Castle, Dorset. The need for lineage, ancestry and for 'history' were always powerful incentives to patrons and their artists.

106. The Etruscan Dressing Room at Osterley Park, Middlesex.
Detail of painted decoration, c. 1775, probably by Pietro Maria Borgnis,
who painted walls, door and ceiling (except the centre roundel).

Many decorations have been attributed, without reason, to Angelica Kauffmann (1741–1807), who arrived in England in 1766. Sir Joshua Reynolds became a great admirer of her talent as a portraitist, and as she was a Foundation Member of the Royal Academy from 1768, she exhibited there for over thirty years. About twelve decorative commissions were given to her, of which the easiest to see are the four roundels representing Design, Painting, Composition and Genius, now in the ceiling of the vestibule of the Royal Academy at Burlington House, Piccadilly. Angelica finally left England for Italy in 1781, the year in which she married for the second time.

Antonio Zucchi (1726–95), Angelica's second husband, was the best known of Robert Adam's decorative painters. He had been employed by Adam in 1757 to engrave plates for the architect's book on the ruins of Diocletian's palace at Spalatro (1764),[31] and at the architect's invitation he later came to England. He settled in London and was much visited there by prospective patrons. Theresa Parker, *née* Robinson, wrote to her brother Frederick on 17 September 1769,[32] asking that he call about the pictures ordered from Zucchi by her husband, John Parker, for the library of their Devon house at Saltram; these paintings are still to be seen there. Adam's

other principal room at Saltram is the saloon, with its Axminster carpet matching the ceiling pattern.

Some of Zucchi's detailed bills survive, for Kenwood and 20 St James's Square, London, and show that he was subjected to the usual supervision of all craftsmen by Robert Adam. Zucchi is, perhaps, the painter most closely identified with the architect and his work is seen, to excellent advantage, in the two houses mentioned above; his paintings of Classical ruins, 1771, in the Music Room at Harewood House, Yorkshire; those illustrating Cupid and Psyche and the Liberal Arts in the Tapestry Room at Nostell Priory, Yorkshire, and those in the centre of the library ceiling at Newby Hall, Yorkshire. At Kenwood, in 1769, Adam and Zucchi had as their patron William Murray, 1st Earl of Mansfield, who as a judge later found for the Adam brothers in the Liardet stucco lawsuit (1778). The brothers had permission to use the stucco invented by John Liardet and with him proceeded at law against a speculative architect, John Johnson, who had infringed their patent.

Zucchi provided many paintings for the magnificent tunnel-vaulted ceiling of the library at Kenwood with its central roundel of 'The Choice of Hercules'. In the *Works in Architecture* Adam records that the stucco work of what he called the 'Great Room' at Kenwood was by Joseph Rose, and

107. *Detail of the Tapestry Room ceiling, 1767, at Nostell Priory, Yorkshire.*
It is painted by Antonio Zucchi with a scene from the story of Cupid and Psyche (centre)
and lunettes representing the Liberal Arts.

108 (opposite). *The saloon, 1768–70, at Saltram, Devon.*
The 'Great Room' designed by Adam still has its Axminster carpet of 1770,
and Antonio Zucchi's painted roundels of mythological subjects.

the paintings 'by Mr Antonio Zucchi, a Venetian painter of great eminence'. He further noted that 'the grounds of the pannels and freeses are coloured with light tints of pink and green, so as to take off the glare of white, so common in every ceiling, till of late'. With its curved ceiling and screen of columns inspired by the examples of Roman antiquity Adam had seen in Italy, the Kenwood library is a magnificent room and undoubtedly influenced the later form of Wyatt's wonderfully linear hall at Heveningham Hall, Suffolk (1778–84).

Michele Angelo Pergolesi (fl. 1762–1801) is said to have been sent by Robert Adam from Rome to England. Only his work at Syon House, Middlesex, is recorded. In the long gallery there are sixty-two pilasters that Pergolesi ornamented between 1765 and 1768 at a total charge of £160 14s, of which £20 was 'a present from His Grace' – the 1st Duke of Northumberland. Some of this payment may have been made because Pergolesi had, under Adam's instructions, attempted at least nine schemes of decoration before they were both satisfied. The architect was mindful of the duke's instructions to him in November 1764 that he would not, 'upon any account, suffer any work to be fixed up at Sion that is not compleatly finished to your satisfaction.'[33]

In 1767 Joseph Bonomi (1739–1808) had come to England from Rome to work for Robert Adam. He married Angelica Kauffmann's niece and, after the troubles of the Adam brothers' speculation in developing terraced houses at the Adelphi on the banks of the Thames (1768–72), he left their office and joined that of Thomas Leverton (1743–1824). However, an important, if eccentric, patron who used Bonomi in his own right was Heneage Finch, 3rd Earl of Aylesford, of Packington Hall, Warwickshire. Bonomi created for him, c. 1786, an important Pompeian Gallery, using the painters Benedetto Pastorini, Giovanni Borgnis and John Francis Rigaud. Joseph Rose junior acted as plasterer and Domenico Bartoli did the scagliola columns and pilasters. With its black and terracotta colouring, partly based on the Greek vases Lord Aylesford collected and on plates in various books on Classical antiquities, it was a room showing archaeological accuracy, and may have influenced the late-nineteenth-century Pompeian Room at Ickworth, Suffolk.

A year or two before Bonomi's scheme, in 1777–80, the Italian painter Vicenzo Valdrè (1742–1814) had painted the Music Room at Stowe, Buckinghamshire, in the Pompeian style. Again, the columns were by Bartoli, and as the 'whole is a highly finished example of the neo-Classical taste, unsurpassed in England' it would be known to Bonomi's painters. The work was Raphaelesque in its layout but Valdrè had studied at the French

Academy in Rome and had a wide knowledge of Classical sources of ornament.

In the late eighteenth century the painted 'landscape room' came into vogue, with walls treated as a continuous landscape seen either from an open pavilion, or a clearing in the woods. There were excellent antique and Renaissance precedents, but it was not seen in a fully developed way in England until the elder George Barret (1728–84), aided by four others, including Cipriani, painted the drawing-room at Norbury Park, Surrey, for William Lock. A trellised pergola opens on to an idealized English landscape and the illusion was heightened in the original scheme by a green carpet, imitating a mown lawn, being laid before it.

'The 'landscape room' had much in common with the 'panorama room'; an excellent early-nineteenth-century example of the latter is the series of large paintings depicting classical ruins in the staircase hall of Bretton Park in south Yorkshire. These works, in their arched grandeur, recall the neo-Classical scene painting which derived from Piranesi, with rearing columns and fallen, broken masonry. The paintings are attributed to the Cremonese painter, Agostino Aglio (1777–1857), who came to England in 1803 after training in Milan and Rome.

Official painting, with the approval of George III, was soon concentrated on establishing what Sir Johsua Reynolds called a 'Great Style'. Neither Reynolds nor Benjamin West was ever able to carry out the aims of their 'movement'. However, in 1800 Thomas Stothard (1755–1834) tried his hand at history painting on the staircase walls at Burghley House, Lincoln-shire, and struggled to contrast his scenes with Verrio's earlier gloomy 'Hell' ceiling – the companion scheme to the adjacent 'Heaven' Room. In oil on plaster Stothard portrayed the 'Horrors of War', the intemperance of the 'Banquet of Cleopatra' and the story of Orpheus and Eurydice, all in a style greatly influenced by Rubens; it was a bold attempt to lift British art from unnoticed provincialism with the bright competence of the assured national artist.

WINDOWS

Perhaps the most significant late-eighteenth-century development that affected the disposition of windows was the use of a curved bay, popularized by the architect brothers, Samuel Wyatt (1737–1807) and his younger brother, James. The canted bay had been used on many earlier occasions, a fine example of which can be seen at Sir Robert Taylor's Thames-side villa, Asgill House, Richmond, 1761–4. The canted and curved bay allowed splendid views in at least three directions. In 1772, James Wyatt exhibited the south-east elevation of Heaton Hall, Manchester, at the Royal Academy. It was probably seen there by several French architects, who used the idea of the bow in at least two Paris *hôtels*. With clever joinery, the wooden frames were kept in a flat plane whilst the stone surrounds were slightly curved.[34]

The bow became a feature of Samuel Wyatt's work: there is a splendid example on the south side of Shugborough Hall, Staffordshire, 1794, matching bows by Thomas Wright of Durham on the ends of the east entrance front. Sash-lighted windows set on the angles gave plenty of natural light.

At Luscombe Castle, Devon, which John Nash designed for Charles Hoare, 1799–1804 (with the siting and landscape by Humphry Repton), all the ground-floor windows came down to floor level, allowing easy access to the garden. It was also possible to step out on to the leads above the conservatory from the windows of the East Bedroom. The Luscombe windows, with their Gothic tracery, are an attractive feature of the house, some placed so that they give a view down the combe overlooking Dawlish to the sea. The front door has panels of stained glass. In country-house terms, these became a speciality of Thomas Willement, 'Heraldic Artist by appointment to George IV'. At Luscombe, the staircase hall was described in 1817 as containing 'an organ by Gray, which with the rich Gothic windows and stained glass give it the appearance of a small chapel.'[35]

Picturesque planning was dependent on the views from such large windows and romanticism flourished in the rich gloom of stained glass, with its ever-changing coloured patterns. Fenestration at its most elaborate was, however, reserved for the conservatories: 'the Greenhouse' by Samuel

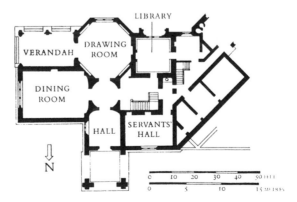

Fig. 15. Luscombe Castle, Devon, ground-floor plan, 1799–1804, by John Nash, from a drawing at Luscombe.

109. A watercolour c. 1807 by A. C. Pugin of the picture gallery at Attingham Park, Shropshire, showing John Nash's proposed oval cast-iron lights.

Pepys Cockerell (1753–1827) at Sezincote, Gloucestershire, c. 1805, is a curving wonder of fifteen arched openings filled with fan-lights and thin glazing, terminating in an octagonal pavilion that was once used as an aviary for exotic birds. The original stonework became badly eroded, so in 1955 a mould was taken of the carving and the whole façade was refaced in reconstituted stone, a process repeated in 1980.

At Sheringham Hall, Norfolk, Humphry Repton and his son, John Adey Repton, provided bow windows on the south front, flanking a colonnade, and on the centre of the east front. In the fenestration Humphry Repton re-introduced a particular type of casement. He said of both the casement and the bow, that they 'introduced a new character as applied to Grecian architecture – which in fact has no more to do with a modern sash than with a large Gothic window'.

There was a considerable interest in the early nineteenth century in top-lighting central halls or galleries that would otherwise have been very gloomy. At Attingham Park, Shropshire, the picture-gallery roof was to have had lights made in cast iron at Coalbrookdale. A watercolour there shows the intended scheme but, probably owing to its impracticability, John Nash provided a different frame in 1807. This roof is the earliest surviving example of such a use for cast iron in England. At Willey Hall (1812) and Oakley Park (1819), both in Shropshire, a few miles away from Attingham, the respective architects Lewis Wyatt and C. R. Cockerell, also had these top-lighting problems under control. At Willey, the hall, some 28 ft high, is lit through the central *lacunaria* of a segmental vault, by a clerestory lantern composed of lunettes above the trusses; at Oakley, there is a glazed dome rising above a ceiling of coffered panels, enabling an even light to fall into the staircase hall, which is rich in Grecian ornamentation.

DOORS

The vistas along the succession of state rooms in country houses had been an important feature from the late seventeenth century. At Holkham Hall, Norfolk, the view depended on the doors in each room being in alignment; a symmetrical balance was achieved by matching the openings with doors in the other two corners of the rooms. However, the fewer doors a room had, the warmer it remained. Robert Adam and his followers had soon discarded pediments over doors, and consoles were used instead to support a decorated cornice above the door. In later years this was refined to incorporate a central tablet with painted or bas-relief decoration, and in the late years of the eighteenth century a reeded architrave enclosed rosettes or pateras at the angles. In the fourth edition of Chambers's *The Decorative Part of Civil Architecture*, edited by J. B. Papworth in 1826, this fact was noted, with the observation that space given to simulated doors might be given instead to decoration.

The door itself was usually six-panelled, and of mahogany, its members being joined with open mortise and tenon joints. Recent examination of the doors in Adam's drawing-room[36] at Lansdowne House shows that the construction of the inner framing was robust but had the usual groove planed on the inside of the frame members for inserting six panels. These had the curious construction of an inner panel of Scots pine veneered on both sides with mahogany. The door furniture was in ormolu and was probably provided by Thomas Blockley (1705–89) of Birmingham who did the same job for Adam at Croome Court, Shardeloes, Saltram, Osterley Park, 20 St James's Square, London, and Harewood House. In the latter, Thomas Blockley's journeyman attended him in 1773 for about ninety days to fit locks and to clean and lacquer door-plates.

110. Ormolu door furniture in the saloon, c. 1768, at Saltram, Devon, possibly provided by Thomas Blockley of Birmingham, a frequent supplier to Adam and his patrons.

In the *Builder's Magazine* of 1774 it was advised that the best form of panels for doors were the plainest, 'that is, a long square, the two or four larger should be long upwards and the other crosswise'. The panels usually had fluted decoration between two shallow mouldings, a rare exception being the doors in the Red Drawing Room at Syon House, Middlesex, which are decked with cut-work patterns in gilded brass, probably an Adam design modified by Nathaniel Bermingham.[37] He had come to England from Dublin and advertised in Mortimer's *London Directory* of 1763 that he was a herald-painter and 'improver of a curious art of cutting out Portraits and Coats of Arms in vellum with the point of a penknife . . .' Bermingham used his vellum template to form the gilt ornament on the doors and also provided the window-shutter knobs at Syon.

At James Wyatt's last house, Dodington Park, Gloucestershire, the magnificent six-panelled drawing-room doors are of mahogany, inlaid with various woods in circles and diamonds. In the dining-room the door frames are of marbled Sienna with bronzed decorations. The firm of Perry had been paid £606 in 1811 for 'bookcases and mahogany doors', presumably for the library, but they may have done more work. At Broughton Hall, Yorkshire, the Durham-born architect, William Atkinson (c. 1773–1839), who began life as a carpenter, added wings and made other alterations for the Tempest family, 1811–13. Atkinson arranged for the Red Drawing Room to be entered through mirror-fronted doors between yellow scagliola columns, a nice conceit that had been anticipated by Henry Holland when

111 (left). *The drawing-room mahogany door leading to the long gallery, c. 1766–7, at Syon House, Middlesex. Ormolu decoration by Nathaniel Bermingham (door) and Diederich Nicolaus Anderson (jamb).*

112 (right). *Door in the Etruscan Dressing Room, c. 1776, at Osterley Park, Middlesex. The six painted panels are presumably by Pietro Maria Borgnis, who painted the rest of the room.*

he was working at Southill, Bedfordshire, for Samuel Whitbread at the end of the eighteenth century. The boudoir there, *Directoire* in style, has a pair of glass doors opening to a dressing-room, which looked, in the words of the Revd Samuel Johnes, who visited it in 1800,[38] 'like a small Temple where had been deposited all the rich offerings from every Country'.

An alternative to the mahogany door, or to those inlaid with other woods, was the painted deal door. This did not have enriched mouldings but panels painted with medallions, flying figures or other light ornament. Grained soft wood was in considerable use from the end of the eighteenth century. It was impossible at the time of the French Revolution to obtain valuable woods – little but deal or beech was to be had; Frederick Crace, speaking to the Royal Institute of British Architects in 1858, said that his father remembered the introduction of these types of wood by French workmen at Carlton House, London. Various woods were copied by veining and graining the surface with simulations of knots, spots and mottles. Maple became popular as a wood to imitate until graining was repudiated as a sham in the 1850s.[39]

CHIMNEYPIECES

In the early years of George III's reign, the heavy types of Palladian chimneypiece were still in use, even though they were unsuited to interiors styled in a more modern way. It was therefore inevitable that Adam, Chambers and Wyatt, concerned with the integrity of their schemes, should introduce stylistic variations to the chimneypiece. These changes must have made even the wealthiest of owners alarmed. If they were concerned to move with the times they either had to buy expensive new marble chimneypieces or have a competent mason refashion an existing one. In 1781 Haig and Chippendale the younger charged Sir Gilbert Heathcote 5s 6d for removing large gilt ornaments from two chimneypieces at his London house in Grosvenor Square, and £10 more for finishing the pilasters, mouldings and friezes with additional antique ornaments.[40]

The Adam chimneypieces of the early 1760s for commissions such as Croome Court, Hereford and Worcester, and Kedleston Hall, Derbyshire, show a determined use of scrolls, columns and caryatid figures. One of the best sculptors at producing them was Joseph Wilton (1722–1803), son of the ornamental plasterer William Wilton, who had wisely sent him to study in Paris, Rome and Florence. Living abroad for over eleven years, he made the acquaintance in the 1750s in Rome of both William Chambers and Robert Adam.[41] In 1755 Wilton returned to England, and continued to associate with both architects as a friend and business colleague for over thirty years. In 1783 he appeared alongside Chambers and Sir Joshua Reynolds in John Francis Rigaud's portrait, now in the National Portrait Gallery, London.

The chimneypiece for the Tapestry Room at Croome Court (now re-erected in the Metropolitan Museum, New York) was provided in 1760 as a 'rich Truss Chimneypiece' by John Wildsmith, but it was Wilton who had the stock to provide the tablet of deep-blue lapis lazuli to be set in the centre of the frieze. However, for the Croome Court gallery, Wilton was in sole charge in 1766 of providing the chimneypiece at a charge of £300: he billed it as a 'large Statuary Chimneypiece composed of Statues

*113. The gallery (originally library), 1761–6, at Croome Court, Hereford and Worcester.
The room was modified by Adam in 1763 to include the statues and bas-reliefs.
The chimneypiece by Joseph Wilton cost £300 in 1766.*

representing Nymphs of Flora, holding a wreath &c'.[42] It was one of his finest achievements.

A caryatid chimneypiece had been used as a type by Isaac Ware in the late 1740s at Chesterfield House, London (this too is now in the Metropolitan Museum of Art, New York). He discussed such chimneypieces in his *A*

Complete Body of Architecture (1756) and it was natural enough that both Adam and Chambers should want to break free and provide alternative designs to them as soon as possible. Adam designed many fine neo-Classical chimneypieces, some incorporating the anthemion motif, as at Osterley Park, Middlesex, others being flanked by Ionic columns with a central tablet, for example, at Shardeloes, Buckinghamshire, and others having richly detailed friezes and shelves supported on console brackets. This type of chimneypiece was popular by the mid-1760s (for example, at Harewood House, Yorkshire) but by 1772 the very delicate kinds of inlaid-marble work, in the style of Pietro Bossi, were becoming even more fashionable and John Hinchcliff, who specialized in providing inlaid marble chimney-pieces (for example at 20 St James's Square, London), was in demand for their supply. Two other leading statuaries were Thomas and Benjamin Carter, who provided some superb chimneypieces at Claydon House, Buckinghamshire, demonstrating their skill in depicting cavorting *putti*.

In 1769 a new inspirational source had come to Adam's table, his friend Giovanni Battista Piranesi's *Diverse maniere d'adornare i cammini* ... They were complex designs but the idea of a dominant frieze with richly grouped figures, heavy swags and classical nymphs in side-panels (as in Piranesi's

114 (left). *Detail of the statuary marble chimneypiece in the State Bedroom, c. 1777, at Osterley Park, Middlesex. It was probably supplied by Joseph Wilton (1722–1803).*

115 (right). *Detail of a statuary marble chimneypiece, c 1765, at Claydon House, Buckinghamshire, by Thomas and Benjamin Carter.*

116. Detail of design for a chimneypiece and wall by Giovanni Battista Piranesi (1720–78), from his Diverse Maniere D'Adornare I Camini, *(1769) Plate 2. Adam took some of his ideas for the Etruscan Dressing Room at Osterley Park from this source.*

Plate 9A) was soon adapted by Adam for the First Drawing Room chimneypiece at 20 St James's Square, London, *c.* 1773. He was working for another significant and well-travelled patron, Sir Watkin Williams Wynn.

As the eighteenth century progressed, the 'continued' form of chimneypiece was less used, although there are many notable examples; by Adam at Harewood House, Yorkshire, and Syon House, Middlesex, and by James Stuart at Shugborough Hall, Staffordshire. There was less attempt to secure rare marbles than in the earlier Palladian years, but the *Builder's Magazine* (1774) noted that 'Siena was common, also the green Anglesea kind and green and white Egyptian'. Painting on marble was also advocated by Adam's draughtsman, George Richardson, who issued his *New Collection of Chimney Pieces* in 1781. The design for the two marble chimneypieces in the Marble Hall at Kedleston, Derbyshire, closely matches one of Richardson's designs. They house superb fire-baskets, perhaps made by Thomas Blockley, who supplied grates for the house in the 1760s and who received larger payments than usual in 1776–7.[43]

Sir William Chambers regarded himself as an accomplished designer of chimneypieces, and produced nine designs in his *A Treatise on Civil Architecture* (1768). There are also a number of very accomplished drawings of chimneypieces by him (mostly in Avery Library, Columbia University). Chambers mostly used Joseph Wilton and Richard Hayward for the execution of his chimneypieces in fine white statuary marble, but at Buckingham Palace (formerly Buckingham House, London) the names of the accomplished Sir Henry Cheere and of Benjamin Carter are in the accounts. They were both capable of sculpting any chimneypiece, no matter how complicated the architect's design.

The lucrative trade in chimneypieces had attracted the attentions of the manufacturers, Matthew Boulton and Josiah Wedgwood. Boulton's cast-tin or pewter ornaments stamped in relief were supplied to builders: when painted, they had the appearance of carving. The demand for friezes and tablets of Classical subjects suggested to Wedgwood that his moulded ware, in plaques and panels designed by John Flaxman and others, could easily be used. They appear, for example at Kedleston, in chimneypieces at 20 St James's Square, London, Berrington Hall, Hereford and Worcester, and others were incorporated in chimneypieces sent out to Catherine the Great's palace, Tsarskoe Selo, at St Petersburg. His enterprise, however, was not welcomed by Chambers, Wyatt and others, and in October 1778 Chambers wrote, with feeling:

I know there are much cheaper at that price than marble, and every way better, but people will not compare things which they conceive to be made out of moulds, or perhaps stamped at a blow like the Birmingham articles, with carving in natural stones where they are certain no moulding, casting, or stamping can be done.[44]

Adam had also provided strong competition to many marble-workers, and to entrepreneurs such as Wedgwood, with his designs for the Carron Iron Company, to be cast in metal: many of these designs and their moulds survive, at the Scottish Record Office and the Falkirk Museum respectively, and there is a wonderful cast chimneypiece by Carron at the Adam family home, Blair Adam, near Kelty.

Additionally, various kinds of stove could warm a room as effectively as an open fire, and Abraham Buzaglo (1716–88), a Moroccan Jew settled in

London, specialized in the manufacture of great cast-iron stoves in the Rococo and, later, neo-Classical styles. There are fine examples of his precisely moulded stoves at Colonial Williamsburg, made in 1770 for the Virginia House of Representatives, and at Knole, Kent, there is a 'Treble Tier Patent Warming Machine' signed and dated 'BUZAGLO 1774'.[45] In 1796 the American Count Rumford also patented his stove, which gave more efficiency to the fireplace by controlling the width of the throat and the arrangement of the brick surround.[46]

The latest stylistic manners were impressed on the early-nineteenth-century *literati* by Thomas Hope (1769–1831), a personal friend of the French architect Charles Percier, who with Pierre-François Fontaine had given precise form to the French Empire period, seeking to achieve the same kind of synthesis as Adam. In Hope's own *Household Furniture and Decoration* (1807) the designs were principally of his Surrey house at Deepdene, which reflected in its interiors his wide knowledge of ornament and housed his extensive collections. Archaeology was one of Hope's main interests and the objects of ancient civilization could be copied as bronzed or gilded griffins, winged sphinxes or lions, Egyptian heads or lyres to deck many a fireplace, its mantel and its hearth.

Finally, there was a long domination in designing chimneypieces and tablets in the late eighteenth and early nineteenth centuries by the Westmacott family. Richard Westmacott the Elder (1747–1808) had published a series of twenty engraved designs for chimneypieces in 1777 and was in demand for his work, which was characterized by supporting figures, bas-relief groups and rich swags of fruit and foliage. The traditions were continued by his son, also Richard (1775–1856), an early pupil of Canova in Rome, who was knighted by George IV after his work at Windsor Castle. He was said to have received £1,244 for the chimneypiece of the Music Room in the Royal Pavilion at Brighton. Lastly, Richard (1799–1872), son of Sir Richard, was active into the late 1850s with marble monuments, reliefs and chimneypieces. The dynasty of the Westmacotts maintained chimneypiece-making as a high art in a period when there was a growing concern to heat a house by other more efficient means.

STAIRCASES

The problem of allocating space between a hall and a staircase continued. In town houses on restricted sites a small hall usually led into a staircase hall, rising, as at Robert Adam's Home House, 20 Portman Square, London,

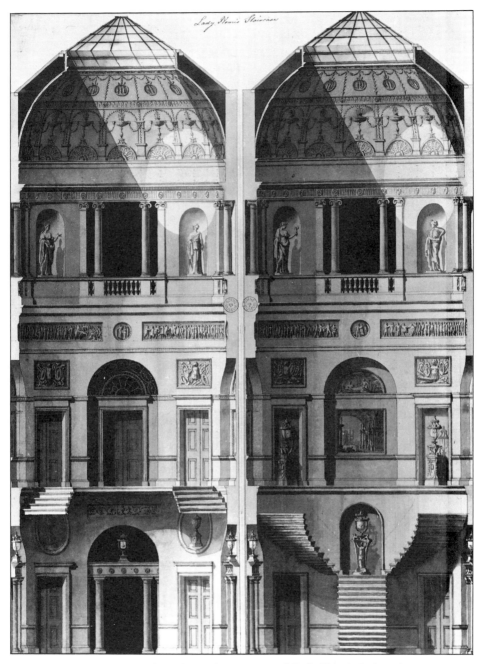

Lady Home's Staircase

117. *Drawing by Robert Adam, c. 1775, of 'Lady Home's Staircase'*
at 20 Portman Square, London. The combined skills of Joseph Rose and Antonio Zucchi
were used to spectacular effect in this circular staircase-well.

118 (left). The staircase, c. 1762, at Lytham Hall, Lancashire, by John Carr.
This is cantilevered with three fluted balusters to each tread,
and Ionic and Corinthian columns to the landing and cove, respectively.
119 (right). The staircase, c. 1765, at The Vyne, Hampshire.
Designed, ingeniously, by John Chute in a long narrow space, with a screen of
fluted columns and stair balusters combining to give it a 'Grecian theatric' effect.

to the full height of the house and lit by a metal-framed skylight. In a great country house the staircase could be allowed to spread itself on a larger scale, perhaps with divided flights and long landings as at Lytham Hall, Lancashire, and in a complex spatial form at The Vyne, Hampshire, designed by John Chute, or with a single flight disposed in an interesting way to attract the eye. This can be seen at, for example, Berrington Hall, Hereford and Worcester (1778), where Henry Holland devised the great staircase hall as one more brilliant exercise in spatial design. Entry to this space is by a door at the foot of the stairs so that the coffered span carrying the landing is first seen in profile. With the staircase to the right there are ever-present sharp contrasts of light and shade. The staircase was to have a 'neat iron baluster capp'd with mahogany' but the iron was disguised to look like bronze. Light poured into a skylight dome, with grisaille medallions in the

120. *The staircase, c. 1768, at Claydon House, Buckinghamshire.*
It has mahogany treads inlaid with various woods probably by Luke Lightfoot.
The ironwork balustrade is so delicately wrought its ears of wheat rustle
as one ascends, past the Classical plaster roundels by Joseph Rose.

angles of the compartmented ceiling below, giving it an added emphasis. There is a slightly old-fashioned feel to the balustrade of Luke Lightfoot's extraordinary staircase at Claydon House, Buckinghamshire, with its ears of wheat that seem to rustle as one ascends.

George Steuart (c. 1730–1806) devised a great circular domed staircase in the late 1780s at Attingham Park, Shropshire. This was replaced by Nash's picture gallery (1805–7). Another staircase by Nash was set in a small rectangular space, divided from the hall by a screen of scagliola columns. At almost the same time, c. 1786, John Carr (1723–1807), the Yorkshire architect, devised a great staircase at Farnley Hall, Yorkshire. This starts as a sedate single flight, but divides at a landing and ascends in two flights to a spacious upper landing, following the pattern he had used successfully twenty years earlier at Lytham Hall. The first landing at Farnley is supported on two Ionic columns, with pilasters on each side wall, the second, at the upper level, has a similar arrangement of Corinthian columns and pilasters supporting an enriched entablature. The staircase is both practical and attractive, with its intriguing form leading the eye up to unknown realms.

The placing of wrought-iron balusters in a staircase had been managed superbly by Jean Tijou at Chatsworth, Derbyshire, in the late seventeenth century. The neo-Classical forms needed in Adam designs in the 1770s also made good use of wrought-iron balusters, which were regularly provided by Thomas Tilston. The late eighteenth century saw the use of cast-iron for structural support, and staircases soon soared higher, in curves that moved out of dark into light and back again with the ease of a bronzed serpent. Small details such as pateras and rosettes could be made in gilded lead or brass and be given the form of Classical medallions, to enhance the strong but delicately styled balusters. At Cound Hall, Shropshire, the staircase rises, daringly, in a series of complex spatial planes that almost seem to defeat its intent.

SERVICES

In 1778 Joseph Bramah (1748–1814), an inventor who had worked first as a cabinet-maker in London, patented a water-closet that was a significant improvement on its gurgling predecessors. A flat trap at the bottom of the pan was operated by a pull handle at the side and water flushed as long as this was raised. An S-bend filled with water had been used in a patent of 1775 by Alexander Cumming, but Bramah's trade was particularly successful because of his willingness to install his necessary devices. He was at Audley End, Essex, for this purpose in 1785, drawing the water supply from tanks placed in the roof, one at each end of the upper storey of the gallery.[47] Outside privies continued to be used alongside inside conveniences and

121 (opposite). The Flying Staircase, c. 1800,
at Cound Hall, Shropshire. The name derives from the 'flyers' –
steps in a flight of stairs that are parallel to each other.

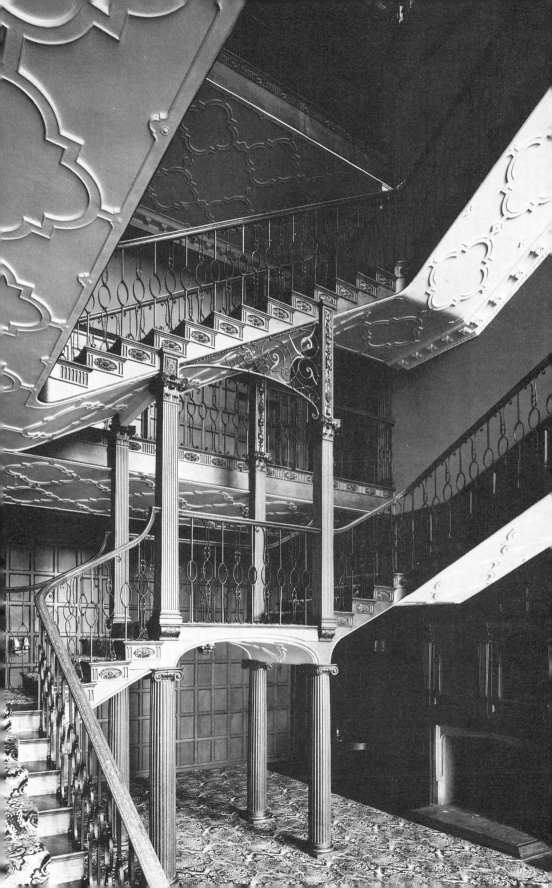

122. *The staircase to the sunken bath at Wimpole Hall,*
Cambridgeshire, designed by Sir John Soane, c. 1791.

there are many payments to joiners and others in house archives for providing new seats and doors to these as well as for the unpleasant task of cleaning them.

Bells in houses to call servants had been in use since the late seventeenth century, and the 'whitesmith' (or tinsmith) Maurice Tobin of Leeds included their maintenance in his overall services to Edwin Lascelles of Harewood House, Yorkshire, in the 1770s. Tobin installed bells in the State Bed Chamber, the dressing-room and the two drawing-rooms at Harewood in 1774.[48] A cabinet-maker of the eminence of Thomas Chippendale only occasionally installed bell systems, but was always ready to provide the fine silk tassels and line for the bell pulls, as well as fixing up hall lanterns with weighted pulleys which allowed them to be lowered for servicing. Chippendale's other commissions included installing fabric roller blinds, which he obtained from a specialist; [49] supplying painted pine or wainscot attic furniture, deal coal boxes, washing mangles, kitchen tables and chairs; fixing up battens for meat hooks; and even providing for Nostell Priory, Yorkshire, on 24 December 1768, in time for Christmas Day, 'A Large strong Elm Chopping block for the kitchen', charged at 10s.[50]

Heating houses became much easier, for those sufficiently wealthy, from about 1790 when hot-air systems were introduced. Hot-water systems and good radiators were not yet available, and there is little doubt more effort was expended on heating walls for kitchen and fruit gardens than on warming the house's chilled occupants. Light was available for gas and oil lamps, but in his *A Collection of Designs for Household Furniture* ... of 1808 George Smith noted that the candle chandelier should still be made in wood, and should have up to twenty-four lights, its dimensions being regulated by the size of the room, provided that the base was at least 7 ft from the ground.

Domestic economy was poised for an upheaval in which improvements could hardly be announced before they were superseded. But much still depended on the uncomplaining service of rows of baize- and cotton-clad servants, hurrying along dark corridors and up back staircases at the insistent tolling of the nodding service bells. One of their duties would be to fill their employers' baths, such as that designed by Sir John Soane at Wimpole Hall, Cambridgeshire.

Six

CONVENIENT, SPACIOUS OR SNUG
1830–1914

THE HOUSE PLAN

Many of the efforts of nineteenth-century house planners were devoted to achieving domestic comfort, even if some of the buildings they created also contained soaring and draughty spaces. Whilst the presence of power in the form of steam and gas helped to overcome the limitations of heating and lighting, ventilation was still crude. Many rooms had open fireplaces giving some radiated heat but the tasks of carrying and replenishing the wood and coal were demanding. However, whilst comfort was an important consideration for the house owners, there was little interest in the new ideas to make houses easier to maintain. The reason for this was quite simple: domestic labour was cheap and plentiful.[1] House plans therefore needed to provide quarters for both people and equipment, allowing areas for privacy and for social occasion, and to do this as efficiently as possible.

John Arkwright, who in 1834 was rebuilding seventeenth-century Hampton Court, Herefordshire, defined the priorities for his class: 'Comfort is the only consideration which had induced me to make any alteration whatever, and that obtained, I care as far as my own taste is concerned, but little for the rest.'[2] The 'rest', for those who wanted comfort, might consist of little more than waxed oak-panelled walls reflected in a cheerful fire, surrounded by deep-buttoned armchairs. But there were also those restless driving souls, in love with imagination and historical associations, intent on creating the great houses of their fevered dreams.

In a careful study of the nineteenth-century and early-twentieth-century house plan[3] Dr Jill Franklin noted that Classical plans outnumbered others and that, although the seventeenth-century double-pile plan was still very popular, three quarters of all plans up to 1890 were for asymmetrical houses.

After 1890, two new plan-types emerged to take their place alongside variations of the double-pile and of the 'Italian villa': the 'butterfly', and the north-corridor plan, both designed as 'sun-trap' plans to give the house maximum sunshine. In the years before the First World War many houses were reduced in size and whilst a few were given an often inconvenient grandeur by Lutyens and others, most were just reasonably convenient, spacious enough for reduced families and, with hissing radiators or spitting coals, even quite snug. But most relied still on the labours of a host of domestic servants: Lady Diana Cooper[4] recalled that the denizens of the deep recesses of a great house such as Belvoir Castle, Leicestershire, were 'dreadfully silent' as they went about their duties: they padded over the high gravelled terraces as watchmen; nudged open doors with their knees as 'coal-men, refilling one's bin with pieces the size of ice-blocks'; or, as water-men, kept 'all jugs cans and kettles full in the bedrooms ... morning or evening' and were ready to bring 'the hot water for the hip baths'.

Dr Franklin classified nineteenth-century house-plans into four groups: (a) those based on Classical prototypes, (b) those founded on historical models, such as the 'H' or 'E' or quadrangular plan, (c) those assembling rooms of all sizes and shapes around a central point, such as a top-lit hall, and (d) those described as 'north-corridor' plans, with reception rooms all facing south, and their variant, the 'butterfly' or 'double sun-trap' plan.

The concerns for symmetry in building a house had been important from the seventeenth century but came under attack in the 1840s. Augustus Welby Northmore Pugin (1812–52), the most renowned architect of his day, had trained in John Nash's office and specialized in Gothic detailing. After being converted to Roman Catholicism in 1835, Pugin produced a number of widely read and quoted publications, publicizing links between his faith and design. In his *True Principles of Pointed or Christian Architecture* (1841)[5] he wrote: 'They must have two of everything, one on each side: no matter if all the required accommodation is contained in one half of the design'. Whatever plan was used, certain principles needed to be followed. In an important book on planning a house, published in 1864, Robert Kerr[6] indicated that: 'the skeleton of the plan' had to be disposed so that rooms were in correct relationship and lines of communication ran from them. Two routes should lead outside (one to the front entrance, the other to the garden), one must go upstairs and another 'vanish' on its way to the service quarters. Kerr stipulated that these routes should be short, direct, uninterrupted, well-lit and well-ventilated. As Dr Franklin later wryly remarked: 'It was the skeleton which ensured that the dinner route was noble, the servants invisible and the boiled cabbage kept at bay'.

The most essential division in the house plan was between the family and its servants. Again, Kerr is precise:[7]

The family constitute one community: the servants another. Whatever may be their mutual regard as dwellers under one roof, each class is entitled to shut its doors upon the other, and be alone ... What passes on either side of the boundary shall be invisible and inaudible on the other.

It was the arrangement of a good plan that satisfied these dictates. All the service rooms were gathered together on one side of the house; this was doubtless convenient, but if the space required were large this would cause problems for the outside elevations. Nevertheless, no architect anxious to please could fail but make it clear at a glance that one part of the edifice was superior to the other. The German observer, Hermann Muthesius, observed in 1904[8] that the superiority of the English house over others lay in the siting and planning of its domestic offices.

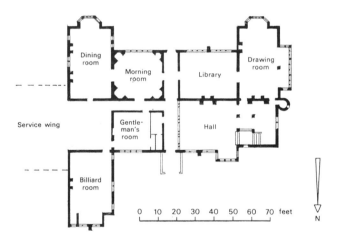

Fig. 16. *Knightshayes, Devon, ground-floor plan, 1869–73, by William Burges.*
(The National Trust)

The plan of the main block needed to deal with two aspects: family life and the housing of guests, with a growing concern in the later nineteenth century for privacy. Few enfilades and few vistas (although there were exceptions to every rule) were needed.

On the ground floor, most house plans incorporated a hall, dining-room, drawing-room, library and study. From the 1870s, when billiards was popular, a room for this might flank (or replace) the library. There were, like most Victorian breakfast menus, many 'extras' which could be had – a

123. Drawing of the Star Parlour at The Vyne, Hampshire, by Martha Chute, 1857, showing its use for relaxation: reading, music and playing games.

breakfast room, music room, smoking room, ballroom, picture gallery or even a chapel. The central core contained shared rooms with those at either side for each sex. The men's quarters were used for smoking, playing billiards, drinking port and talking politics, the women's, in particular, the drawing-room, for tea and polite conversation with the 'carriage callers', needlework and, the supreme accomplishment of ladies, music at the piano or the harpsichord.

Brooding over the plans themselves were all those black frock-coated gentlemen, good husbands but with plans for further improvements on their minds. They garnered money, attended to their estates, coal-mines and factories, and forced architects and craftsmen to be competent in order to survive, and to improve their skills. Their wives tended to be content with less – winter gardens or *boiseries* (carved panelling) on the drawing-room doors.

In the smaller house the same principles of separating functions applied. It was in the long terraces that there could be similarity of plan. It is easy to overlook that the humble terrace house had its grander counterparts: the Bath crescents and terraces designed by John Wood and his son; John Nash's Carlton House Terrace, London and George Basevi's Belgrave

Square. These grand terrace houses were only 28 or 30 ft wide but had rooms piled up into five storeys. It is always salutary to look at the backs of houses and in, for example, Marlborough Buildings, Bath (c. 1790), owing to different levels of land, the backs rise like cliffs, with clinging later accretions built out to give more room. Rooms had to be placed at the head or on one or both sides of the staircase landings. The large rooms were at the back: at The Paragon, Bath, the houses of uniform main façades were built on a strip of land sloping between two roads with a 40 ft difference in their levels. At the rear, great vaults support hanging gardens entered from the basements of the houses.[9]

In the 'Artizans' Labourers' and General Dwelling Estate' at Noel Park, Hornsey, of 1833, there were five classes of small house. A small garden at the front prefaced all five types, which were built on a thin linear strip-site and, had two main rooms on the ground floor and two bedrooms on the first floor. In classes 1 and 2, the long hall led through to a kitchen and scullery sited at the back of the second parlour. In classes 3, 4 and 5, this second parlour was turned into the kitchen, with only class 3 having an additional scullery. All houses had a small back garden, with an outside privy.

In most very small town dwellings[10] it was necessary to go through the living-room-cum-kitchen to get to the back of the house, which was, of course, inconvenient. Coal was tipped through a grating into a basement and there was frequently only an outdoor toilet. The two-storeyed single-pile house — that is, of one room deep — was common until the mid nineteenth century. The stairs were behind the front door. A development to create more spacious accommodation was to have a four-roomed house that was two rooms deep; there are many examples of this design in Lancashire.

The early back-to-back houses, warm and snug (at least to their occupants), were common to all the northern industrial towns. The front door led straight into the living-room, with a narrow flight of stairs in a back corner. This rose through two storeys to an attic. Lavatories were placed in groups at the end of a row, accessible only from outside. As Stefan Muthesius has noted 'the essential characteristic of the back-to-back was that it had no back'.[11] This led to groups of houses being placed around courts, with tunnels through from the fronts. As nearly all these housing arrangements were of high density, inconvenient and of low standard, they have been swept away in large numbers. A visit to the North of England Open-Air Museum at Beamish, Durham, or the Black Country Museum at Dudley, Hereford and Worcester, is often the only way to see furnished pit cottages, or other cottages lived in by many categories of the working classes. They have been removed in large numbers as living conditions improved, or, where they remain, have been extensively altered for the same reason. Larger houses, described in detail in nineteenth-century periodicals such as the *Builder's Magazine*, thus attract attention at the expense of research into humbler dwellings.

ROOMS AND THEIR USES

In two volumes on house architecture, published in 1880, J. J. Stevenson[12] had much to say about the drawing-room, which he thought should be designed for conversation 'to favour the forming of the company into separate groups'. 'Unity of plan', he lectured, 'is an error', but many late Victorian and Edwardian drawing-rooms were wide, crammed, glittering and certainly united.

If possible, the drawing-room was placed so that it had the best view and received the south-east, or southern sun. The advantage of a south-east siting was that the full glare of the sun had passed by the time the

124. Detail of the design by William Burges for the morning room, c. 1868,
at Knightshayes Court, Devon. The walls were to be partially panelled in ebonized wood,
framing tiles with a frieze above 'illustrating the Heroes and Heroines of the Fairytales'.
(Victoria and Albert Museum, London, No. E97–2, 102, 9)

125. *The library at Stourhead, Wiltshire, in 1898, showing the lattice-work ceiling (repainted 1962) and the chimneypiece bought from Wavendon in 1913: fixed points in a scene of over-furnishing.*

late-afternoon carriage-callers came to tea. It was a room to be treated with some reverence. The young Augustus Hare, staying in 1851 with his tutor and many other pupils in an 'ugly brick villa ... in the pretty village of Southgate, about ten miles from London', noted that: 'a dinner-bell rings at half-past one, and the others come in from the drawing-room whither they adjourn before dinner, with the penalty of a penny if they lean against the mantelpiece, as they might injure the ornaments.'[13]

Hare's tutor, the Revd Charles Bradley, might choose to retreat from the niceties of afternoon tea, or the Greek grammar whisperings of his pupils, to his library. This was, however, frequently only a second sitting-room, a fact Loudon had commented on as early as 1833 in his *Encyclopedia*. Mrs Catherine Gore, in her novel *The Diamond and the Pearl* (1849), wrote that the family spent their mornings in the library and that there were: 'half a dozen work-tables and writing-tables being in play in various nooks of the room, with a praiseworthy activity of small-talk and Berlin wool.'[14]

But the library was normally a male preserve: it was, as Robert Kerr said in his book on planning the gentleman's house (1864): 'a sort of Morning Room for Gentlemen'. It housed all the richly gold-tooled bindings in 'Russia' or goat-skin, and often had (as at Alnwick Castle, Northumberland, where Anthony Salvin equipped the library, 1854–65, with the help of Italian decorators), a smell 'as odorous as a private chapel'. But the nineteenth-century English gentleman was not a great reader, and in many small town houses there was no library at all. However, all such houses had a dining-room, over which the owner presided, with an envious precision of etiquette and observance of precedence. As this attitude moderated in the 1870s there was a gradual move towards the company sitting at circular dining-tables, which could be extended with extra leaves. A good example was designed for Sir William, later Lord Armstrong, at Cragside, Northumberland,[15] by Richard Norman Shaw (1831–1912), one of the most influential domestic architects of the later Victorian period. It was made in oak by James Forsyth, along with a recessed sideboard and two settles for the sides of the inglenook. The effect was, of course, overpoweringly

126. *The dining-room, 1870–72, on the north-west side of Cragside, Northumberland, designed by Norman Shaw. Panelled in light oak with an inglenook fireplace, fireback and firedogs, and dated 1872. The sideboard was made by John Forsyth.*

masculine, and most dining-rooms had this dark sombre appearance, exaggerated by their facing north or east. Dining in the sun was considered unpleasant until Edwardian times and Kerr pompously noted: 'Inasmuch as where there may be no state whatever in the habits of the family, there will be at least a little of that quality occasionally, in the act of proceeding to and from dinner.'

Apart from a study or business room – sometimes called a 'justice room' because many gentlemen were 'justices of the peace' – and perhaps a breakfast or morning room, there were other rooms on the ground floor for playing billiards, smoking, or the storing of guns. The number of surviving late-eighteenth-century billiard tables by the Lancaster and London firm of Gillows shows how the game had increased in popularity from its fifteenth-century origins. The table itself, with its richly decorated oak frame, encasing the baize-covered slate bed, became a miniature expression of the Gothic style. Gradually, the billiard room became less of a male preserve: in November 1899 Maud Lyttelton recorded in her journal[16] that, during her stay at Holkham Hall in Norfolk, she used to read by the fire in the billiard room while the men played. Many women also came to enjoy a game of mixed billiards.

127. The billiard room at Lanhydrock House, Cornwall,
with its Burroughes and Watts table, installed in the rebuilding,
after the fire of 1881.

Smoking was often forbidden in many mid-nineteenth-century houses and as cigar-smoking became popular many hostesses found the pervasive smoke intolerable. When H. H. Emerson painted[17] Lord Armstrong and even the Prince of Wales (later Edward VII) smoking cigars at Cragside, Northumberland, they were outside on the terrace. It had, however, been recognized that such a 'solution' was not always possible so smoking rooms remained, although they were separated from other parts of the house. At Castle Carr, near Halifax, the billiard room[18] opened out into the smoking room and these, together with the library, were in a wing of their own.

As shooting parties became more organized, from the 1860s onwards, it proved no longer convenient to clean guns in the butler's pantry. Kerr considered that a gun room was 'indispensable in a country house of any pretensions'. There was a gun room on the second floor at Cragside, Northumberland, but it was usual for it to be easily accessible from the grounds — so much so that Lady Carbery's 'uncle Philip' even made a proposal of marriage there; despite the unusual location for a young lady, it was successful.[19]

The Victorian conservatory was not usually regarded as a room of the house and many writers ignored it. However, at Flintham, Nottinghamshire, the Italianate palm house by Thomas Hine (1853–7) is an integral part of Lewis Wyatt's building, having vistas through it from two floors. Normally, conservatories, with their filigree architecture, were ill-suited to being placed adjacent to the solid frame of the house, and their warm, moist air was considered by some to be dangerous to health. Nevertheless, many were connected to the house by corridors and some even opened into the drawing-room. At Harlaxton, Lincolnshire, in about 1840, William Burn put a large double conservatory on the south-east of that great extravagant house. This was heated by its connection to the house's hot-air system, which was fed by coal and wood brought on a small service railway to the top of the house, where it was lowered to various collection points. It was a sanctuary for plants that could not survive outdoors. The Edwardian idea of a conservatory was to give some protection to plants and to open the room to sun and air, using it in the summer months as an 'outdoor' dining- and sitting-room.

From medieval times the hall had been the main room that was entered first, and its placing therefore affected the planning of the house at an early stage. In the Victorian house the hall was often regarded as a large family sitting-room, suitable for musical evenings. There are many Victorian views of families gathered around the imposing fireplace or piano in the hall. At Wallington, Northumberland, the hall was a space used frequently for tea, which had not been the intention of its architect, John Dobson (1787–1865), of Newcastle. He designed it in 1853 as an open courtyard and it was only roofed in 1855, at the suggestion of Ruskin, who painted its piers, helped by Pauline, Lady Trevelyan and her friends.

One of the grandest halls is A. W. N. Pugin's 'medieval' hall at Scarisbrick Hall, Lancashire, which lies on the south front and has two great canted bays supporting oriels and a tall lantern providing light. The hall has the inscription: 'This hall was built by me, Charles Scarisbrick, MDCCCXLII, Laus Deo'.[20] I prefer it to the great space created by Anthony Salvin (1799–1881) in his last major house, Thoresby Hall, Nottinghamshire, 1863–75. Here, the basement hall has a staircase that rises to the light of the arcaded great hall, and to the principal rooms on the *piano nobile* level. It runs 70 ft across the north front, with four reception rooms at its back, on the south side. One of its lavish rivals is Thomas Allom's strictly Gothic hall (entered from a vaulted entrance hall) of 1862 at Highclere Castle, Hampshire, a house of 1840–50 designed by Sir Charles Barry. Thomas Allom (1804–72) was an accomplished draughtsman and took over at Highclere at Barry's death in 1860.

The hall was usually the place for the staircase to rise from, but at Knightshayes Court, Devon, designed by a good medievalist, William Burges (1827–81), and built in 1869–74, the teak staircase was at first hidden from the hall behind a screens passage (removed in about 1914). It was an effective imitation of early traditions by Burges for patrons who were anxious to re-create, in their own minds at least, a vision of themselves as medieval lords, served by a docile peasantry.

The architect Richard Norman Shaw was an ardent advocate of a house having a good hall, and at The Hallams, Shamley Green, Surrey, 1894, he created a grand one rising through two storeys with a gallery 'looking down into the hall from amidst the tie-beams'.[21] He had restored the hall at Ightham Mote, Kent, in 1872 with new panelling, doors and fireplace, whilst at Cragside the entrance hall he created led up past richly tiled walls to a top-lit picture gallery.

The upstairs areas of a house were usually simpler to plan than the ground floor, as bedrooms could be reached from a landing or corridor. The principal bedroom needed a dressing-room, and should, Kerr thought, not be less than 24 ft by 18 ft in size. These modest dimensions were frequently exceeded, the size being partly governed by the size of reception rooms and the position of bearing walls below. The ceiling could be as high as 14 or 15 ft in order that four-post beds should have adequate head space, and that the great dressed windows and satinwood wardrobes might be

128. *The great hall at Knightshayes Court, Devon, looking west. The hall 'is an*
extravagant imitation of the medieval tradition' by William Burges, 1869–74.
It is dominated by the teak chimneypiece, teak staircase and arch-braced roof.

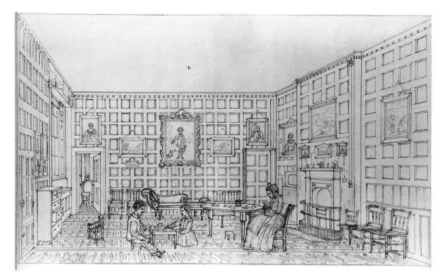

129. Drawing of 'The Nursery' at The Vyne, Hampshire, by Martha Chute,
c. 1857, showing a formal panelled room with fireguard and furniture
a little too grand for robust use.

disposed correctly, and not dwarf the draped toilette and brass-inlaid writing-table. Such bedrooms had, as one visitor of 1852 put it: 'all the perfection of comfort'.[22] Rooms for guests or single members of the family were either on the second floor, or above a wing. The long bachelor's wing at Cannon Hall, Yorkshire, had its neat array of grained deal doors to the corridor, and windows looking out to a back court. Reached by a backstairs, these bachelors' rooms were usually very comfortable, with their open fireplaces − a male 'sanctum', although smaller and lower than the best bedrooms in the house.

As early as 1833 J. C. Loudon had indicated in his *Encyclopedia* that nurseries should be 'on the bedroom floor, in a retired part of the house' and that they should be 'light and airy apartments'.[23] This arrangement was rarely followed from about 1860, when the nursery area was often over a service wing, convenient for the preparation of food and for keeping noisy children out of the way of adults. By Edwardian days, the nursery had become incorporated into the main block, in an area hitherto given over to the principal bedrooms. At Eaton Hall, Cheshire, in the 1880s, the second floor of a private wing was allotted to the children, set above the first-floor quarters of the Duke and Duchess of Westminster. This second floor had its schoolroom, day- and night-nurseries and six other bedrooms.[24] The wing, with its moderate scale, meant that family life could be separated from the vast spaces of Waterhouse's house, which the *Daily Telegraph* described in 1899 as 'one of the most princely and beautiful mansions that these islands contain'.

The duke and his second wife, 'Katie' Cavendish, were deeply religious. There were prayers each morning in the private chapel, attended by the whole household. After prayers, the household filed out, in order of rank. A list[25] of the Eaton staff in the later nineteenth century shows 346 servants, divided between inside and outside duties. Apart from a chef, there was a head kitchen maid, two kitchen maids, two scullery maids and a kitchen porter. The housekeeper controlled the head housemaid, nine other maids, the sewing, scullery and the two still-room maids, and the Duchess of Westminster's two ladies' maids. In addition, the total included fourteen people who dealt with laundry, three coachmen and twelve grooms dealing with the horses and coaches (as well as thirty men and boys working for the head groom), forty gardeners, seventy foresters, forty farm workers and seventeen tradesmen. The house steward controlled two grooms of chambers, a valet, under-butler, three footmen, a pantry boy, a hall usher, a night watchman and an odd-job man. It was a mighty team, able to serve and feed their master, his wife and their family and guests, and themselves be housed, fed and paid. Kerr summed it up: 'Every servant, every operation, every utensil, every fixture should have a right place and no right place but one.'

These 'right places' needed to be in a servants' wing[26] at one side of the house, and considerable thought was given to their planning. The design emphasized the hierarchical division of servants themselves: the principal triumvirate of butler, housekeeper and cook needed spaces for their 'departments' of upper and lower servants. At Thoresby Hall, Nottinghamshire, there was even a small room for a lower servant to wash vegetables. Male and female servants had rigidly segregated sleeping quarters and, whilst this did not guarantee propriety, eagle-eyed Victorian housekeepers did their utmost to make it difficult for one to visit the other. Separate staircases to their quarters were included frequently by the designing architect. Great ingenuity in these arrangements can be found at Penrhyn Castle, Gwynedd, Wales, designed by Thomas Hopper (1776–1856) in the neo-Norman style, *c.* 1820–45.

Apart from the great commissions that brought lustre to their names, many nineteenth-century architects concerned themselves with designing small houses. There was also a spate of books published, in addition to Loudon's influential *Encyclopedia* (1833), which helped the process, in particular, J. B. Papworth's *Rural Residences* (1818) and Charles Parker's *Villa*

Rustica (1832). S. H. Brooks in his *Designs for cottage and villa architecture* (1839) gave almost entirely asymmetrical designs in the Elizabethan, Gothic, Moorish and Grecian styles. Others, such as Henry Roberts, devoted themselves to developing plans for healthy dwellings for the labouring classes (1862, 1867), while Ernest Newton (1882) and Richard Norman Shaw (1878) made sketches for cottages and country residences that were to be constructed in the cement-slab system of W. H. Lascelles, patented in 1875.

Two of the most significant nineteenth-century houses were designed by Philip Webb (1831–1915), who had worked for George Street in Oxford as his chief assistant. There he met William Morris, who was also in Street's office, and after setting up his own architectural practice in London he joined Morris's new London firm in 1861. With Morris, he founded the Society for the Protection of Ancient Buildings in 1877. First, in 1859–60, Webb designed The Red House, Bexleyheath, Kent, for Morris, in a curious blend of Gothic and farmhouse, following Morris's instruction to use 'the style of the thirteenth century'. The simple L-shaped exterior hides a very rich interior, with stained glass by Edward Burne-Jones and Webb himself, and coloured wallpaper and oak furniture by Morris, some painted with medieval scenes. There was a writing-room, and a dining-room with wooden panelling, a built-in Gothic sideboard and a brick fireplace with tiled sides. The large drawing-room had a built-in settle, the top of which was a tiny minstrels' gallery.

The Red House, as planned by Philip Webb, owes much to Butterfield and to Street's use of the Gothic style for their patrons. Both William Butterfield (1814–1900) and George Edmund Street (1824–81) were associated with the Ecclesiological Society. This had been re-formed in 1845 at Cambridge and in numerous publications its members gave prescriptions for building churches of varying sizes and elaboration as well as arguing over narrow doctrinal symbolism. Their magazine, *The Ecclesiologist*, published from 1841 to 1868, was one of the most important forums for such discussion. Butterfield and Street provided many honest, informally planned brick houses with steep gables and dormers, or groups of buildings incorporating the church, school, vicarage and curate's house, sometimes arranged around a courtyard. The Red House is an excellent essay in this 'parsonage manner'.

Philip Webb's second important house (which was almost his last) was built at Standen, near East Grinstead, Sussex, in the years 1892–4 for a solicitor client, J. S. Beale. The tight, comfortable core of small hall, drawing-room, dining-room and study is flanked on the west by a large billiard

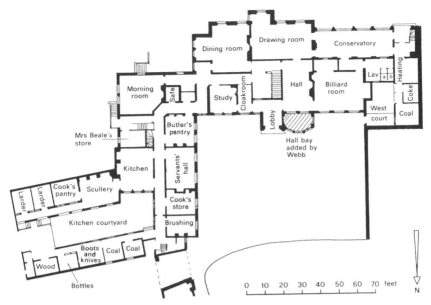

Fig. 17. Standen, West Sussex, ground-floor plan showing the asymmetrical 'double-pile' form, 1892–4, by Philip Webb, based on a plan in the Royal Institute of British Architects Library.

room, a conservatory and the heating services. A long low service wing stretches away to the north and east. This gave too many corridors, and in the 1910 *Country Life* description it was felt that the plan had 'an irregularity almost wayward'. It was traditional, vernacular in every sense and more varied and relaxed than any comparable house.

The blend of careful thought with a search for a style continued into the twentieth century. The neo-Georgian manner had its ardent exponents and there are fine individual houses in a variety of styles by Charles Francis Annesley Voysey, M. H. Baillie Scott and, notably, Sir Edwin Landseer Lutyens.[27] C. F. A. Voysey (1857–1941) liked low rooms and said 'spaciousness and ample superficial areas are essential qualities in a good hall, the effect of which excessive height tends to destroy'. He outlined his method of design as follows:

Put down all the requirements in tabulated order of importance then all conditions, from which two lists you will be able to formulate a third of materials. Then ask the everlasting why are we doing all this....

If a home was wanted for hospitality and large-hearted generosity the doors 'will be wide in proportion to height, to suggest welcome'. The offices for servants should be 'cheerful and not shabby and dark'. This manner of working was 'the exact opposite of the usual method which is to seek the books and museums ... or worse still the example of foreigners ... Forms that are stolen not only make us ridiculous but leave our faculties starved and our characters degrading.'[28]

In Voysey's designs for small houses he brought everything together under a simple sweeping roof, and in the larger houses put the offices in separate blocks. It was a process that produced houses of elegant and lasting quality, related organically to their surroundings.[29]

This spirit of believing the house should relate well to its site, encouraged by a careful blend of traditional materials, is exemplified in the brilliant work of Sir Edwin Landseer Lutyens (1869–1944).[30] He was born in Surrey and had been a pupil of Sir Ernest George, who with his partner, the garden designer Harold Peto, used brick and stone with great skill in a variety of 'early' styles. Lutyens's partnership with the noted gardener, Gertrude Jekyll (for whom he had built Munstead Wood, Surrey, in 1896), led to many elaborate achievements. Whilst Lutyens could create a fine Classical house at Heathcote, Ilkley, or The Salutation, Sandwich, he could also produce the gaunt yet romantic pile of Castle Drogo in Devon (1910–30) for Julius Charles Drewe of the Home and Colonial Stores.

Drewe was an outstanding example of energy and enterprise and his shops flourished so well that he retired at the early age of thirty-three. He then started to realize his dream of establishing himself as a landed country gentleman. What is seen today at Castle Drogo is about a third of what was intended, all set out on top of a hill at the tip of a granite spur. The entrance tower is of solid granite, replete with arrow slits and machicolated parapets on the two turrets. When the portcullis was lowered, Mr Drewe could retreat into his Edwardian castle. Granite and oak are everywhere within, with cross-over vaults, saucer domes, and some ceilings soaring into near Baroque scale 27 ft above. Yet the castle has its comforts, with a wood-panelled drawing-room and dining-room, and a great range of kitchen and domestic offices, all subtle experiments in geometry, and with the advantage that the fittings (even the teak draining-boards and long plate-rack) were designed by the architect.

Mackay Hugh Baillie Scott (1865–1945),[31] having served an apprenticeship with Charles Davis in Bath, set up in practice at Bedford in 1901. The interiors of his houses relied on built-in furniture, friezes and 'panels' of fabrics, and wall-panels for their effect. He also 'revived' the nineteenth-century use of the hall as a social place. According to Baillie Scott's description in his 1906 *Houses and Gardens* (which illustrates his own work)

*130 (left). The vaulted granite stairway and, transom and mullion window,
at Castle Drogo, Devon. Sir Edwin Lutyens built this house in 1910–30
for Mr Julius Drewe, whose portrait by C. M. Hardie R.A., is at the head of the stairs.*

*131 (right). The kitchen at Castle Drogo c. 1915, with its circular beech table,
was designed by Lutyens. Light enters through lunette windows in the roof.*

the hall should 'be a room where the family can meet together – a general
gathering-place with its large fireplace and ample floor space. It must no
longer be a passage.' He further recommended that rooms 'which do not
demand a strict division from the hall should be divided from it by folding
or sliding doors, or even by curtains, so that they share in its spaciousness
and appear rather as recesses than rooms claiming a separate individuality.'

Baillie Scott's fine house, Blackwell, at Bowness-on-Windermere, 1898–9,
built for Sir Edward Holt, has a panelled dining-room with a deep
peacock frieze, a white-painted drawing-room and a two-storey hall, with
an ingenious arrangement of low alcoves and a balcony surrounded by
black-and-white timbering. In 1904 Hermann Muthesius thought Blackwell
'one of the most attractive creations that the new movement in house-
building has produced'.

In all building ventures the attitude and requirements of the owners were very important and were neglected at an architect's peril. In 1891 Margaret Helen McEwan of the Scottish brewing family married the Hon. Ronald Greville, a friend of the Marlborough House circle. In 1906 she and her husband purchased the Polesden Lacey estate in Surrey and the house was substantially remodelled for her by the creators of the new Ritz hotel, the Anglo-French architects Mèwes and Davis.

Mrs Greville was a well-known hostess, a clever woman with little time for those of shallow mind and from the death of her husband, in 1908, until the outbreak of the Second World War, invited distinguished guests to stay for long periods. The dining-room at Polesden Lacey was the setting for the fabled creations of Mrs Greville's French chef, and the carved and gilt panelling, *c.* 1700, in the drawing-room had once adorned an Italian palace. In *Down the Kitchen Sink* (1974) Beverley Nichols describes the scene at Polesden Lacey during a weekend party at tea-time. In the small drawing-room, or 'Tea Room', with its painted *boiseries* (carved panelling) in the Louis XVI style, the ceremony was about to take place. The 'political house' had stopped, for tea and for gossip.

Tea is at 5 o'clock ... and not 5 minutes past ... which means that the Spanish ambassador, who has gone for a walk down the yew avenue hastily retraces his steps, and that the Chancellor of the Exchequer hurries down the great staircase, and that the various gentlemen rise from their chaise-longues ... and join the procession to the tea-room. The tea-pots, the cream-jugs, the milk-pots and the sugar basins are of Queen Anne silver; the tea-service is Meissen; and the doyleys, heavily monogrammed, are of Chantilly lace.

When Mrs Greville died in 1942 she bequeathed the house to the National Trust.

DECORATED WALLS
AND CEILINGS

Numerous patent compositions for stucco were described in the dictionaries of architecture and building magazines issued in the early nineteenth century. The various fireproof cements that largely superseded plaster or stucco did not crack or swell, dried or hardened rapidly, and could be painted almost at once: they were correspondingly popular.

132 (opposite). The saloon, c. 1782, at Kingston Lacy, Dorset.
The coved ceiling, cornice and frieze were probably painted by Cornelius Dixon in 1790.
The Aubusson carpet was purchased by Henry Bankes at the 1823 Fonthill sale.

As the century progressed aesthetes paid attention to Pugin's dictates, in his *True Principles of Pointed or Christian Architecture* (1841): 'there should be no features about a building which are not necessary for convenience, construction or propriety', and 'all ornament should consist of enrichment of the essential construction of the building.' Embellishments of plaster, stucco, composition and papier mâché continued in forms reminiscent of earlier styles of decoration. But an entrepreneur, C. F. Bielefeld, who had published several books on papier mâché[32] began to make fibrous slabs, with which the ceiling of the Reading Room at the British Museum was lined. Additionally, White and Parlby patented a method of producing papier mâché ornaments direct from moulds in 1858.

It was competition that rendered plasterwork less desirable, although there had been some flamboyant essays in the late years of the 1830s, dominated by Francis Bernasconi's skilful use of 'Gothic compo'. His was the only firm in England capable of dealing with William Burn's commission at Harlaxton, Lincolnshire, c. 1838 for Gregory Gregory (1786–1854). Burn had taken over there from Anthony Salvin, who had been in Munich and Nuremberg in 1835[33] and may well have sought out Bavarian stuccoists. However, Bernasconi's involvement is more likely. The Cedar Staircase at Harlaxton is a prodigious display of decorative virtuosity, unparalleled in any nineteenth-century English house. It has great console brackets incorporating supports to the upper landing in the form of male figures and is covered in *putti* seen in various poses – bearing great cockleshells, or swinging daringly on the cascade of bellying stucco drapery with its tasselled cords and festoons.

One later interior that did rival Harlaxton was the Green Drawing Room of Dorchester House, Park Lane, London, built in 1848–63 by Lewis Vulliamy (1791–1871), a pupil of Sir Robert Smirke. Alfred Stevens decorated it in fresco for the millionaire collector R. S. Holford, who also used Vulliamy a few years later to build Westonbirt in Gloucestershire (1864–72). The plans of both were lavish and needed a commercial prince's fortune to sustain.

At the end of the nineteenth century, however, the imitation of earlier types of plaster – particularly the heavy, foliage-decked ceilings of the 1670–90 period – was much practised by architects and craftsmen, and revived interest in the use of plasterwork. Two leading firms were those of George Jackson and George Bankart; Bankart was the author of *The Art of the Plasterer* (1908), and had worked for the talented designer and craftsman, Ernest Gimson (1864–1920), and for the architect, Sir Robert Lorimer (1864–1929), who had done so much to revive the building crafts in

133. *The staircase well at Harlaxton Manor, Lincolnshire,*
with exuberant plasterwork attributed to Francis Bernasconi, c. 1840.

Scotland. At Barnett Hill, near Wonersh, Surrey, Arnold Mitchell (1863–1944) designed a house for Frank Cook of the firm of Thomas Cook. The staircase hall rises to a great lantern which was copied from that in the seventeenth-century Ashburnham House, Westminster. It is surrounded by Bankart's heavy foliated plasterwork in an Edwardian form of seventeenth-century Baroque, and the viewer gazes upwards through a succession of oval voids.

One of the grandest Victorian town houses was Barry's Bridgewater House for Francis Egerton, 1st Earl of Ellesmere, designed in 1845 and completed in 1854. Sir Charles Barry (1795–1860) had been awarded the gold medal of the Royal Institute of British Architects in 1850. He was already well known for his rebuilding of the Houses of Parliament, for various London clubs, and for great country houses remodelled from earlier ones, such as the Duke of Sutherland's Trentham Hall, Staffordshire (1834–57), and Kingston Lacy, Dorset (1835–9). Within a short distance of St James's Palace, Bridgewater House was on a prime site. All the decoration on both floors was derived from Raphael's *Logge*, and was executed by J. Götzenberger, who had come to England a little before 1844. At Lancaster House (also known as York House and Stafford House), nearby in Stable Yard, Barry had made far-reaching alterations from the late 1830s. The gallery had a lantern on palm-tree supports (which are really ventilation shafts) and old master canvases by Guercino and Veronese took the place of work by lesser painters.

At the accession of Queen Victoria in 1837 a break had come in the long history of decorative painting in England. The Houses of Parliament were almost complete and a long debate ensued on the painted decoration. Under the chairmanship of Prince Albert, a committee considered various candidates, settling eventually for John Gregory Crace (1809–89), who came from a long line of decorative artists, and disappointing many other painters, for example, Benjamin Robert Haydon (1786–1846), who had long wanted the commission. Crace supervised the decoration not only of the new Houses of Parliament, but also of the Great Exhibition of 1851.[34]

The most outstanding collaboration of the years 1857–60 was the decoration of the Debating Room of the Oxford Union Society Building by Dante Gabriel Rossetti with a team of his Pre-Raphaelite Brotherhood friends: Edward Burne-Jones, William Morris, Val Prinsep, Arthur Hughes, John Roddam Spencer-Stanhope and John Hungerford Pollen. The paintings[35] are now faded and hardly visible, but their style had an effect on at least one country-house interior. The designer of the Debating Room at

Oxford, Benjamin Woodward, was asked, in 1856, along with Pollen, to work for the 8th Marquis of Lothian at Blickling Hall, Norfolk. They formed a new morning room, with a wonderful beamed and painted ceiling (which survives above a later suspended one); painted Celtic interlace on the ceiling of Lady Lothian's sitting-room; and decorated the long gallery with a huge, hooded marble chimneypiece, carved in 1860 to Pollen's design, and an elaborate frieze. This frieze was painted in a Renaissance white-vine interlace 'inspired' – as John Maddison has noted in the guide book to Blickling (1987) – 'perhaps, by the fifteenth-century Suetonius manuscript, which is one of the greatest treasures of the Blickling library.'

Apart from the wide use of stucco wallpaper and paint, other materials were used, to a lesser extent, to decorate walls. William Bankes acquired gilded leather in Venice for the Spanish Picture Room at Kingston Lacy, Dorset. In 1849 he wrote from Venice: 'I have at length purchased hangings of gilded leather sufficient, I trust, for the whole walls, but as the quantity runs very close, I want the utmost precision in the dimensions.' The leather is tooled and painted, as an elaborate book-binding, and has been restored recently to its original bright colours. When the German art historian, Dr Waagen, visited Kingston Lacy in 1857 he wrote: 'I know no other collection in England containing so many valuable pictures of the Spanish School.'[36] They hang in the richest of settings, beneath a seventeenth-century Venetian ceiling adapted to the size of the room.

In 1857 Giles Gilbert Scott had written of a revival in making stamped leather, but it did not take the place of the older Dutch, Italian and Spanish leathers. Likewise, leather paper only gradually replaced the use of sewn skins. Not everyone wanted leather, although they liked its appearance. When Lord Beaumont was building Carlton Towers, Yorkshire, in 1873–5, he adopted an alternative in his Venetian Drawing Room. His architect, J. F. Bentley (1839–1902) covered the upper parts of the walls with moulded plaster, which had a pattern of pomegranates gilded to look like stamped leather.

From the middle of the nineteenth century, machine-printed wallpaper was available and its relative cheapness made it easy to apply a new surface quickly. The twenty-four order books of the Cowtan firm from 1824 to 1938[37] survive at the Victoria and Albert Museum, London, and show the development of wallpapers for specific parts of a house: flocks for drawing-rooms, sitting-rooms, dining-rooms and libraries; marble papers with a gloss finish for halls, staircases and passages; moiré papers imitating watered silks for bedrooms, although flocks of a small design, and often red, green or blue in colour, were also in use. Bedrooms could be papered with floral and

*134. The great parlour, 1893, at Wightwick Manor, Wolverhampton, West Midlands.
This principal room by Edward Ould has a deep plaster frieze by C. E. Kempe
telling the story of Orpheus and Eurydice. Chandeliers from Morris & Co. were made
by W. A. S. Benson. The date '1893' appears over the inglenook fireplace.*

chintz designs and small pattern repeats were suitable for servants' rooms, attics and garrets. The paintwork was usually coloured to match the ground colour of the papers.[38]

The repetition of ornament by machine was, of course, totally unacceptable to an acute observer such as John Ruskin (1819–1900): 'In good design all imitation by machinery is impossible. No curve is like another for an instant.'[39]

Nevertheless, William Morris, who also eschewed the products of the machine, produced many wallpapers, of which there are some good examples *in situ*, at Wightwick Manor, Wolverhampton, along with many chairs covered in his printed linen fabrics, and tapestry. In the billiard room the Pimpernel wallpaper was the design used by Morris for his dining-room at Kelmscott House, Hammersmith. The dining-room at Wightwick has the

Wild Tulip paper, a ground-floor passage the Daisy paper (the first Morris wallpaper design) and so on, through to the Acanthus Room and the Pomegranate Passage, named after further Morris papers. They take their place around a very distinguished group of works by many associated with the Pre-Raphaelite Brotherhood and the Morris firm, such as Walter Crane, William de Morgan and W. A. S. Benson.

The architect C. F. A. Voysey produced designs for at least eleven wall-paper manufacturers, as well as designing carpets and rugs, tiles and textiles. His earliest wallpaper design was in 1883, his last in July 1930, with the bird and the heart as recurring motifs. In a lecture at Manchester in 1895 Voysey said:

An additional reason for aiming at flatness in wall-coverings is that found in the fact that an attempt at realism provokes comparison with nature which is distressing in proportion to the beholder's appreciation of the subtle beauties of real life; whereas, in conventional ornament, the life of the designer is brought in and should form a very living and additional attraction.[40]

Voysey was exceptional in concentrating on the small details of his houses, and this enhances the pleasure of seeing them.[41]

Another popular decoration was wall-panelling; there was a vogue for re-erecting eighteenth-century French panelling at houses such as Waddesdon, Buckinghamshire, built for the Rothschild family (1874–89). Coloured carvings and panelled walls contributed to the jewel-like richness characteristic of interiors by William Burges; his Summer Smoking Room at Cardiff Castle is one of the most elaborate. In Lady Bute's bedroom at nearby Castel Coch (1875–81) Burges made a domed ceiling, lavishly decorated with painted flowers, leaves, animals and oriental motifs: a unique polychromatic statement of great beauty.

WINDOWS

The revival of interest in Gothic architecture in the nineteenth century had a considerable effect on the tracery patterns of windows, and upon glass-painting. Stained and painted glass windows were in great demand, to indicate to onlookers the owner's heraldry and lineage and even, as at Cliffe Castle, Keighley, Yorkshire, c. 1880, to show the Victorian Butterfield family in Elizabethan dress. Mr Butterfield was a Keighley textile manufacturer with French connections and pretensions. These found expression in glass, metal and soaring vistas and not least in his winter-garden, with its 65-ft dome.

The outstanding stained-glass artists in the nineteenth century were Thomas Willement, William Morris & Co., C. E. Kempe, John Hardman and Clayton and Bell.[42] It was Thomas Willement (1786–1871) who restored heraldic glass to a place of dignity; his best-known work is the memorial window in the great hall at Hampton Court Palace, but there is a remarkable pastiche of thirteenth-century glazing by him in the hall at Penrhyn Castle, Gwynedd, in Wales. It was put up in 1837, when Willement was also working at Mamhead in Devon, and has roundels depicting the zodiac. Stained glass also came within the many accomplishments of the Crace family. The south windows at Bolton Abbey, Yorkshire, the shooting lodge of the Dukes of Devonshire, have an inscription: 'These windows were ordered by William Spencer, Duke of Devonshire, John G. Crace, fecit 1853.' They cast a coloured light as bright as the serried ranks of dead feathered pheasants.

The work of C. E. Kempe (1837–1907)[43] varies in quality, but good examples of his painted (not stained) glass can be seen at Wightwick Manor, Wolverhampton. One group of windows there came from his own house, Old Place, Lingfield, Sussex. These include a Kempe panel of 'Summer', from William Morris's *Earthly Paradise*, showing a maiden in a long flowing dress, holding a basket of flowers and a spray of leaves and standing on the square tiled floor of a classical loggia. John Richard Clayton (1827–1913) and Alfred Bell (1832–95) cooperated to produce many fine windows, following medieval precedents, but their work is mostly in churches.

William Morris (1834–96) had as considerable an effect on the craft of stained glass as he did on the other decorative arts. With his friends Edward Burne-Jones (1833–98) and Dante Gabriel Rossetti (1828–82) steadily producing cartoons for him, the Morris firm gained a considerable reputation for its glass.[44] Their superb achievements can be seen in the windows (c. 1876) of the chapel of Castle Howard, Yorkshire. There, with frescoes by pupils of C. E. Kempe, woodwork by local craftsmen, and with the ceiling a copy of that designed by Holbein for the Chapel Royal, St James's Palace, High Church ornamentation within a private house was manifest for the pious to contemplate.

The firm whose glass was most often intended for country houses was John Hardman & Co. of Birmingham. They had been persuaded by the architect A. W. N. Pugin in the mid 1840s to expand into making windows, alongside their premier achievements in metalwork. John Hardman (1811–67) had first joined with Pugin in 1838 to make church fittings and ecclesiastical metalwork for St Mary's Church, Derby, dedicated in October

1839, and was then much in demand by Catholic architects for liturgical pieces. His partner was William Powell, whose son, John Hardman Powell (1827–95), was Pugin's pupil. He provided the richly-coloured stained glass depicting scenes from the life of the Virgin Mary in the private chapel of Arundel Castle, Sussex, which Charles Alban Buckler (1824–1905) had designed for the 15th Duke of Norfolk in the 1880s. He is also depicted, rather surprisingly, with his patroness Anne Scarisbrick (sister of the owner Charles Scarisbrick) in his staircase window in E. W. Pugin's new wing of the 1860s at Scarisbrick Hall, Lancashire.

Throughout the eighteenth century there were various excise duties imposed on glass and a window tax levied on houses with more than six windows, from 1823. Both were eventually abolished (glass in 1845 and windows in 1851) but the law then regulated the minimum size of windows for small rooms.[45] This concern with size did not affect the large house. The manufacture of sheet and plate glass, which was efficient since the 1830s, allowed the use of large panes of plate glass to be set into robust sash-windows. Webster and Parkes wrote in 1844: 'The abundant introduction of light, by means of large panes of glass, adds a cheerfulness formerly unknown.'[46]

This statement was, in spirit, taken much to heart by C. F. A. Voysey. In his terrace houses in Hans Road, Knightsbridge (1891–2), he introduced as much light as he could, particularly on the staircase. He also set windows in great semicircular frames, and on the west side at Broadleys, Windermere (1898), positioned three bow windows to break up the roof line, with the centre one lighting the upper areas of the galleried hall.

DOORS

One of the richest interiors, using superb, heavy, decorated doors is A. W. N. Pugin's Scarisbrick Hall, Lancashire (1836–45). Whilst much that was good there was sold in sales in 1860–61 and 1963 (with only some 'fixtures' eventually returned), there is still enough to amaze the eye. The King's Room in the west wing (by A. W. N. Pugin, 1836–9) has six-inch-thick arched doors leading to the Red Drawing Room. They are deeply and flamboyantly carved with a swirling Gothic pattern, and have a rich carved moulding at the centre. All around is panelling in the same style topped with paintings of kings and queens and a ceiling with gilt ribs and gold stars on a blue ground. The ornament resembles plates in Pugin's own *Details of Antient Timber Houses* ... (1837).

135. *The chimneypiece of white statuary and Siena marble, 1865,*
in the Picture Gallery at Weston Hall, West Midlands.

In the dining-room at Kingston Lacy, Dorset, designed by Sir Charles Barry in the 1830s, the panels of the four pairs of double doors are of carved boxwood. They were started in 1849 in Venice by Vicenzo Favenza, who took some four years to carve them, copying the cupids playing on different instruments or singing from works by Donatello, Sansovino and Luca della Robbia. After a fire, from which the doors were rescued, Walter Ralph Bankes (1853–1904) panelled the room in oak and cedarwood and set the doors back in position.

Door panels were a good place for a rich display of inlaid or painted decoration, and of opulent lock-plates and hinges. At Bear Wood, near Wokingham, Berkshire, which John Walter, proprietor of *The Times*, built from 1865–74, there are sliding doors between the drawing-room and the morning room on the west side of the huge pile and adjacent to a top-lit picture gallery. A rich strapwork border on the doors surrounds an excessively dense oval panel of birds, foliage, music and musical instruments. The doors were seemingly made on the estate: John Walter had his own brick-kilns, from which the bricks for the house came, and his own carpentry and joinery shops.[47] At Harlaxton Manor, Lincolnshire, Anthony Salvin, followed by William Burn and David Bryce, had set a lavish style for a lavish patron, Gregory Gregory. The lock-plate in Rococo style (*c.* 1844) is notable, and is signed by Gibbons of Wolverhampton. At Carlton Towers, Yorkshire, J. F. Bentley designed the door handles to the huge oak double doors of the Venetian Drawing Room, *c.* 1875. The plates are a floral design in filigree metal screwed to the doors by twelve screws in each border. They were the small detailed finishing touches that a good architect saw carried out to his satisfaction.

The alternatives to heavy Gothic doors were those which had glass panels in the upper stage, or those made of cheaper woods, such as deal, and then painted white or stone colour.

<hr />

CHIMNEYPIECES

The open fire continued in popularity throughout the nineteenth century but was supplemented by central-heating systems using steam, hot air or hot water. It is not to my purpose to list every lavish chimneypiece, but there are excellent examples at Chatsworth, Derbyshire – described by the *Illustrated London News* (9 December 1843) as having 'splendid figures as side accompaniments'. They were designed by Sir Jeffry Wyatville and executed by Richard Westmacott, R. A. He was a successful sculptor and

136. The drawing-room, 1883–4, on the south-east corner of Cragside, Northumberland. Norman Shaw's last addition to Cragside with the double-storey chimneypiece designed by his assistant, W. R. Lethaby, and executed in Italian marbles by Farmer and Brindley.

provider of chimneypieces to many owners. The chimneypiece was a dominant feature particularly in a large, two-storey room, such as at Weston Hall, West Midlands, and they were well suited to the display of heraldry and ornament. The principal feature of the drawing-room at Arundel Castle, Sussex, is the large heraldic chimneypiece, 1875, carved in Painswick stone by Thomas Earp, with the arms of the 15th Duke of Norfolk impaling those of his first wife, Lady Flora Hastings. The northern home of the Duke of Norfolk is Carlton Towers, Yorkshire, built by J. F. Bentley, 1873–5. The chimneypiece in the Venetian Drawing Room is decorated with heraldry and panels of Flora and the Four Seasons by N. H. J. Westlake. A large shield supported by the Stapleton talbots carries thirty-six armorial quarterings. The yellow embossed fireplace tiles are by William de Morgan.

Perhaps the most imposing experiment in Renaissance styling, however, is the enormous alabaster overmantel and inglenook in the drawing-room at Cragside, Northumberland. It is worthy of an Italian *palazzo* but was designed *c.* 1883–4 by Robert Norman Shaw's pupil, W. R. Lethaby (1857–1931).

Lethaby had been responsible a year or two earlier for designing doorways, fireplaces and other details at Flete, Devonshire, which had been designed as a whole by Shaw and built for Henry Bingham Mildmay, 1878–83. In Shaw's own design of 17 June 1875[48] for the chimneypiece in the drawing-room at Sutton Place, Guildford, Surrey, there were plans to provide panels of Japanese silk and squares of mirror in the overmantel and canopy. It was all to be 'mainly made of dark stained black wood and French polish'd – not to be too costly'. The opening below was 5 × 4 ft, lined with Dutch tiles, and the shafts and mouldings, were 'to be the same as previous chimneypieces'. Japanese leather was put on the dado, and Morris's Daisy Blue paper above. The sides of the fire opening could then be lined with old Dutch tiles, or, as at Carlton Towers, Yorkshire, with tiles decorated by incised or relief flower-patterns produced by potters such as William de Morgan.

STAIRCASES

In the mid-nineteenth century the dominant position of the entrance hall in a house meant that the staircase was not immediately visible. Grand social occasions were on the ground floor, and there was little reason to build the imposing staircases common fifty years before. Nevertheless, many impressive staircases were still in evidence, for example, that at Kingston Lacy, Dorset, which imitates the style of the staircase in the original seventeenth-century house on this site. In his book on planning a house (1864), Robert Kerr rather dogmatically asserted that while oval or circular staircases 'were imposing on paper ... winders ought never to be used'. It was a statement that met with approval in the building magazines and whilst there was a pair of circular staircases installed at the Rothschild house, Waddesdon Manor, they were soon out of favour when the Prince of Wales broke his leg on one of them.[49]

A staircase with an open newel and quarter-landings was considered appropriate for most houses, but there were those that started in one flight and returned in two. Where there was a galleried hall, as at Mentmore, Buckinghamshire, built for Baron Meyer Amschel de Rothschild by Sir Joseph Paxton and G. H. Stokes in 1850–55, this type was usual, but other staircases were also needed: a private one for the owner, or a family staircase. Some houses also had separate access to the bachelors' wing, and

137. The staircase second flight, c. 1837–8, at Kingston Lacy, Dorset, designed by Sir Charles Barry and executed in Carrara marble, worthy of an Italian palazzo and therefore rising to the state rooms on the piano nobile.

if those for the use of servants were included, the total might be up to six or seven. Most staircases were given some sort of carpeting, although in many, stone steps were left plain. Those that lead from the Stone Hall at Arundel Castle, Sussex, to rooms above are very handsome. They do what all Baroque staircases did: lead from a small space (in Arundel's case, a vaulted undercroft) up into the vast and impressive void − 50 ft high and 133 ft long − of the Barons' Hall.

An octagon staircase with a central shaft reminiscent of that in the York Minster Chapter House is in Burges's Cardiff Castle, and has few equals in its form. At Bear Wood, Berkshire, the clever design produces a sense of great height as the onlooker can gaze through one space to a higher one, whilst George Myers's staircase at Horsted Place, Sussex, was the one exhibited by A. W. N. Pugin at the 1851 Exhibition. However, my favourite nineteenth-century staircase remains that at Harlaxton Hall, Lincolnshire, with its cedar riches and Bernasconi stuccoes. It does what good staircases should do: take the breath away, not in the ascent, but at the sheer rising opulence of it all.

By 1900 the grand staircase was less in evidence, and one staircase was considered sufficient for most houses. There is still an austere grandeur in the granite staircases by Lutyens at Castle Drogo, Devon, and in the marble stairs at Heathcote, Ilkley, Yorkshire. Those by C. R. Ashbee (1836−1942) display an enviable simplicity: at 39 Cheyne Walk, Chelsea (1899−1901), with a frieze by C. F. Varley, Ashbee provided a simple straight-balustered flight of stairs that has as much elegance as one by Voysey. It is an example of the standard of domestic work practised by these interesting artisans, which has rarely been equalled. At the point where design and invention were set to the greatest advantage it was inevitable that convenience had also come, at last, to reign.

In considering the appearance of the English house interior from the medieval period onwards certain factors have stood out. Whilst early houses were often designed with defence in mind there was a growing concern with convenient arrangement and with comfort. It helped daily life if rooms were easy of access, warm and well-lighted. Decoration in paint, plaster and carved wood, with a lavish use of fabrics, wallpaper and tapestries could aid this, even when the search for style was quixotic. The sprite-like curves of Rococo decoration might have enhanced plasterwork, chimney-pieces, overmantels and gilded furniture, but it was the later insistence

138. A design for a drawing-room by Waring and Gillow, London, c. 1900.

on proportion and linear values, mixed with a greater concern for colour, which gave rooms a balance and distinction rarely achieved previously, or since.

The early nineteenth century found house-owners striving to achieve domestic efficiency. Central-heating, colza oil lamps and Joseph Bramah's water-closets could have provided this. However, these innovations existed in large rambling interiors, which still required a host of domestic staff. Jane Austen's writings often stress the word 'comfort', and all levels of society enjoyed it in varying measure.

In the twentieth century there has been a slight rejection of clutter, intimacy, and privacy in some interior settings. For the American architect, Frank Lloyd Wright (1867–1959), the interior took second place to the exterior, and there were those for whom dwellings were machines not homes. Perhaps Dr Johnson had the correct assessment of the house interior when he wrote: 'To be happy at home is the ultimate result of all ambition.'

NOTES

CHAPTER ONE

1. W. A. Pantin, 'Medieval English town-house plans', *Medieval Archaeology*, VI-VII, 1962–3, pp. 202–39.
2. Margaret Wood, *The English Medieval House*, 1965, Chapter 5.
3. Penelope Eames, 'Documentary evidence concerning the character and use of domestic furnishings in England in the fourteenth and fifteenth centuries', *Furniture History*, VII, 1971, pp. 41–60.
4. J. T. Smith, 'Medieval Roofs: A Classification' in *Studies in Domestic Medieval Architecture*, 1975, pp. 44–83; Cecil A. Hewett, *English Historic Carpentry*, 1980, p. 320.
5. J. G. Hurst, 'Wharram Percy, Yorkshire', *Medieval Archaeology*, I, II, III, 1957, 1958, 1960; Wood, *op. cit.*, p. 389.
6. I have used the edition of *Vitruvius* translated by M. H. Morgan, Harvard, 1914. See Book II, v and Book VII, ii and iii; Marion E. Blake, *Ancient Roman Construction in Italy*, Washington D.C., 1947, p. 320.
7. L. F. Salzman, *Building in England Down to 1540: A Documentary History*, Oxford 1967, Appendix A, pp. 355–412.
8. T. B. James, A. M. Robinson and Elizabeth Eames, *Clarendon Palace* ... Society of Antiquaries of London, Research Report XLV, 1988.
9. Elizabeth Eames, 'A tile pavement from the Queen's Chamber, Clarendon Palace, dated 1250–2', *Journal, British Archaeological Association*, 3rd series, XX-XXI, 1957–8, pp. 95–106.
10. T. Hudson Turner, *Some Account of Domestic Architecture in England*, Oxford, 1851, I, p. 235, quoting the *Liberate Roll*, 36 Henry III.
11. *Chronica Majora* V, p. 481 (Rolls Series).
12. Salzman, *op. cit.*, p. 160.
13. E. Clive Rouse and A. Baker, 'Longthorpe Tower', *Archaeologia*, XCVI, 1955, pp. 1–34.
14. E. W. Tristram, *English Medieval Wall Painting*; G. H. Cook, *The English Medieval Parish Church*, 1954, pp. 195–202.
15. Hugh Braun, *The Story of the English House*, 1965, Chapter 5.
16. A list is given in Wood, *op. cit.*, pp. 118–20.

17. John Harvey, *Gothic England . . ., 1300–1550*, 1947, p. 130, Plates 141–2.

18. Olive Cook, *The English House Through Seven Centuries*, 1968, p. 35.

19. Wood, *op. cit.*, p. 122.

20. J. T. Smith, 'Stokesay Castle', *Archaeological Journal*, CXIII, 1956, pp. 211–14.

21. J. W. F. Hill, *Medieval Lincoln*, 1948, pp. 208–20.

22. Hewett, *op. cit.*, gives several drawings of early door leaves in English parish churches.

23. J. A. Repton, *Norwich Cathedral*, Farnborough, 1965, p. 34.

24. Literature on early fireplaces is scarce and reference still needs to be made to L. A. Shuffrey, *The English Fireplace*, 1912. He illustrates the Conway fireplaces, Figs. 30–1; see also Sydney Toy in *Archaeologia*, LXXXVI, 1937, pp. 163–92, Wood, *op. cit.*, pp. 273–6 and Alison Kelly, *The Book of English Fireplaces*, 1968.

25. W. H. Godfrey, *The English Staircase*, 1911; E. F. Sekler, 'The development of the British Staircase', University of London, Courtauld Institute, Ph.D. thesis, 1954.

26. Hewett, *op. cit.*, drawings, pp. 222–3.

27. Mark Girouard, *Life in the English Country House*, 1978, p. 38.

28. U. J. Holmes, *Daily Living in the Twelfth Century*, University of Wisconsin Press, 1953.

29. L. Wright, *Clean and Decent: The Fascinating History of the Bathroom and the Water Closet*, 1960, p. 70.

CHAPTER TWO

1. Maurice Howard, *The Early Tudor Country House: Architecture and Politics, 1490–1550*, 1987, Chapter 4, 'The Courtyard and the Household'.

2. H. M. Colvin, ed., *The History of the King's Works*, Vol. IV, Pt. II, 1982, pp. 222–34. A conjectural plan is given on p. 226.

3. *Ibid.*, For a more detailed examination of evidence see Simon Thurley. 'Henry VIII and the Building of Hampton Court: A Reconstruction of the Tudor Palace,' *Architectural History*, 31, 1988, pp. 1–57.

4. Neville Williams, *Henry VIII and his Court*, 1971, p. 94.

5. Howard, *op. cit.*, p. 29.

6. Strode's diary is printed by John Hutchin, *History of Dorset*, 3rd ed., 1861–73, IV, pp. 5–7, and noted by Arthur Oswald in his account of Chantmarle, *Country Life*, CVII, 1950, pp. 1966–71.

7. For a full discussion of de l'Orme's work see Anthony Blunt, *Philibert de l'Orme*, 1958. The Anet frontispiece is now in the courtyard of the École des Beaux Arts in Paris.

8. Sir John Summerson, ed., 'The Book of Architecture of John Thorpe', *Walpole Society XL*, 1966; Mark Girouard, ed., 'The Smythson Collection of the Royal Institute of British Architects', *Architectural History*, V, 1962; *ibid.*, *Robert Smythson and the Elizabethan Country House*, 2nd edn., 1983.

9. Malcolm Airs, *The Making of the English Country House, 1500–1640*, 1975, pp. 5–7.

10. David Knowles, *The Religious Orders in England, The Tudor Age*, 1959, III, 'Suppression and Dissolution', pp. 291–402.

11. Mark Girouard, 'Elizabethan Architecture and the Gothic Tradition', *Architectural History*, VI, 1963, p. 30.

12. *Ibid.*, pp. 32–33, and Fig. 6.

13. Rosalys Coope, 'The Long Gallery', *Architectural History*, 29, 1986, pp. 49–50.

14. *Ibid.*, p. 50 and fn. 72; W. R. D. Harrison and Viscount Chandos, *Carvings, Oak Gallery, The Vyne, Hampshire*, Sherborne St John, 1979.

15. Sacheverell Sitwell, *British Architects and Craftsmen*, 1948, p. 28.

16. Girouard, 1983, *op. cit.*, Chapter 4.

17. Coope, *op. cit.*, p. 60.

18. Howard Colvin and John Newman, eds., *Of Building, Roger North's Writings on Architecture*, Oxford, 1981, pp. 135–6.

19. John Newman, 'Copthall, Essex', in Howard Colvin and John Harris, eds., *The Country Seat* (1970).

20. Girouard, 1983, *op. cit.*, pp. 81–108.

21. *Ibid.*, p. 108.

22. Lindsay Boynton and Peter Thornton, 'The Hardwick Hall Inventories of 1601', Furniture History Society, *Journal*, VII, 1971.

23. Hilary Wayment, 'The Stained Glass in the Chapel of The Vyne', *National Trust Studies*, 1980, pp. 35–48; 'The Stained Glass of the Chapel of The Vyne and the Chapel of the Holy Ghost, Basingstoke', *Archaeologia*, CVII, 1982, pp. 141–52.

24. Airs, *op. cit.*, pp. 97–8.

25. For details of stone use, see Salzman, *op. cit.*, p. 131, and Alec Clifton-Taylor, *The Pattern of English Building*, 2nd edn, 1972, Chapters 2–4.

26. Ernest Law, *History of Hampton Court Palace*, 1885, 1, p. 363.

27. Clifton-Taylor, *op. cit.*, pp. 178–80.

28. William Horman, *Vulgaria*, ed. M. R. James, Roxburghe Club, 1926, XXIX.

29. W. H. St J. Hope, *Cowdray and Easebourne Priory*, 1919, p. 121.

30. W. Harrison, *The Description of England*, ed. G. Edelen, Ithaca, 1968, p. 321.

31. Exchequer receipts, 1531–2, quoted by Salzman, *op. cit.*, p. 258.

32. Colvin, *King's Works, op. cit.*, pp. 132–5.

33. Francis W. Reader, 'The Use of the Stencil in Mural Decoration', *Archaeological Journal*, XCV, 1938, Part 1, pp. 112–25 and XCVII, 1940, pp. 88–95.

34. Edward Croft-Murray, *Decorative Painting in England*, I, 1962, Plates 17–20 as by Toto del Nunziata, but E. K. Waterhouse, *Apollo*, 1963, p. 342 thought Nicolò Bellin a more likely attribution.

35. Francis W. Reader, 'Tudor Domestic Wall-Paintings', two articles in *Archaeological Journal*, XCII, 1935, and XCIII, 1936. See also his study of lesser houses in Buckinghamshire, *Royal Archaeological Institute Journal*, LXXXIX, 1933.

36. Margaret Jourdain, *English Interior Decoration, 1500–1830*, 1950, Plate 21.

37. Elsie Matley-Moore, 'Wall paintings recently discovered in Worcestershire', *Archaeologia*, LXXX, 1940, pp. 281–8.

38. David N. Durant and Philip Riden, eds., *The Building of Hardwick Hall, Part 2, The New Hall, 1591–98*, Derbyshire Record Society, IX, 1984, p. xviii.

39. Geoffrey Beard, *Decorative Plasterwork in Great Britain*, 1975, Chapter 2; *ibid., Stucco and Decorative Plasterwork in Europe*, 1982, Chapter 1.

40. H. Avray Tipping, *English Homes*, Period II, *Early Tudor, 1485–1558* and Period III, Vols. 1 and II, *Late Tudor and Early Stuart, 1558–1649*, (1929–).

41. Durant and Riden, *op. cit.*, pp. lxviii and lxxix.

42. Thomas Percy, ed., *The Northumberland Household Book*, 1770, p. xvii.

43. A brief balanced account of English stained glass in C. Woodforde, *English Stained and Painted Glass*, Oxford, 1954.

44. Red Lodge, Bristol; Bradfield House, Devon; Bradninch Manor, Devon; Broughton Castle, Oxon; Cotehele, Cornwall; Maxstoke, Warwickshire; Sherborne Castle, Dorset; Sizergh Castle, Cumbria, Inlaid Room (now Victoria and Albert Museum, London); Stockton House, Wiltshire; Thame Park, Oxon.

45. Anthony Wells-Cole, 'An Oak Bed at Montacute: A Study in Mannerist Decoration', *Furniture History*, XVII, 1981, pp. 1–19.

46. Martin Biddle, 'A "Fontainebleau" Chimney-piece at Broughton Castle', in Howard Colvin and John Harris, eds., *The Country Seat*, 1970, pp. 9–12.

47. Nikolaus Pevsner, 'Old Somerset House', *Architectural Review*, 1954, CXVI, pp. 163–7. Plate 17 illustrates the Holbein drawing.

48. Andrea Palladio, *I Quattro Libri Dell'Architettura*, Venice 1570, Book I, Chapter xxviii.

49. Durant and Riden, *op. cit.*, p. 259.

CHAPTER THREE

1 Sir John Summerson, *Inigo Jones*, 1966; and as Surveyor-General in Howard Colvin, ed., *The History of the King's Works, 1485–1660 Part 1*, III, 1975.

2. H. L. Bradfer-Lawrence, 'The Building of Raynham Hall', *Norfolk Archaeology*, xxiii (1929), pp. 93–105; John Harris, *The Palladians*, 1981, p. 47.

3. Sir John Summerson, *Architecture in Britain, 1530–1830*, 7th edn, 1983, pp. 89–98.

4. John Harris, *The Design of the English Country House, 1620–1920*, 1985, p. 9.

5. R. T. Gunther, ed., *The Architecture of Sir Roger Pratt*, 1928, p. 24.

6. Howard Colvin and John Newman, eds., *Of Building: Roger North's Writings on Architecture*, 1981, p. 69.

7. Andor Gomme, in *The Cambridge Guide to the Arts in Britain*, IV, 1990.

8. Eric Mercer, *English Vernacular Houses: A study of traditional farmhouses and cottages*, 1975, p. 1.

9. Mark Girouard, *Life in the English Country House*, 1978, p. 152.

10. Rudolf Wittkower, 'Inigo Jones, Architect and Man of Letters', Royal Institute of British Architects, *Journal*, lx, 1953, pp. 84–5.

11. Howard Colvin, 'The South Front of Wilton House', *The Archaeological Journal*, cxl, 1955, pp. 181–90.

12. Rudolf Wittkower, *Architectural Principles in the Age of Humanism*, 1962, pp. 129–32.

13. Sir William Chambers, MS, 'Description of Wilton'. Royal Institute of British Architects Library, London.

14. Rudolf Wittkower, *Palladio and English Palladianism*, ed. Margot Wittkower, 1974, pp. 76–7.

15. *Country House Floors, 1660–1850*, Temple Newsam Country House Studies, No. 3, Leeds, 1987, pp. 8–10.

16. Anthony Blunt, *Art and Architecture in France, 1500–1700*, 1973, p. 89.

17. Christopher Morris, *The Illustrated Journeys of Celia Fiennes c. 1682–c. 1712*, 1984, pp. 83–4.

18. For Watson and Selden, see Geoffrey Beard, *Craftsmen and Interior Decoration in England, 1660–1820*, 1981, pp. 284, 289.

19. Lawrence Stone, 'The Building of Hatfield House', *The Archaeological Journal*, CXII, 1955, pp. 98–128.

20. P. J. Drury, 'The Evolution of Audley End, 1605–1745', *Architectural History*, 23, 1980, pp. 5–6.

21. Morris, ed., *op. cit.*, p. 140.

22. E. S. de Beer, ed., John Evelyn, *Diary*, 1955, I, p. 29.

23. Geoffrey Beard, 'William Winde and Interior Design', *Architectural History*, 27, 1984, pp. 150–9.

24. David Green, *Grinling Gibbons*, 1964.

25. Geoffrey Beard, 'Some English Wood Carvers', *Burlington Magazine*, CXXVII, October 1985, pp. 686–94.

26. I have used the analysis of the Belton archives and inventories made for the National Trust by Mrs Rosalind J. Westwood (typescript, East Midlands Regional Office).

27. Royal Commission on Historical Monuments: *Westmorland*, 1936, p. 227.

28. Edward Croft-Murray, *Decorative Painting in England 1537–1837*, 1962, I, p. 208; Per Palme, *The Triumph of Peace: A Study of the Whitehall Banqueting House*, 1957; Sir Roy Strong, *Britannia Triumphans: Inigo Jones, Rubens and Whitehall Palace*, 1980, notes specialist articles.

29. E. K. Waterhouse, *Apollo*, April 1963, p. 344 advances other names. See also Margaret Whinney and Oliver Millar, *English Art, 1625–1714*, Oxford, 1957, XII for a summary of the main achievements of the painters, given in detail by Croft-Murray, *op. cit.*

30. *Surtees Society*, 55, 1872, pp. 361–2.

31. Croft-Murray, *op. cit.*, Vol. I gives all painters to c. 1720.

32. Howard Colvin, ed., *The History of the King's Works*, V, 1976, p. 320.

33. Kent County Record Office, MS, U.269, A1/1, 'A Booke of severall Accompts of Tho: Earle of Dorsett', 1607.

34. Mark Girouard, *Robert Smythson and the Elizabethan Country House*, 1983, pp. 21–2.

35. *Country Life*, 8 September 1966.

36. At Devon County Record Office. See also *Country Life*, 2 March 1940, pp. 222–5, and *Transactions, Devonshire Association*, XLIX, 1917 and 89, 1957, pp. 124–44.

37. Pratt noted the prices of 'Hubart's Plaster heades' in a memorandum of 1664 about Clarendon House, and may have used something similar and readily available at Coleshill, Gunther, *op. cit.*, p. 157.

38. Warwick County Record Office. The plaster-work entry was not noted in the description of Warwick Castle (recording the payments for cedar boards etc.) in *Victoria County History, Warwickshire*, 1969, VIII, p. 460.

39. Geoffrey Beard, *Decorative Plasterwork in Great Britain*, 1975, p. 229.

40. Kerry Downes, *Hawksmoor*, 2nd edn, 1979, p. 1.

41. Geoffrey Beard, 'Edward Goudge: The beste master in England', *National Trust Studies*, 1979, pp. 20–7.

42. Howard Colvin, 'Letters and Papers relating to the rebuilding of Combe Abbey, Warwickshire, 1681–1688', *Walpole Society*, L, 1984, pp. 248–309, and plates from *Country Life* XXVI, 1909, pp. 794–840, for interiors stripped twenty years later.

43. John Harris, 'The Building of Denham Place', *Records of Buckinghamshire*, XVI, Part III, 1957–8, pp. 193–6.

44. Christopher Sandford, 'Notes on Eye Manor', *Transactions of the Woolhope Club*, 1952, pp. 24–7; *Country Life*, 15 September 1955.

45. Beard, 1979 (note 41, above), p. 21.

46. Wittkower, *op. cit.* (note 14, above), pp. 158–9.

47. H. J. Louw, 'The Origin of the Sash-Window', *Architectural History*, 26, 1983, pp. 49–72, based on his doctoral thesis, Oxford, 1981.

48. Peter Thornton, *Seventeenth Century Interior Decoration in England, France and Holland*, 1978, pp. 81–5.

49. Gunther, ed., *op. cit.*, p. 295.

50. John Dunbar, 'The Building-activities of the Duke and Duchess of Lauderdale, 1670–82', *Archaeological Journal*, CXXXII, 1975, p. 225.

51. Sir Balthazar Gerbier, *Counsel and Advice to all Builders*, 1664, pp. 18–19.

52. Howard Colvin, 'The Architect of Thorpe Hall', *Country Life*, 6 June 1952.

53. The door-case can be seen at Thorpe Hall in John Cornforth and Oliver Hill, *English Country Houses: Caroline, 1625–85*, 1966, Plate 167.

54. Beard, *op. cit.*, (note 23, above, and Colvin, *op. cit.* (note 42, above).

55. Mercer, *English Vernacular Houses*, *op. cit.*, (note 8, above), Plates 104–5, and gazetteer, pp. 137–227.

56. Eric Mercer, *English Art, 1553–1625*, 1962, p. 118.

57. Harris, *op. cit.*, (note 4, above), pp. 78–9.

58. Several French chimney pieces from Barbet's book and Jean Le Pautre's *Cheminées à la moderne* (1661) and his *Cheminées à l'Italienne* (1665) are given in Thornton, *op. cit.* (note 48, above), Plates 65–70.

59. H. A. Tipping, *English Homes, Late Stuart 1649–1714*, Period IV, Vol. 1, 1929, pp. 1–22.

60. H. A. Tipping, *Country Life*, 29 July 1919, p. 116.

61. This was done under the supervision of the late John Fowler. He was attacked vigorously in *The Times* by the late Ralph Edwards. See John Cornforth, *The Inspiration of the Past*, 1985, p. 213, and *Country Life*, 10 June 1971, p. 1431.

62. June Seymour, 'Edward Pearce: Baroque Sculptor of London', *Guildhall Miscellany*, No. 1, 1952; H. M. Colvin, *A Biographical Dictionary of British Architects, 1600–1840*, 1978, pp. 635–6.

63. Tipping, *op. cit.*, (note 59, above) pp. xi, xxxvi.

64. Tipping, *op. cit.*, p. 165; see also Colvin (note 42, above).

65. James Parker, 'A Staircase by Grinling Gibbons', *Bulletin*, Metropolitan Museum of Art, New York, June 1957, pp. 229–36.

66. Francis Thompson, *A History of Chatsworth*, 1949, pp. 123–5.

67. Morris, *Fiennes, op. cit.*, (note 17, above), p. 105.

68. Colvin and Newman, *op. cit.*, (note 6, above), p. 134.

69. Girouard, *op. cit.* (note 9, above), Chapter 9, 'Early Country-House Technology'.

CHAPTER FOUR

1. A synthesis of Vanbrugh's career, with references to further reading, is my *The Work of John Vanbrugh*, 1985.

2. W. S. Lewis, ed., *The Yale Edition of Horace Walpole's Correspondence*, New Haven, 1960, Vol. 20, pp. 103–4.

3. Michael McCarthy, 'The Building of Hagley Hall', *Burlington Magazine*, April 1976, pp. 214–25.

4. Sir John Summerson, 'The Idea of the Villa', The Cantor Lectures, Royal Society of Arts, London, No. CVII, 1959 (*Journal of the Royal Society of Arts*, July 1959, p. 570).

5. Eric Mercer, *English Vernacular Houses*, 1975, p. 74.

6. Walter Ison, *The Georgian Buildings of Bath*, 1948, pp. 105–13.

7. Tim Mowl and Brian Earnshaw, *John Wood, Architect of Obsession*, Bath, 1988.

8. Sir John Summerson, *Georgian London*, 1962, p. 67.

9. Illustrated in colour in Temple Newsam House, Leeds, *Country House Floors 1660 to 1850*, Leeds, 1987, Plate 1a. The conclusion of work in 1744 has been established recently from the house archives.

10. W. E. Minchinton, 'The Trade of Bristol in the XVIIIth Century', *Bristol Record Society*, XX, 1957; H. S. K. Kent, 'The Anglo-Norwegian Timber Trade in the Eighteenth Century', *Economic History Review*, VIII, 1955, pp. 62–74.

11. The Beningbrough parquet is illustrated in H. A. Tipping and Christopher Hussey, *The Work of Sir John Vanbrugh and His School, 1699–1736*, English Homes, Period IV, Vol. II, 1928, p. 229; King's Weston, see *Architectural History*, 10, 1976, Plate 32.

12. Christopher Hussey, *English Country Houses: Early Georgian, 1715–1760*, 1955, p. 111.

13. *Country House Floors, op. cit.*, p. 34.

14. *Country Life*, 15 February 1919, p. 171. The house was demolished *c.* 1920; some of the rooms were re-erected at the Philadelphia Museum; Geoffrey Beard, *Craftsmen and Interior Decoration in England, 1660–1820*; Edinburgh 1981, p. 173.

15. *Country Life*, 2 January 1953, p. 36.

16. The text is given as Appendix 3 in Mowl and Earnshaw, *op. cit.*

17. Geoffrey Beard, 'Some English Wood Carvers', *Burlington Magazine*, October 1985, pp. 690–1.

18. Desmond Fitz-Gerald, *The Norfolk House Music Room*, Victoria and Albert Museum, 1973.

19. Lindsay Boynton, 'Luke Lightfoot, ?1722–1789', *Furniture History*, II, 1966, pp. 7–17.

20. Vertue's *Notebooks* were published by the Walpole Society in five volumes between 1929 and 1938. A full index to them was given in *Walpole Society*, XXIX, (1940–2).

21. Edward Croft-Murray, *Decorative Painting in England, 1537–1837*, I, 1962, p. 273.

22. *Country Life*, 13 January 1966, pp. 58–61; 27 January, pp. 188–90; 13 February, pp. 224–7.

23. Ingrid Roscoe, 'The Decoration and Furnishing of Kirtlington Park', *Apollo*, January 1980, pp. 22–9.

24. Anthony Wells-Cole, *Historic Paper Hangings*, Temple Newsam House, Leeds, 1983.

25. Oxfordshire County Record Office, Dillon MSS I/p/3h, cited in Geoffrey Beard, *Decorative Plasterwork in Great Britain*, 1975, pp. 201–2.

26. Geoffrey Beard, *Italian Stuccoists in Yorkshire*, York Civic Trust, 1985.

27. R. W. Ketton-Cremer, *Felbrigg*, 1962, pp. 131–43.

28. Book IV, Chapter 23, p. 467.

29. Rudolf Wittkower, 'Pseudo-Palladian Elements in English Neoclassicism', in *Palladio and English Palladianism*, ed. Margot Wittkower, 1974, pp. 158–9.

30. Geoffrey Beard, *Georgian Craftsmen and their Work*, 1966, pp. 48–9.

31. Print Room, 41, 100, 77; first noted by Dr Eileen Harris.

32. Geoffrey Beard and Helena Hayward, 'The Interior Design and Furnishings at Woburn Abbey', *Apollo*, June 1988, pp. 393–400.

33. T. Friedman, ed., 'The Man at Hyde Park Corner: Sculpture by John Cheere, 1709–1787', Temple Newsam House, Leeds, catalogue, 1974.

34. Victoria and Albert Museum, Department of Prints and Drawings, 93, c. 27.

35. Peter Leach, *James Paine*, 1988, pp. 153–61 for his chimneypieces.

36. William Collins (1721–93) provided many of Aesop's *Fables* panels, as a pupil of Sir Henry Cheere. The Cheere workshop was very large and obviously relied on 'sub-contracting'. J. T. Smith in *Nollekens and his Times* (1828) says that Collins was 'Gainsborough's friend ... and the most famous modeller of chimney tablets of his day'.

37. Leach, *op. cit.*, pp. 50–1.

38. Mark Girouard, *Life in the English Country House*, 1978, Chapter 7, 'The Social House: 1720–70'.

39. C. H. and M. I. Collins Baker, *The Life and Circumstances of James Brydges, First Duke of Chandos*, Oxford, 1949, pp. 169–70.

40. Herbert Davis, ed., *Pope: Poetical Works*, Oxford 1966, pp. 319–20.

41. Collins Baker, *op. cit.*, Chapter 8.

CHAPTER FIVE

1. John Brooke, *King George III*, 1972.

2. John Harris, 'Le Geay, Piranesi and International Neo-classicism in Rome, 1740–1750', in *Essays in the History of Architecture presented to Rudolf Wittkower*, 1967.

3. John Fleming, *Robert Adam and his Circle in Edinburgh and Rome*, 1962, pp. 160–1.

4. Peter Leach, *James Paine*, 1988, p. 59.

5. Sir John Summerson, 'The Classical Country House in 18th century England', *Journal of the Royal Society of Arts*, CVII (1959), pp. 539–87.

6. Leslie Harris, *Robert Adam and Kedleston: The Making of a Neo-Classical Masterpiece*, The National Trust, 1987, p. 11.

7. *The Works in Architecture of Robert and James Adam, Esquires*. I, 1778, Preface.

8. Marcus Binney, *Sir Robert Taylor: From Rococo to Neo-Classicism*, 1984, Plate 56.

9. Antony Dale, *James Wyatt*, 1956; John Martin Robinson, *The Wyatts: An Architectural Dynasty*, 1979.

10. J. Mordaunt Crook, 'The pre-Victorian architect: professionalism and patronage', *Architectural History*, 12, 1969, p. 64.

11. J. Wilton-Ely, 'Soane and the Architectural Model', *Architectural History*, 11, 1968, p. 6.

12. Sandra Blutman, 'Country House Design Books, 1780–1815', *Architectural History*, 11, 1968, p. 27.

13. Dorothy Stroud, *The Architecture of Sir John Soane*, 1961, p. 27; J. Mordaunt Crook, *The Greek Revival*, 1972, p. 115.

14. John Fowler and John Cornforth, *English Decoration in the 18th Century*, 1974, p. 213.

15. General C. H. Aspinall-Oglender, *Admiral's Widow*, 1942, p. 54.
16. Lady Llanover, *Autobiography and Correspondence of Mrs Delaney*, 1861–2, VI, p. 400.
17. Treve Rosoman, 'The Chiswick House Inventory of 1770', *Furniture History*, XXII, 1986, pp. 81–102.
18. Maurice Tomlin, 'The 1782 Inventory of Osterley Park', *ibid.*, pp. 106–29.
19. Humphry Repton, *Red Book* for Sheringham, 1812 (preserved at the house).
20. Damie Stillman, *The Decorative Work of Robert Adam*, 1966, p. 26.
21. Arthur T. Bolton, *The Architecture of Robert and James Adam*, 2 vols., 1922; Geoffrey Beard, *The Work of Robert Adam*, 1978.
22. Leslie Harris, *op. cit.*, p. 14.
23. Ian Bristow, 'The Lansdowne Room in the Context of Robert Adam's Work', Philadelphia Museum of Art, *Bulletin*, 82, Nos. 551–2, Summer 1986, p. 14.
24. Bristow, *op. cit.*, p. 15.
25. Derek Buttle, 'James Wyatt and the Early Greek Revival', in W. A. Singleton (ed.): *Studies in Architectural History*, II, York, 1956, pp. 82–3.
26. *Country Life*, 4 November 1954, p. 1577.
27. British Museum, 1955–4–16–13, reproduced, *British Museum Quarterly*, XXI, 1957, pp. 14–15.
28. Edward Croft-Murray, 'Three Famous State Coaches', *Country Life*, Coronation Number, 1953, pp. 80–87; Harris, John, *Sir William Chambers*, 1970, pp. 80–82.
29. British Library, Add. MS. 41133.
30. Harris, *Chambers, op. cit.*, Plate 90; since 1985 in the Victoria and Albert Museum, Department of Prints and Drawings.
31. John Fleming, 'The Journey to Spalato', *Architectural Review*, CXXIII, 1958, pp. 103–7.
32. Leeds Archives Dept., Studley Royal MSS., Robinson letters, 14776.
33. Alnwick Castle Archives, U.I. 46.
34. Heaton Hall, Manchester, Bicentenary Exhibition Catalogue, 1972, p. 43. Wyatt's elevation was partly a recasting of Adam's Kedleston front published in *Vitruvius Britannicus*, IV, 1767.
35. *Guide to Teignmouth, Dawlish and Torquay*, 1817.
36. Cornelius van Horne in Philadelphia Museum of Art, *Bulletin*, 82, Nos. 551–2, Summer 1987, pp. 40–1, 45, fn. 22.
37. Geoffrey Beard, *Craftsmen and Interior Decoration in England, 1660–1820*, 1981, p. 246; *Country Life*, 30 July 1943.
38. Francis Watson and others, *Southill*, 1951.
39. Gilbert Scott, *Remarks on Secular and Domestic Architecture*, 1857, p. 76.
40. *The Fashionable Fireplace, 1660–1840*, Temple Newsam House, Leeds, Country House Guides, 3, 1985, p. 8.
41. John Fleming, *Robert Adam and his Circle in Edinburgh and Rome*, 1962, p. 133.
42. Stillman, *op. cit.*, p. 66.

43. Leslie Harris, *op. cit.*, p. 63.
44. Ann Finer and George Savage, *Selected Letters of Josiah Wedgwood*, 1965; letter of 6 October 1778.
45. *The Fashionable Fireplace* (cf. note 40, above) p. 64.
46. J. A. Thompson, *Count Rumford of Massachusetts*, New York, 1935, pp. 109–10. I am indebted to Mark Girouard for this reference.
47. J. D. Williams, *The Restoration of Audley End, 1762–1797*, Chelmsford, 1966, p. 32.
48. Mary Mauchline, *Harewood House*, Newton Abbot, 1974, p. 93.
49. Christopher Gilbert, *Thomas Chippendale: His Life and Work*, 1978, I, p. 59.
50. *Ibid.*, p. 188.

CHAPTER SIX

1. Witold Rybczynski, *Home: A Short History of an Idea*, 1986, Chapter 7.
2. *Country Life*, 28 July 1973, p. 582.
3. Jill Franklin, *The Gentleman's Country House and Its Plan, 1835–1914*, 1981.
4. Diana Cooper, *The Rainbow Comes and Goes*, 1958, pp. 36–7.
5. Pugin's *True Principles* ed. Marina Henderson, 1973, p. 63.
6. Robert Kerr, *The Gentleman's House, or how to plan English residences from the Parsonage to the Palace*, 1864, p. 173.
7. *Ibid.*, p. 75.
8. Hermann Muthesius, *Das Englische Haus*, Berlin, 3 vols., 1904–5, abridged English edn, ed. Dennis Sharp, 1979, p. 95.
9. Walter Ison, *The Georgian Buildings of Bath*, 1948, pp. 105–110.
10. Stefan Muthesius, *The English Terraced House*, 1982, p. 87.
11. *Ibid.*, p. 107.
12. J. J. Stevenson, *House Architecture*, 1880, II, p. 57.
13. Augustus Hare, *The Years with Mother*, 1896, I, p. 66.
14. C. Gore, *The Diamond and the Pearl*, 1849, I, p. 288.
15. Andrew Saint, *Richard Norman Shaw*, 1976, p. 71, Plate 49.
16. In my collection.
17. Mark Girouard, *The Victorian Country House*, 2nd edn, 1979, Plate XXVI.
18. Franklin, *op. cit.*, p. 57.
19. Mary Carbery, *Happy World*, 1941, p. 99.
20. Girouard, *op. cit.*, pp. 112–3.
21. Saint, *op. cit.*, p. 111.
22. Mrs Edward Twistleton, *Letters Written to Her Family, 1852–1862*, 1908, p. 132.
23. J. C. Loudon, *Encyclopedia of Cottage, Farm and Villa Architecture*, 1833, p. 802.
24. Gervas Huxley, *Victorian Duke, The Life of Hugh Lupus Grosvenor, First Duke of Westminster*, 1967, p. 142.
25. Huxley, *op. cit.*, p. 138.
26. Franklin, *op. cit.*, pp. 90–106; Girouard, *op. cit.*, pp. 29–31.
27. Gavin Stamp and André Goulancourt, *The English House, 1860–1914*, 1986 is an excellent, well-illustrated survey.

28. *Journal of Decorative Art*, XV, 1895, pp. 82–90, cited in John Brandon-Jones and others, *C.F.A. Voysey, architect and designer, 1857–1941*, 1978, p. 20.

29. Joanna Symonds, *Catalogue of drawings by C. F. A. Voysey in the Drawings Collections of the Royal Institute of British Architects*, Gregg, Farnborough, 1976.

30. A. S. G. Butler, *The Architecture of Sir Edwin Lutyens*, 3 Vols., 1950; Christopher Hussey, *The Life of Sir Edwin Lutyens*, 1950. (Both reprinted 1984.)

31. James Kornwolf, *M. H. Baillie Scott and the Arts and Crafts Movement*, 1972.

32. Notably C. F. Bielefeld, *On the Use of the Improved Papier-mâché in Furniture, in the Interior Decoration of Buildings, and in Works of Art*, 1850.

33. Jill Allibone, *Anthony Salvin, Pioneer of Gothic Revival Architecture*, 1988, Chapter 4.

34. Edward Croft-Murray, *Decorative Painting in England, 1537–1837*, II, 1970, p. 78.

35. K. L. Goodwin, *Journal of the William Morris Society*, II, no. 3, Winter 1968.

36. Anthony Mitchell, *Kingston Lacy*, The National Trust, 1987, pp. 31–8.

37. Victoria and Albert Museum, London, E1862–1946.

38. Anthony Wells-Cole, *Historic Paper Hangings*, Temple Newsam House, Leeds, Country House Guides, I, 1983, p. 44.

39. E. T. Cook and A. Wedderburn, *The Works of John Ruskin*, Vol. VI, 1906, p. 333.

40. *Journal of Decorative Art* (cf. note 28, above).

41. Voysey catalogue (cf. note 28, above), article on 'Pattern Design' by Elizabeth Aslin, p. 97.

42. M. Harrison, *Victorian Stained Glass*, 1980.

43. Lady Mander, 'The work of C. E. Kempe', *Apollo*, February 1973.

44. A. C. Sewter, *The Stained Glass of William Morris and his Circle*, 1974, I, pp. 68–72.

45. Girouard, *op. cit.*, p. 21; Muthesius, *op. cit.*, p. 49.

46. T. Webster and Mrs W. Parkes, *An Encyclopedia of Domestic Economy*, 1844, p. 45.

47. *Country Life*, 17 and 24 October 1968.

48. Saint, *op. cit.*, p. 119.

49. Franklin, *op. cit.*, p. 74.

——— GLOSSARY ———

A glossary of architectural terms in a useful format is that by John Harris and Jill Lever, *Illustrated Glossary of Architecture, 850–1830* (1966). There is one for cabinet-making and upholstery terms in Geoffrey Beard, *The National Trust Book of English Furniture*, 1985.

ACANTHUS. Plant with thick, scalloped leaves used as part of the decoration of a Corinthian capital, and in some forms of leaf carving.

ANGLE CHIMNEY. A chimney placed in the angle of a room.

APRON. Horizontal piece of timber in wooden, double-flighted stairs for supporting the carriage pieces. Firmly fixed into the wall.

APSE. Vaulted, semi-circular or polygonal end of a chancel, chapel or room.

ARABESQUE. Surface decoration using combinations of flowing lines, tendrils, etc., interspersed in a light and fanciful way with vases, animals, etc.

ARCH. A curved span across an opening.

ARCHITRAVE. The lowest of the three main parts of the entablature (q.v.) of an order.

ATLANTES. Male counterparts of caryatids (q.v.).

BALUSTER. Small pillar or column, and (in staircases) a turned or carved wood or moulded metal member.

BALUSTRADE. Series of balusters supporting a handrail (q.v.).

BASE of a room. The lower projecting part. It consists of two parts, the lower of which is a plain board adjoining the floor, called the plinth, and the upper of one or more mouldings. The plinth is sometimes tongued into a groove in the floor.

BATTEN. A scantling or piece of timber from 2 to 6 in. broad, used in the boarding of floors and upon walls to receive the laths on which plaster is laid or the canvas over which paper or fabric was mounted.

BAY WINDOW. Angular or curved projection of a house with space given to ample fenestration.

BEAD. A moulding whose section is circular.

BOARD. A piece of timber of undefined length more than 4 in. broad and not more than $2\frac{1}{2}$ in thick. Boards wider than 9 in are called planks. Fir boards were called deals (q.v.).

BRACKET. Small supporting piece of wood or stone to carry a projecting horizontal such as a gallery.

BRACKETING. Preparing the timber framework ribs to cornices, etc., to carry plaster mouldings.

CANTILEVER. Blocks inserted into the wall of a building for supporting a balcony, staircase, eaves of a house, etc.

CAPITAL. Head or top part of a column.

CARTOUCHE. A tablet with an ornate frieze enclosing an inscription.

CARYATID. Stone or wood representation of the female figure used instead of a column to support an entablature or mantel-shelf. *See* ATLANTES.

CHAMFER. A surface made by cutting across the square angle of a stone block, piece of wood, etc., at an angle of 45° to the other two surfaces.

CHEVRON. Norman stone-moulding forming a zigzag pattern.

COFFERING. The decoration on a ceiling in sunk squares or polygonal ornamental panels.

COLONNADE. Range of columns. Painted occasionally in feigned form (e.g., 'Heaven Room', Burghley House, Lincolnshire).

COMPARTMENT CEILING. One divided into panels, which are usually surrounded by mouldings.

CONSOLE. Bracket with a compound curved outline.

CORNICE. In Classical architecture, the upper section of the entablature. Also a projecting feature in wood or plaster along the top of a wall or arch.

COVE. The quadrantal profile between the ceiling of a room and its cornice.

CUPOLA. Small circular or polygonal domed turret supported on a drum (q.v.) and often surmounted by a lantern (q.v.). Sometimes applied to the underside or ceiling part of a dome.

CUT STRING STAIRS. Stairs which have the outer string cut to the profile of the steps.

CYMA. A moulding taking its name from its contour, resembling that of a wave. The *cyma recta* is hollow in its upper part and swells below; the *cyma reversa* has the upper part swelled and the lower hollow. Also called an *ogee*.

DADO. The part of the pedestal of a column between the base and the cornice, and applied to that part of a room's panelling representing the pedestal.

DEAL. Usually restricted to the wood of the fir tree cut up into thicknesses in the areas from whence deals were exported, viz. Christiana, Drammen. They were purchased by the *hundred*, which contained 120 deals. Yellow deal was obtained from the Scotch fir (*Pinus sylvestris*). White deal was the product of the Norway spruce (*Abies excelsa* or *communis*).

DISTEMPER. Whiting mixed with size or other soluble glue and water with which walls and ceilings were painted.

DRAUGHT. The representation of a building on paper by means of plans, elevations and sections, drawn to a scale.

DRUM. Circular or polygonal vertical wall of a dome or cupola.

ENTABLATURE. In Classical architecture the horizontal members above a column (architrave, frieze and cornice). All three vary according to the different orders.

FESTOON. Carved garland of flowers and fruit suspended at each end.

FINIAL. The topmost (ornamented) feature of a gable, roof, canopy, etc.

FLOATED WORK. Plastering rendered perfectly plane by means of using a long rule with a straight edge, a wood or metal rectangular trowel, called a float.

FLUTING. Vertical channelling in the shaft of a column.

FOLIATED. Carved with leaf shapes.

FRAME, FRAMING. The rough timberwork of a house, or any pieces of wood fitted together with mortises and tenons, are said to be *framed* (doors, sashes, etc).

FRESCO. Wall-painting on wet plaster in which it becomes permanent.

FRESCO-SECCO. Wall-painting on dry plaster, wetted just before working on it.

FRIEZE. Middle division of a Classical entablature (q.v.) between the architrave (q.v.) and cornice (q.v.).

FRIEZE PANEL. The upper panel but one of a six-panelled door.

GEOMETRICAL STAIRCASE. That in which the flight of stone steps is supported by the wall at only one end of the steps.

GILDING. The practice of applying gold leaf. Done in oil-size on woodwork and in water-size on plastering. Water gilding can be burnished. The gold leaf was supplied in books of 25 leaves and in various thicknesses designated 'single', 'double' and 'thirds'.

GRISAILLE. A type of painting usually in various tones of grey as for *trompe l'œil* reliefs, etc.

GUILLOCHE. An ornament in the form of two or more bands or strings twisting over each other, so as to repeat the same figure, in a continued series.

GYPSUM. Crystals of calcium sulphate. Subjected to heat to expel the water of crystallization, it forms plaster of Paris, and when water is applied to it assumes a solid form. Alabaster is a form of gypsum.

HAMMER-BEAM. A beam projecting at right angles from the top of the wall to carry braces or struts of a roof structure.

HANDRAIL of a stair. A rail raised upon balusters to assist in ascending and descending stairs.

HEADWAY of stairs. The distance, measured perpendicularly, from a given landing place or stair to the ceiling above.

HOLLOW NEWEL. An opening in the middle of a staircase. In the hollow newel, or well-hole, the steps are only supported at one end by the surrounding wall of the staircase, the ends next to the hollow being unsupported.

ICONOGRAPHY. The subject matter of works of the visual arts.

INDIA PAPER. Hand-painted Oriental wallpaper.

INLAYING. Work in which a material is substituted for the surface of another which has been cut away.

JAMB. The straight side of a doorway, window or archway.

JOIST. The timber to which the boards of a floor or laths of a ceiling are nailed.

KING-POST. The centre upright post in a trussed roof which connects the tie-beam and collar beam with the ridge beam.

LANTERN. In architecture, a small circular or polygonal turret with windows all round, surmounting a roof or cupola.

LATH. A thin 4- or 5-foot-long piece of wood, $1\frac{1}{2}$ in wide, nailed to joists and used in plastering to give a frame to which the applied material can adhere.

LINENFOLD. Tudor panelling carved with a representation of linen laid in vertical folds in each panel.

LINTEL. Horizontal beam or stone over an opening.

LOGGIA. A recessed colonnade.

LOUVRE. Opening to let smoke escape from a central hearth.

LOZENGE. Diamond-shape.

MARBLING. Painted work simulating the veining of marble.

MORTISE. A recessed cutting within a piece of timber to receive a projecting piece (*tenon*) on the end of another piece of timber, in order to fix the two together at a given angle.

MOULD. A pattern or contour by which any work is to be wrought. Used by masons, glaziers and plasterers, and of various materials, e.g., plasterers used iron, wood and wax moulds at various periods.

MULLION. Vertical post or upright dividing a window into two or more 'lights'.

NEWEL. Central post in a circular or winding staircase. The principal post when a flight of stairs meets a landing.

NICHE. A shaped recess in a wall or screen, often made for carved urns or figures.

OGEE. A moulding, the same as the *cyma reversa* (*see* CYMA).

OPEN-WORK. Any kind of work with interstices in its substance, as in open-work of iron, etc.

ORIEL. A bay window on an upper floor only.

PAPIER-MÂCHÉ. Paper rendered to a pulp which, having other ingredients mixed with it, is pressed into moulds, and thus ornaments are formed of it.

PARQUETRY. Inlaid work, made of thin plates or veneers of hard woods, secured to a framing of deal to form flooring.

PAVING. Stone from various sources (Portland, Purbeck, Bremen) used for flooring.

PEDIMENT. A low pitched triangular gable used above a portico and over doors and windows. Can be of *broken* form in which the centre portion of the base is open, or *open* form where the centre portion of the sloping sides is left out.

PENDANT. An elongated boss hanging from a ceiling made in wood, stone or plaster.

PENDENTIVE. Concave triangular spandrel used to lead from the angle of two walls to the base of a circular dome.

PIANO NOBILE. Principal storey of a house, usually the first floor state rooms.

PIETRA DURA. Ornamental inlay by means of thin slabs of stone practised especially at Florence from the sixteenth century onward.

PILASTER. A flat pier attached to a wall, having a base and a capital: sometimes fluted.

PORPHYRY. A very hard stone, of the nature of granite. It is harder than marble and takes a fine polish. It is found in purple, red, black, green and variegated shades.

PORTICO. Centrepiece of a house supported by detached or attached columns and surmounted by a pediment.

PRIMING. In painter's work, the first colouring of the work, which forms a ground for the succeeding coats.

PURBECK STONE. A species of stone obtained from the Purbeck Hills in Dorset of a very hard texture, used for paving.

QUADRANGLE. An inner courtyard.

QUEEN-POST. Two struts placed symmetrically on a tie or collar-beam.

RAFTER. Roof timber sloping up from the wall-plate to the ridge. A roof contains principal and common rafters, the principal usually corresponding to the main bay divisions of the space below.

RUSTICATION. Chamfers (q.v.) or grooves round the face edges of individual stones to create shadows.

SCAGLIOLA. Plaster and colouring matter mixed to imitate marble – in the case of columns it is laid thinly on laths over a wooden framework.

SCARFING. The joining of two pieces of timber together transversely, so that the two appear as one.

SCREENS PASSAGE. Passage between the entrances to the service areas (kitchen, buttery, etc.) and the screen separating it from the Hall.

SIENA MARBLE. An attractive yellow form of marble veined with grey.

SOFFIT. The underside of an arch, vault, cornice, etc.

SOLAR. The upper living-room in a medieval house.

SPANDREL. A 'triangular' space between the curve of an arch and the mouldings enclosing it.

SPRINGING. The level at which an arch rises from its supports.

STAIR WELL. *See* WELL-HOLE.

STATUARY MARBLE. Pure white marble, such as that quarried in Italy at Carrara, and used by sculptors and carvers for their best works.

STRAPWORK. Stylized representation of geometrically arranged leather straps copied from Renaissance decoration.

STRING BOARD. In wooden stairs, the board next to the well-hole which receives the ends of the steps, often a place for applied carvings.

STUCCO. 'Plasterwork' in a mixture containing gypsum, sand, marble-powder and water, or variations thereof, and modelled around wood or metal armatures.

SUPPORTER. Human or animal figures either side of a shield of a coat of arms.

SWAG. An ornamental festoon of flowers, foliage or fruit, fastened at each end and often hanging down in the centre.

TENON. A projecting rectangular prism formed on the end of a piece of timber to be inserted into a mortise (q.v.) of the same form.

TERM. A trunk, pilaster or pillar, often in the form of the frustum of an inverted obelisk, with the bust of a man, woman or satyr on the top. Fashioned to a high level of craftsmanship by the carvers of marble chimneypieces.

TERRACOTTA. Unglazed burnt clay.

TIE-BEAM. Beam connecting the two slopes of a roof across its foot to prevent spreading.

TOP RAIL. The uppermost rail of a piece of framing or wainscoting, as its name suggests.

TRACERY. Intersecting ribwork in the upper part of a window or used 'blind' on arches, vaults, etc.

TRANSOM. A structural member dividing a window horizontally.

TREAD. The horizontal part of the step of a stair.

VENEER. A thin leaf of wood of a superior quality for covering furniture etc., made of an inferior wood. In use in England in the seventeenth and eighteenth centuries.

VENETIAN WINDOW. Window with three openings, of which the central one is arched and wider than the outside ones.

VOLUTE. A spiral scroll which forms the principal feature of the capital (q.v.) of the Ionic order in Greek and Roman architecture.

WAINSCOT. The oak, deal or cedar lining of walls in panels.

WALL-PLATE. Timber laid longitudinally on the top of a wall as a support for other members fixed thereto.

WELL-HOLE. In a flight of stairs, the space left in the middle beyond the ends of the steps, also called STAIR WELL.

—— BIBLIOGRAPHY ——
(Place of publication is London unless otherwise stated)

—— 1. GENERAL ——

AGIUS, Pauline, *Ackermann's Regency Furniture and Interiors*, 1984.

AIRS, Malcolm, *The Making of the English Country House, 1500–1640*, 1975.

ALLEN, Barbara Sprague, *Tides in English Taste, 1619–1800*, 2 Vols., 1937 (reprinted New York, 1969).

AMERY, Colin, *Period Houses and Their Details*, 1974.

ASLET, Clive, *Last of the Country Houses (1890–1939)*, 1982.

ASLIN, E., *The Aesthetic Movement: Prelude to Art Nouveau*, 1981.

BARLEY, Maurice, *English Farmhouses and Cottages*, 1983.

BEARD, Geoffrey, *The Work of Robert Adam*, Edinburgh, 1978.

BOASE, T. S. R., *English Art, 1800–1870* (*The Oxford History of English Art*, X) 1959.

BROWN, R. J., *Timber Framed Buildings of England*, 1986.

BRUNSKILL, R. W., *Illustrated Handbook of Vernacular Architecture*, 1970.

—— *Traditional Buildings of Britain*, 1981.

See also CLIFTON-TAYLOR, Alec, *and* BRUNSKILL, Ronald.

BURKE, Joseph, *English Art, 1714–1800* (*The Oxford History of English Art*, IX), 1976.

CLARK, Kenneth, *The Gothic Revival*, 2nd edn, 1950.

COLVIN, H. M., *A Biographical Dictionary of British Architects 1600–1840*, 1978. (The 1st edn of 1954, *English Architects 1660–1840*, contains many carpenters etc., excluded from the 2nd edn.)

COLVIN, H. M., ed., *History of the King's Works*, 6 Vols, 1976–83 (surveys the Middle Ages to 1851). The standard history of the building and maintenance of royal palaces.

COOK, Olive, *The English House through Seven Centuries*, 1968.

COOPER, N., *The Opulent Eye: Late Victorian and Edwardian Taste in Interior Design*, 1980.

CORNFORTH, John, *English Interiors 1790–1848: The Quest for Comfort*, 1979.

—— *The Inspiration of the Past: Country-House Taste in the 20th Century*, 1985.

CORNFORTH, John, and Oliver HILL, *English Country Houses: Caroline, 1625–85*, 1966.

CORNFORTH, John, *see* FOWLER and CORNFORTH.

CROOK, J. Mordaunt, *The Greek Revival: Neoclassical Attitudes in British Architecture, 1760–1870*, 1972.

DOWNES, K., *English Baroque Architecture*, 1966.

DUTTON, Ralph, *The English Interior, 1500–1900*, 1948.

FOWLER, John, and John CORNFORTH, *English Decoration in the 18th Century*, 1978.

GIROUARD, Mark, *Life in the English Country House: A Social and Architectural History*, 1978.

—— *The Victorian Country House*, 2nd edn, 1980.

—— *Robert Smythson and the Elizabethan Country House*, 2nd edn, 1983.

—— *Sweetness and Light: The 'Queen Anne Movement', 1860–1900*, 1984.

GOTCH, J. A., *The Growth of the English House*, 1928.

GREEN, David, *Blenheim Palace*, 1951.

HARRIS, John, *Sir William Chambers: Knight of the Polar Star*, 1970.

—— *The Palladians*, 1981.

—— *The Design of the English Country House, 1620–1920*, 1985.

—— *The Artist and the Country House*, revised edn, 1986.

HARRIS, Richard, *Timber-framed Buildings*, 1980.

HARVEY, John, *The Master Builders: Architecture in the Middle Ages*, 1971.

HILL, Oliver, see CORNFORTH, John and Oliver HILL.

HONOUR, Hugh, *Chinoiserie: The Vision of Cathay*, 1961.

—— *Neo-Classicism*, 1975.

HOOK, J., *The Baroque Age in England*, 1976.

HOWARD, Maurice, *The Early Tudor Country House: Architecture and Politics, 1490–1550*, 1987.

HUSSEY, Christopher, *English Country Houses: Early Georgian*, 1965 (2nd edn); *Mid-Georgian*, 1956; *Late Georgian*, 1958. Reissued in facsimile by the Antique Collectors' Club, Woodbridge.

JACKSON-STOPS, G., and J. PIPKIN, *The Grand Tour: The English Country House*, 1985.

JERVIS, Simon, *High Victorian Design*, 1984.

—— *Dictionary of Design and Designers*, 1986.

JOURDAIN, Margaret, *English Interior Decoration, 1500–1830*, 1950.

LAMBOURNE, L., *Utopian Craftsmen: The Arts and Crafts Movement*, 1980.

LEACH, Peter, *James Paine*, 1988.

LEES-MILNE, James, *English Country Houses: Baroque, 1685–1715*, 1970.

LLOYD, Nathaniel, *A History of the English House*, 1931 (reprinted 1975).

MACAULAY, James, *The Gothic Revival, 1745–1845*, 1975.

McCARTHY, Michael, *The Origins of the Gothic Revival*, 1987.

MERCER, Eric, *English Art, 1553–1625* (*The Oxford History of English Art*, VII), 1957.

—— *English Vernacular Houses*, 1975.

MORRIS, C., ed., *The Illustrated Journeys of Celia Fiennes*, 1981.

MUTHESIUS, Hermann, *The English House*, ed., Dennis Sharp, 1979.

MUTHESIUS, S., *The English Terrace House*, 1982.

PILCHER, D., *The Regency Style, 1800 to 1830*, 1947.

RICHARDSON, Sir Albert, *An Introduction to Georgian Architecture*, 1949.

ROBINSON, John Martin, *The Latest Country Houses, The Continuation of a British Tradition, 1945–83*, 1984.

SALZMAN, L. F., *Building in England down to 1540: A Documentary History*, Oxford, 1967.

SERVICE, A. ed., *Edwardian Architecture and its origins*, 1975.

—— *Edwardian Interiors*, 1982.

STAMP, Gavin, *The English House, 1860–1914*, 1985.

STILLMAN, Damie, *The Decorative Work of Robert Adam*, 1966.

—— *English Neo-Classical Architecture*, 2 Vols., 1988.

SUMMERSON, Sir John, *Architecture in Britain, 1530–1830* (Pelican History of Art, 7th edn), 1983.

—— *Georgian London*, revised edn, 1988.

THOMPSON, Francis, *A History of Chatsworth*, 1949.

THOMPSON, Paul, *The Work of William Morris*, 1967.

THORNTON, Peter, *Seventeenth-Century Interior Decoration in England, France and Holland*, 1978.

—— *Authentic Decor, the Domestic Interior, 1620–1920*, 1984.

TIPPING, H. Avray, *English Homes* (9 Vols., covering the period from Norman times to 1820), 1921–37.

TURNOR, Reginald, *The Smaller English House, 1500–1939*, 1952.

WATKIN, David, *Thomas Hope and the Neo-Classical Idea*, 1968.

—— *English Architecture, A Concise History*, 1979.

—— *The Royal Interiors of Regency England*, 1984.

WHINNEY, Margaret, and Oliver MILLAR, *English Art, 1625–1714* (*The Oxford History of English Art*, VIII), 1957.

WILSON, M., *William Kent, 1685–1748*, 1984.

WITTKOWER, R., *Palladio and English Palladianism*, ed. M. Wittkower, 1974.

WOOD, Margaret, *The English Medieval House*, 1953.

2. CRAFTSMEN,
—— TRADES AND TECHNIQUES ——

ARKELL, W. J., *Oxford Stone*, 1947.

AYRTON, Maxwell, and Arnold SILCOCK, *Wrought Iron and Its Decorative Use*, 1929.

BANKART, G. P., *The Art of the Plasterer*, 1908.

BEARD, Geoffrey, *Georgian Craftsmen and Their Work*, 1966.

—— *Decorative Plasterwork in Great Britain*, 1975.

—— *Craftsmen and Interior Decoration in England, 1660–1820*, Edinburgh, 1981. Gives lists of craftsmen and their work.

—— *Stucco and Decorative Plasterwork in Europe*, 1983.

—— *The Work of Grinling Gibbons*, 1989.

BRIGGS, M. S. A., *A Short History of the Building Crafts*, Oxford, 1925.

CLIFTON-TAYLOR, Alec, *The Pattern of English Building*, 4th edn, 1986.

CLIFTON-TAYLOR, Alec, and Ronald BRUNSKILL, *English Brickwork*, 1978.

CLIFTON-TAYLOR and A. S. IRESON, *English Stone-Building*, 1983.

CROFT-MURRAY, Edward, *Decorative Painting in England, 1530–1837*: (1) *Early Tudor to Sir James Thornhill*, 1962; (2) *The Eighteenth and Early Nineteenth Centuries*, 1970.

DAVEY, N., *A History of Building Materials*, 1961.

ENTWISTLE, E. A., *The Book of Wallpaper, A History*, 1954.

—— *A Literary History of Wallpaper*, 1960.

GLOAG, John and Derek BRIDGWATER, *A History of Cast Iron in Architecture*, 1948.

GODFREY, W. H., *The English Staircase*, 1911.

GOODISON, Nicholas, *Ormolu: The Work of Matthew Boulton*, 1974.

GREEN, David, *Grinling Gibbons, His Work as Carver and Statuary, 1648–1721*, 1964.

HARRIS, John, *English Decorative Ironwork, 1610–1836*, 1960.

HELLYER, S. Stevens, *The Plumber and Sanitary Houses*, 1877.

HEWETT, C., *English Historic Carpentry*, 1980.

IRESON, A. S., see CLIFTON-TAYLOR, Alec and A. S. IRESON.

JOURDAIN, Margaret, *English Decorative Plasterwork of the Late Renaissance*, 1926.

KELLY, Alison, *Decorative Wedgwood in Architecture and Furniture*, 1965.

—— *The Book of English Fireplaces*, 1968.

LISTER, Raymond, *Decorative Wrought Iron in Great Britain*, 1960.

—— *Decorative Cast Ironwork in Great Britain*, 1963.

LLOYD, N., *History of English Brickwork*, 1925 (reprinted 1983).

MEGSON, B., *English Homes and Housekeeping, 1700–1960*, 1968.

O'DEA, E., *The Social History of Lighting*, 1958.

OMAN, C., *Wallpapers and Wallpaper Designs in the Victoria and Albert Museum*. 2nd revised edn, expanded by J. Hamilton, 1982.

PURCELL, Donovan, *Cambridge Stone*, 1967.

SUGDEN, A. V., and J. L. EDMONDSON, *A History of English Wallpaper, 1509–1914*, 1925.

Temple Newsam House, Country House studies, Leeds: (I) *Historic Paper Hangings*, 1983; (II) *The Fashionable Fireplace 1660–1840*, 1986; (III) *Country House Floors*, 1987.

TURNER, Laurence, *English Decorative Plasterwork*, 1927. Useful for its illustrations.

PERSONAL NAMES INDEX

Abbott family, 104–5
Accres, Thomas, 35, 38, 62, 63
Adam, James, 189, 191 *see also* Adam, Robert
Adam, Robert, 172, 175, 188–9, 191–9,
   203–7, 209, 211–15, 222, 225–30
Adams, John, 66
Aglio, Agostino, 219
Aiscough, Robert, 118
Albert, Prince Consort, 260
Allom, Thomas, 248
Amigoni (or Amiconi), Jacopo, 162
Anderson, Diederich Nicolaus, 224
Archer, Thomas, 143
Arkwright, John, 238
Artari, Giuseppe, 162, 167, 170
Ashbee, C. K., 271
Aslet, Clive, x
Atkinson, William, 223
Aubrey, John, 29, 79, 94

Bagutti, Giovanni, 162, 167, 168
Baillie Scott, M. H., 253, 254–5
Baily, John *and* Joseph, 211
Ballechouse, John, 49, 64
Bankart, George, 258
Bankes, Walter Ralph, 267
Bankes, William, 261
Barbet, Jean, 122, 123
Barlow, Francis, 112
Barret, George, 219
Barry, Sir Charles, 159, 248, 260, 267, 270
Bartoli, Domenico, 218
Basevi, George, 241
Beard, Geoffrey, ix
Beckford, William, 209
Bell, Alfred, 264
Bellin, Nicolò, 47, 53, 60
Bellucci, Antonio, 162
Benson, W. A. S., 262, 263
Bentley, J. F., 261
Bentley, J. W., 267, 268
Berain, Jean, 124
Bermingham, Nathaniel, 223, 224

Bernasconi family, 210–11, 258, 271
Bernini, Giovanni Lorenzo, 139, 174
Bibiena family, 188
Bielefeld, C. F., 258
Binks, Thomas, 25
Blockley, Thomas, 222, 223, 229
Bonomi, Joseph, 218
Boromini, Francesco, 174
Borgnis, Giovanni, 218
Borgnis, Giuseppe Mattia, 164
Borgnis, Pietro Maria, 215, 224
Bosse, Abraham, 122
Bossi, Pietro, 227
Boulton, Matthew, 229
Bourchier, Archbishop Thomas, 75, 76
Bradbury, Robert, 108, 133
Bramah, Joseph, 185, 234, 272
Brettingham, Matthew, 172, 189, 191
Brooks, S. H., 252
Brown, Lancelot 'Capability', 172
Browne, Thomas, 60
Brownlow, Sir Thomas, 83–4
Bryce, David, 267
Bucke, John, 84, 128
Bucket, Rowland, 84, 128
Buckler, Charles Alban, 265
Burges, William, 240, 243, 249, 263, 271
Burn, William, 267
Burne-Jones, Sir Edward, 252, 260, 264
Burridge, John, 104
Butterfield, William, 252
Buzaglo, Abraham, 229–30

Campbell, Colen, 141–7, 155, 167, 169, 172,
   181–2, 189
Carpenter, Edmund, 92
Carr, John, 167, 232, 234
Carter, Benjamin, 227, 229
Carter, Thomas (joiner at Ham House), 116,
   130
Carter, Thomas, the elder (sculptor),
   180–81

Carter, Thomas, the younger (sculptor), 180–81, 227, 229
Carwitham, John, 150
Caus, Isaac de, 79, 115
Chambers, Sir William, 79, 145, 179, 187, 188–9, 192–4, 195, 206, 213–14, 222, 223, 227, 229
Charles II, king, 69, 96–7, 108
Cheere, Sir Henry, 180, 229
Cheere, John, 180
Chippendale, Thomas, 236
Chute, John, 39, 143–4, 232
Cibber, Gabriel, 83
Cipriani, Giovanni Battista, 211, 213–14, 219
Clark, Thomas, 172
Clayton, John Richard, 264
Clayton, Thomas, 167, 171
Cleare, Richard, 117, 132
Clement, William, 45
Clerment, Andien de, 165
Cleyn, Francis, 93
Crane, Walter, 263, 264
Cockerell, C. R., 203, 222
Cockerell, Samuel Pepys, 221–2
Codman, Ogden, ix
Collins, John, 97–8
Collins, Thomas, 192, 194, 206
Collins, William, 191
Colt, Maximilian, 121
Cornforth, John, ix, x
Cort, Cornelius, 95
Cortese, Giuseppe, 167, 169
Cosin, John, Bishop of Durham, 95
Cooter, Peter de (Balthazar), 51
Cousin, René, 97, 98
Cowtan (wallpaper manufacturers), 261
Crace, Frederick, 224–5
Crace, John Gregory, 260
Crunden, John, 178
Cuer family, 121
Cumming, Alexander, 234
Cuneot, John, 156

Dale, Richard, 36
Daviler, Charles Augustine, 82–3, 146, 150
Davis, Charles, 254
Davis, William, 90
de Bruyn, Abraham, 53, 102, 103, 104
de Bruyn, Nicholas, 55
de Critz, Emanuel and John, 94
de Morgan, William, 263
de Rossi, Domenico, 174
de Vos, Marten, 53, 55, 56, 85
de Vries, Jan Vriedeman, 27, 53, 58, 64, 102
de Whitt, Giles, 121
Deane, Anthony, 113
Delvaux, Laurent, 169

Devall, John, 180
Dietterlin, Wendel, 27, 53, 85, 102
Dininckhof, Bernard, 58
Dixon, Cornelius, 256
Dobson, John, 248
Doe, Robert, 178
Du Cerceau, Jacques Androuet, 27, 37
Dungan, Richard, 102–4
Dunsterfield, George, 113

Earp, Thomas, 268
Eboral, Thomas, 154
Eginton, Francis, 201
Elizabeth I, queen, 53, 55
Evelyn, John, 63, 88, 94, 151

Favensa, Vicenzo, 267
Fiennes, Celia, 83, 88, 132, 137, 152
Flaxman, John, 229
Flitcroft, Henry, 172, 174
Fontaine, Pierre-François, 230
Forsyth, James, 245
Fowler, John, ix
Franklin, Dr Jill, x, 238

Gardom, John, 135
Gedde, Walter, 80, 115
Gentileschi, Orazio, 93
George III, king, 187, 219
George IV, king, 187
George, Sir Ernest, 254
Gerbier, Sir Balthazar, 93, 116
Gibbons, Grinling, 70, 88–9, 90, 92, 124, 132, 135, 155, 159
Gibbons of Wolverhampton, 267
Gibbs, James, 143, 146, 154, 155, 167, 170, 178
Gimson, Ernest, 258
Girouard, Professor Mark, x, 32, 37, 164, 184
Gomme, Professor Andor, 72
Gooderick, Matthew, 94, 101, 116–17
Götzenberger, J., 260
Goudge, Edward, 101, 109, 110–11, 113
Gravelot, Hubert-François, 164
Green, George, 172
Greville, Margaret H. and Hon. Richard, 256
Griffin, William, 30
Grove, John and John II, 113
Gunby, Francis, 104

Hallett, William, 186
Hardman, John, 264
Hare, Augustus, 244
Harington, Sir John, 23, 68
Harlow, Henry, 80, 116
Harrison, William, 44

Hauduroy, Samuel, 102
Hawksmoor, Nicholas, 110, 140, 143, 148, 153
Haydon, Benjamin Robert, 260
Hayman, Francis, 164
Hearst, Randolph, 47, 58
Henderson, James, 169
Henry III, king, 11, 13
Henry VI, king, 17
Henry VII, king, 16, 24, 25, 32, 45, 52
Henry VIII, king, 32, 45, 51
Herland, Hugh, 4
Highmore, Thomas, 160
Hill, Sir Roger, 112
Hinchcliff, John, 227
Hine, Thomas, 247
Hogarth, William, 164, 184, 189
Holbein, Hans, the younger, 47, 63, 264
Holland, Henry, 195, 214, 223, 232
Holmes, Benjamin, 183
Holmes, George, 101
Hone, Galyon, 57
Hooke, Robert, 143
Hope, Thomas, 230
Hopper, Thomas, 251
Horman, William, 43
Houlbert, John, 113
Hughes, Arthur, 260
Hurlbutt, Roger, 87

Ibeck, Joseph, 135
Ireson, Nathaniel, 150

Jackson, George, 258
James II, king, 97
James, John, 143
Jekyll, Gertrude, 254
Johnson, John, 217
Johnson, Dr Samuel, 199, 273
Joli, Antonio, 178
Jones, Inigo, 70, 71, 73–4, 79, 82, 93–4,
    114–15, 122–3, 131, 145, 172, 178
Jordaens, Jacob, 93
Jourdain, Margaret, ix

Kauffmann, Angelica, 211, 215, 218
Kempe, C. E., 262, 264
Kent, William, 155, 162–4, 172, 178, 182, 184
Kerr, Robert, 239–40, 245, 246, 248, 251, 269
Kinward, Thomas, 116

Laguerre, Louis, 98–100, 135, 158–9
Langley, Batty, 131, 150, 183, 184
Lanscroon, Gerard, 97
Lascelles, W. H., 252
Lauderdale, John, 1st Duke of, 115
Le Blond, Jean, 152
Lee, James, 102

Lemyinge (or Liminge), Robert, 121
Leoni, Giacomo, 167
le Pautre, Jean, 134
Lethaby, W. R., 268, 269
Leverton, Thomas, 214, 218
Liardet, John, 217
Lightfoot, Luke, 156–8, 177, 233
Lloyd Wright, Frank, 273
Lobb, Joel, 90
Lorimer, Sir Robert, 258–60
Loudon, J. C., 244, 250, 251
Louw, Dr J. H., 115, 116
Luti, Benedetto, 162
Luttrell, Colonel Francis, 111
Lutyens, Sir Edwin Landseer, 239, 253, 254,
    255, 271

Maine, Jonathan, 90
Mansard, Jules-Hardouin, 139
Mansfield, Samuel, 109
Marcer, John, 53
Marlborough, Sarah, Duchess of, 141, 158, 184
Marot, Daniel, 124, 174
Martin, Edward, 109–10
Mary II, queen, 124
May, Hugh, 72, 88, 96, 113, 139
Mercier, Eric, 72
Miller, Sanderson, 143
Mills, Peter, 107, 117
Mitchell, Arnold, 260
Moreton, William, 36
Morris, Robert, 179
Morris, William, 49, 252, 260, 262–3, 264, 269
Moxon, Joseph, 86, 134
Muthesius, Herman, 240, 255
Muthesius, Stefan, 242

Nash, John, 222, 234, 239, 241
Nash, Joseph, 84
Neale, John, 165
Nedeham, John, 45
Newton, Ernest, 252
Norman, Samuel, 174
North, Roger, 34, 71, 122–4, 137
Nunziata, Toto del, 47

Okey, Charles, 83
Orton, Robert, 55
Ould, Edward, 262

Paine, James, 150–51, 166, 171–2, 181,
    183–4, 189, 191, 206
Palladio, Andrea, 37, 65, 70, 71, 73, 74, 79–
    80, 104, 106, 114, 143, 172, 181, 189, 191
Papworth, J. B., 251
Parker, Charles, 251–2
Parker, Thomas, 150

Parker, William, 112
Pastorini, Benedetto, 218
Paxton, Sir Joseph, 269
Peacham, Henry, 104
Peake, Robert, 102
Pellegrini, Giovanni Antonio, 158, 160–61
Percier, Charles, 230
Pergolesi, Michele Angelo, 211, 218
Perritt, Thomas, 167, 172
Petiver, James, 109
Peto, Harold, 254
Petre, Sir William, 28
Pettifer, James, 108, 133
Pevsner, Sir Nikolaus, 15
Phillips, Henry, 88
Pierce (or Pearce), Edward, the elder, 94, 132–3
Pierce, Edward, the younger, 112, 113, 118, 119, 132–5
Piranesi, Giovanni Battista, 188, 208, 219, 228
Plot, Robert, 134
Pollen, John Hungerford, 260–61
Pope, Alexander, 101, 185–6
Portington, William, 85
Powell family, 265
Powis, William Herbert, 1st Earl of, 97
Pratt, Sir Roger, 71, 83, 87, 106, 107, 113, 115, 131
Primaticcio, Francesco, 95
Prinsep, Val, 260
Pugin, A. W. N., 239, 248, 258, 265, 271

Raphael, Sanzio, 54, 94, 162, 213, 260
Rebecca, Biagio, 211, 213–14
Repton, Humphry, 200–202, 220, 221
Repton, John Adey, 221
Revett, Nicholas, 206, 208, 213
Reynolds, Sir Joshua, 215, 219
Ricci, Marco, 158, 160–2
Ricci, Sebastiano, 158, 162
Richards, Godfrey, 80
Richards, James, 155–6, 174, 176, 182
Richardson, George, 191, 204, 228
Rigaud, John Francis, 218, 225
Roberts, Henry, 252
Roberts, Thomas, 170
Robinson, John Martin, x
Robinson, Sir Thomas, 142
Rochefoucauld, François de la, 194
Rodes, John and Christopher, 56, 66
Rose, Joseph (& Company), 172, 193, 204, 205, 206, 207, 209, 210, 217, 218, 233
Rossetti, Dante Gabriel, 260, 264
Rothwell, William, 211
Roubiliac, Louis-François, 165
Rubens, Sir Peter Paul, 71, 92–3
Ruskin, John, 262

Rydge, Richard, 45
Rysbrack, John Michael, 178–9

Salvin, Anthony, 245, 258, 267
Salzman, L. R., 11
Samwell, William, 116
Sandys, Sir William, 27, 32, 39
Savino, Guido de, 42
Scamozzi, Vincenzio, 73, 106, 114, 122, 172
Scheemakers, Peter, 169
Scott, Giles Gilbert, 261
Selden, John, 83, 90
Serena, Francesco, 167
Serlio, Sebastiano, 27, 63, 71, 79–81, 102, 104, 106, 114, 144, 145, 172
Shaw, Richard Norman, 245, 252, 268, 269
Shrewsbury, Elizabeth, Countess of (Bess of Hardwick), 32–3, 37, 38, 56–7, 63
Sims, John, 118
Sitwell, Sir Sacheverell, 32
Sleter, Francesco, 162
Smirke, Sir Robert, 210, 258
Smith, Abraham, 55
Smith, Francis, 142–3, 152, 153–4, 167, 183
Smith, George, 237
Smith, William, 142–3
Smythson, John, 83
Smythson, Robert, 27, 29, 32, 34, 37, 63, 82
Snidall, Richard, 56
Soane, Sir John, 195–6, 211, 236, 237
Somerset, Charles Seymour, 6th Duke of, 137
Spencer-Stanhope, John Roddam, 260
Stanley, Simon, Charles, 169–70
Stanton, William, 84, 110, 112
Stanyan, Edward, 104
Steuart, George, 234
Stevens, Albert, 258
Stevenson, J. J., 243
Stokes, G. H., 269
Stone, Nicholas, 82
Stothard, Thomas, 219
Street, George, 252
Strode, Sir John, 26
Stuart, James 'Athenian', 206, 208, 212–13
Summerson, Sir John, 71, 146
Swan, Abraham, 184

Talman, William, 140, 143, 192
Taylor, Sir Robert, 144, 194, 219
Tempesta, Antonio, 94
Thompson, Christopher, 150
Thornhill, Sir James, 153, 158–60, 161
Thornton, Peter, x
Thornton, William, 124, 173–4
Thorp, John, 146
Thorpe, John, 27, 75, 85
Tiepolo, Gianbattista, 160

Tijou, Jean, 135, 234
Tilston, Thomas, 234
Tobin, Maurice, 236
Toogood Arthur, 108
Townshend, Sir Roger, 70, 74
Tradescant, John, 126–8
Turner, Lawrence, 109

Valdré, Vicenzo, 218–19
Van Dyck, Sir Anthony, 93, 118
van Ersell, John Baptist, 95
Vanbrugh, Sir John, 140–41, 143, 146, 148, 160, 167, 168
Vardy, John, 178
Varley, C. F., 271
Vassalli, Francesco, 148, 167, 170
Verrio, Antonio, 70, 90, 95, 101, 134, 158, 160, 219
Vertue, George, 83, 110, 133, 214
Visentini, Antonio, 208
Vitruvius, 11
Voysey, C. F. A., 253–4, 263, 265
Vulliamy, Lewis, 258

Wagg, Thomas, 182
Walpole, Horace, 39, 143, 183, 192, 209, 210
Ware, Isaac, 114–15, 124, 131, 144, 151, 172–3, 178, 181, 189, 198, 226–7
Waterson, Merlin, x
Watson, Samuel, 83, 91
Webb, John, 32, 79, 108, 122, 123, 131, 143
Webb, Philip, 252, 253
Wedgwood, Josiah, 229
Welldon, William and John, 182, 184
Wells-Cole, Antony, 152
West, Benjamin, 219
Westlake, N. H. J., 268

Westmacott family, 230, 267
Wharton, Edith, ix
White and Parlby (company), 258
Whiting, Thomas, 117
Whitney, Geoffrey, 104
Whittle, James, 174
Wightwick, G., 196
Wildsmith, John, 225
Willcox, Jonathan, 110, 118
Willement, Thomas, 220, 264
William III, king, 69–70, 84, 97, 100
Wilton, Joseph and William, 225–6, 227
Winde, Captain William, 88, 101, 110–12, 116, 118, 132, 134–5
Wolfe, Renold, 54
Wolsey, Cardinal Thomas, 25, 26, 32, 45, 52–3, 63
Wood, John, the elder and younger, 145, 153, 155, 241
Woodward, Benjamin, 261
Wotton, Sir Henry, 71, 126
Wren, Sir Christopher, 70, 88, 106, 108, 109–10, 116, 124, 139–41, 155, 192
Wright, Richard, 57
Wright, Thomas, 220
Wyatt, George, 195
Wyatt, James, 172, 194, 206, 208–10, 214, 218, 219–20, 223, 225
Wyatt, Jeffrey see Wyatville, Sir Jeffrey
Wyatt, Lewis, 222, 247
Wyatt, Samuel, 219–20
Wyatville, Sir Jeffrey, 96, 194–5, 267

Young, Thomas, 90

Zucchi, Antonio, 211, 215–18

GENERAL INDEX

National Trust properties are asterisked ★
Page numbers of illustrations are in **bold** *type*

Abbotsbury, Dorset, 3
Abbott's Parlour, Thame Park, Oxfordshire, 45
Adelphi, London, 218
★Alfriston Clergy House, Sussex, **12**
Alnwick Castle, Northumberland, 57, 209, 245
Amesbury House, Wiltshire, 108
Anet, Château of, 27, 82
★Anglesey Abbey, Cambridgeshire, **8**
Arbury Hall, Warwickshire, 64, 109–10
Arlington Street (22), London, 183
Arundel Castle, Sussex, 265, 268, 271
Asgill House, Richmond, Surrey, 219–20
★Ashleworth, Gloucestershire (tithe barn), 3
Astley House, Lancashire, 113
★Attingham Park, Shropshire, **221**, 221–2, 234
Auchterhouse, Dundee, 105
Audley End, Essex, 74, 84, 105–6, 199, 214, 234
Aydon Castle, Northumberland, 20

★Baddesley Clinton, Warwickshire, 24, 31, 64
Barnett Hill, Wonersh, Surrey, 260
Barnstaple, Devon, 104
Baroque style
  chimneypieces, 178–81
  doors, 175–8
  floors, 146–53
  house plans, 139–46
  painted walls and ceilings, 158–66
  plastered and stuccoed surfaces, 166–72
  staircases, 181–4
  windows, 172–5
Bath, Avon, 145, 241, 242
bathrooms, 184–6 *see also* privies; water-
  closets
Beamish, Durham, Open-Air Museum, 242
Bear Wood, Wokingham, Berkshire, 267, 271
Beere, North Tawton, Devon, 11
Belgrave Square, London, 241
bell-systems, 236
★Belton House, Lincolnshire, 83, 90, 91, 110,
  112, 143, 152, 166

Belvoir Castle, Leicestershire, 239
★Beningbrough Hall, North Yorkshire, 124,
  152, 173–4, **174**
Benthall Hall, Shropshire, **64**
Berkeley Square (44), London, 182–3
★Berrington Hall, Hereford and Worcester,
  229, 232
billiard rooms, 208, 240, 246
Bishop Auckland, Durham, Bishop's Palace, 95
Black Country Museum, Dudley, 242
Black Death (1348), 2
Blackwell, Bowness-on-Windermere, 255–6
Blair Adam, Kelty, 229
Blair Castle, Perth, 171
Blenheim Palace, Oxfordshire
  'bagnio', 184
  painted walls and ceilings, 99, 158–9, 160
  plans of, 141–2
★Blickling Hall, Norfolk, 76, 104, 121, **128**,
  261
Bolsover Castle, Derbyshire, 71, 80, 83, 95,
  104
Bolton Abbey, Yorkshire, 264
Boothby Pagnell Manor House, Lincolnshire,
  17
Boston Manor, Brentford, **103**, 104
Bradfield House, Devon, 58
★Bradley Manor, Devon, 16, **29**
Bradnick Manor, Devon, 58
Bretton Park, Yorkshire, 219
★Bredon, Hereford and Worcester (tithe barn),
  2, 3, 5
bricks, 42
Bridewell Palace, London, 63
Bridgewater House, London, 260
Broadleys, Windermere, 265
Broughton Castle, Oxfordshire, 9, 23, 60
Broughton Hall, Yorkshire, 223
Buckingham Palace, London, 229
★Burghley House, Lincolnshire
  chimneypieces, 63
  floors, 44, 83
  staircase, 66

*Burghley House, Lincolnshire—*contd.*
  walls and ceilings, 97–8, 99–100, 109, 110,
    140, 219
Burlington House, Piccadilly, 162, 215
Burton Agnes Hall, East Yorkshire, 9, 32, 128

'cabinets', 74, 82, 93
Cannon Hall, Yorkshire, 250
Cannons, Middlesex, 162, 184, 186
*Canons Ashby, Northamptonshire, 48, **49**,
    80, 94, 105, 116
Cardiff Castle, 263, 271
Carlisle Cathedral, **46**
Carlton House, London, 187
Carlton House Terrace, London, 241
Carlton Towers, Yorkshire, 261, 267, 268,
    269
Carron Iron Company, 229
Carshalton House, Surrey, 184
Cassiobury Park, Hertfordshire, 135, 139
Castle Ashby, Northamptonshire, 128
Castle Bromwich Hall, Warwickshire, 88, 118
Castle Carr, Halifax, 247
Castle Coch, Cardiff, 263
*Castle Drogo, Devon, 254, **255**, 271
Castle Hedingham, Essex, 17
Castle Howard, Yorkshire
  ceilings, 160
  chapel, 264
  floors, 146, **147, 148,** 151
  mausoleum, 148–50
  plans of, 140–42, **141**
  stucco, 168
  Temple of the Four Winds, 148, **149,** 167
ceilings
  medieval, 15–17
  nineteenth century, 256–63
  painted, 16, 39, 92–102, 158–66, 211–19
  plastered, 102–13, 203–6
central heating, 272
Chantmarle, Dorset, 26
chapels, 6, 36, 39–41
Chatsworth, Derbyshire
  Baroque front, 140
  chapel, 83, **99**
  chimneypieces, 125, 267
  hall, 99
  staircases, 135–7, 234
  state rooms, 99
  water-supply, 137
  walls and ceilings, 47, 97, 98, 160
  windows, 116
  wood-carving, 90, **91**
  Wyatville's work, 195, 211
Chesterfield House, London, 206, 226
Chetham's Hospital, Manchester, 15
Cheyne Walk (39), Chelsea, 271

chimneypieces
  bolection moulded, 125
  corner, 122–3
  eighteenth century, 225–30
  firebaskets, 229
  Georgian, early, 178–81
  'Holbein', 63
  medieval, 32, **33, 35, 38**
  mirror glass, 124
  nineteenth century, 267–9
  seventeenth century, 121–6
  stoves, 229–30
  Tudor, 53, 60–65, **61**
Chinese style, 156, 189
Chippenham Park, Newmarket, 88
Chiswick House, Middlesex, 156, 163,
    199–200
Cholmondeley Hall, Cheshire, 153
Chute Lodge, Wiltshire, 194
*Clandon Park, Surrey, 178, **179**
Clarendon House, Piccadilly, 83
Clarendon Place, Wiltshire, 11, 13–14
Clarke Hall, Wakefield, 113
*Claydon House, Buckinghamshire, 151–2,
    156, **157, 158,** 210, **227**
Clenston Manor, Dorset, **52**
Clevedon Court, Avon, 6
Cliffe Castle, Keighley, Yorkshire, 263
Cobham Hall, Kent, 64, 117, 121
Coleshill House, Berkshire, 71, **72,** 83, 107,
    108, 131–2
Combe Abbey, Warwickshire, 101–2, 112,
    132, 135
comfort in houses, 1, 27, 28, 47, 238, 271
*Compton Castle, Devon, 6, 18, 67
Compton Place, Sussex, **169, 182**
Compton Wynyates, Warwickshire, 15
conservatories, 220–21, 247
Conway Castle, North Wales, 20
Copthall, Essex, 36
*Cotehele, Cornwall, 6–7, **7,** 24, **25**
Cound Hall, Shropshire, 234, **235**
Covent Garden, London, 145
Cowdray House, West Sussex, 43, 56
*Cragside, Northumberland, 245–6, **245,** 247,
    248, **268,** 269
Crewe Hall, Cheshire, 84
Cromwell House, Highgate, London, 128
Croome Court, Hereford and Worcester, 143,
    172, 222, 225–6, **226**
Crowcombe Court, Somerset, 150, 153
Cusworth Hall, Yorkshire, 151, 206

Danson Hill, Bexleyheath, 194
Davenport House, Shropshire, 152, 154–5
Deepdene, Surrey, 230
Delgatie Castle, Aberdeenshire, 16

Denham Place, Buckinghamshire, 112
distemper, 165
Ditchley Park, Oxfordshire, 178, 180
Doddington Park, Gloucestershire, 211, 223
Doncaster Mansion House, 171
doors
  arches, **19**
  eighteenth century, 222–5
  farmhouse, 118
  medieval, 17–20, 39
  painted deal, 224–5
  Palladian, 175–8
  seventeenth century, 116–21
  Tudor, 58–9
Dorchester House, Park Lane, London, 258
'double-pile' plan, 70, 71–3, 143, 238–9
drawing rooms, 198, 243–4, **272**
Duddingstone, Edinburgh, 192
Dulwich Picture Gallery, 211
*Dunster Castle, Somerset, **87**, 111–12, **112**,
  131, 135, **136**
Durham Castle, 18–19
Durham Cathedral, 19, 43
*Dyrham Park, Avon, 102, 124

*East Riddlesden Hall, Yorkshire, **5**, 92, **114**,
  125–6
Eastnor, Hereford and Worcester, 210–11
Easton Neston, Northamptonshire, 153
Eaton Hall, Cheshire, 250–51
Ecclesiological Society, 252
eighteenth-century styles
  chimneypieces, 225–30
  doors, 222–5
  house plans, 189–98
  painted walls and ceilings, 211–19
  plastered walls and ceilings, 203–6
  rooms, 198–203
  staircases, 230–34
  windows, 219–22
Eltham Lodge, Greenwich, 72
Eye Manor, Hereford and Worcester, 113

Farnley Hall, Yorkshire, 234
Fawley Court, Buckinghamshire, 112
*Felbrigg Hall, Norfolk, 166, **170**, 172
fireplaces see also chimneypieces, 6, 9, 20–21,
  60, 73
Flemish craftsmen, 45, 97
Flete, Devon, 269
Flintham, Nottinghamshire, 247
floors
  Baroque, 146–53
  carpeting, 151
  deal, 151
  floorcloths, 153
  glacis, 44, 80

inlaid, 152
medieval, 11–13
painted, 152
seventeenth century, 42–4
Tudor, 42–4
Fonthill Abbey, Wiltshire, 209
Forde Abbey, Dorset, 104, **105**, 107, 132
fortified houses, 8, 16, 24, 26, 271
Frocester, Gloucestershire, 3

galleries, 32–4, 76
garderobes, 23 see also privies; water-closets
gatehouses, 24, 26
Gilling Castle, Yorkshire, 47, 48, 49, **51**, 58
Glamis Castle, Teyside, 105
glass, 57, 115 see also windows
  medieval scarcity, 17
  sheet and plate, 265
  stained, 17, 39, 57, 220, 263–4
Glastonbury Abbey, Somerset, 3, 22
Golden Farm, Somerset, 104
Gothic architecture, 9, 17, 29, 37
'Gothic compo', 258
Gothick Revival, 19, 209–11, 239, 248, 263,
  265, 267
Gower House, Whitehall, 192
*Great Chalfield Manor, Wiltshire, 16
*Great Coxwell, Gloucestershire (tithe barn),
  3
Great Witley, Hereford and Worcester, 162
Greek ornament, 206–9, 213
Greenwich Hospital, 160
Grimsthorpe Castle, Lincolnshire, 148, **173**
gun rooms, 247
Gunnersbury House, Middlesex, 108

Haddon Hall, Derbyshire, 6, 21, 22, 46, 80
*Hagley Hall, West Midlands, 143–4
Hallams, The, Shamley Green, Surrey, 248
halls
  eighteenth century, 192–4, 198
  medieval, 3–6, 15, 17
  nineteenth century, 247–8, 254, 269
  screen passages, 6–8, 15, 30–31, 74, 248
  screens, 15, 22, **29**, 84
  seventeenth century, 84
  Tudor, 70
*Ham House, Surrey, 74, 76, 80, 88, 93, 101,
  115–16, **125**, **130**, 135
Hampstead Marshall, Berkshire, 110
Hampton Court, Herefordshire, 238
Hampton Court Palace
  bricks, 42
  chapel, 45
  chimneypieces, 124
  gallery, 32
  gatehouse, 25–6

Hampton Court Palace—*contd.*
  great hall, 6, 45
  plans of, 25
  walls and ceilings, 52–3, **53**, 100–101
  windows, 116, 264
  Wolsey apartments, 45
  wood-carving, 88
*Hanbury Hall, Hereford and Worcester, 153, 160, **161**
Hans Road, Knightsbridge, 265
*Hardwick Hall, Derbyshire
  chapels, 39–40
  chimneypieces, **62**, 63–4
  floors, 44
  gallery, 32, 34–6, **35**, 49, 62
  great chamber, 37–9, **38**, 48, 50–51
  hall screen, 30
  kitchen, 67
  plasterwork, **55**, 55–6
  stone staircase, 66
  water supply, 68
  windows, 29, 56–7
Harewood House, Yorkshire, 143, 217, 222, 227, 228, 236
Harlaxton Manor, Lincolnshire, 247, 258, **259**, 267, 271
Harmondsworth, Gloucestershire, 3
Harvington Hall, Hereford and Worcester, 47
*Hatchlands, Surrey, 205
Hatfield House, Hertfordshire, 70, 74, 76, 84, 102–4, 121, 126, 128, **129**
Heath House, Wakefield, 182
Heathcote, Ilkley, 254, 271
heating systems, 237, 238, 267
Heaton Hall, Manchester, 208, 214, 220
Hemingford Grey Manor House, Cambridgeshire, 17
Hengrave Hall, Suffolk, 57
Herrington, Somerset, 104
Heveningham Hall, Suffolk, 194, 214, 218
Highclere House, Hampshire, 248
Hill Hall, Essex, 48–9
Holkham Hall, Norfolk, 165, **171**, 172, 176, 183, 189, **190**, 222
Holme Lacy, Hertfordshire, 113
Holyroodhouse, Edinburgh, 113
Horseheath Hall, Cambridgeshire, 113, 131
Horstead Place, Sussex, 271
*Horton Court, Avon, 18
Houghton Hall, Norfolk, 143–4, 146–8, 163, 172, 174, 178, 189
house plans
  Baroque, 139–46
  eighteenth century, 189–98
  medieval, 3–9
  nineteenth century, 238–43
  seventeenth century, 70–73

terrace houses, 145–6, 241–3
town houses, 144–6
Tudor, 24–9, 70
villas, 13
  with wings, 186, 189, **190**
Hulne Priory, Northumberland, 209

*Ickworth, Suffolk, 201, **202**, 218
*Ightham Mote, Kent, 18, 30, **31**, 39, **41**, 48, 248
Ingatestone Hall, Essex, 28
inventories, 199–200

Jew's House, Lincoln, 18

*Kedleston Hall, Derbyshire, 189–92, **190**, **191**, 199, 203, 205–6, 225, 229
Kelmscott House, Hammersmith, 262
Kensington Palace, 116, 124, 159, 163, **164**
Kenwood, Hampstead, 217–18
Kimbolton Castle, Cambridgeshire, 160
King's College, Cambridge, 39, 46
King's Weston, Bristol, 152
*Kingston Lacy, Dorset, 71, 87, **257**, 260, 261, 267, 269, **270**
Kirkstall Grange, Leeds, 189
Kirtlington Park, Oxfordshire, 165
kitchens, 21–3, 67, 184–5
Kiveton, Yorkshire, 135
*Knightshayes Court, Devon, 240, **243**, 248, **249**
*Knole, Kent, **75**, 75–6, 80, 84–5, **85**, 102–4, **120**, 121–2, **127**, 128, 230

*Lacock Abbey, Wiltshire, 19, 30
Lancaster House, London, 260
landscape rooms, 219
Langleys, Essex, 46
*Lanhydrock House, Cornwall, 104, **106**, **246**
Lee Priory, Kent, 210
Leeds Castle, Kent, 117
*Little Morton Hall, Cheshire, 36, 48, **50**, **54**
Longleat, Wiltshire, 34, 37, 195, 211
Longthorpe Hall, Northamptonshire, 17
Longthorpe Tower, Northamptonshire, 23
Loseley Park, Surrey, 47, 53, 60, **61**, 64
Lowther Castle, Cumbria, 98, 210
Luscombe Castle, Devon, **220**
Lydiard Tregoze, Wiltshire, 143
*Lytes Cary, Somerset, 36–7
Lytham Hall, Lancashire, **232**, 234

Magdalen College, Oxford, 46
Mamhead, Devon, 264
marble, 42–3, 79, 82–4, 90, 121–2, 150, 181, 225–30
  scagliola, 125, 149, 202, 218

Marlborough House, London, 93, 99
Mawley Hall, Shropshire, 152, 154, 155, **182**, 183
medieval buildings, 1–23
Melbourne House, Piccadilly, 192
Melbury House, Dorset, 56
Mentmore, Buckinghamshire, 269
Mereworth, Kent, 144, 146, 162, **163, 176**
Mersham Le Hatch, Kent, 203, **205**
Milton Abbey, Dorset, 206
*Montacute, Somerset, 29–30, **30**, 32, 34, 58, **59**
Moor Park, Hertfordshire, 162
*Mottisfont Priory (Abbey), Hampshire, 27–8, **28**
Munstead Wood, Surrey, 254

neo-Classicism, 187–9, 213
Nettlecombe Court, Somerset, 105
Newby Hall, Yorkshire, 203, 217
Newmarket Palace, 70, 122
nineteenth-century building, 238–69
Noel Park, Hornsey, 242
Nonsuch Palace, Surrey, 26, 47, 51, 53, 60, 166
Norbury Park, Surrey, 219
Norfolk House, London, 156, 206
*Nostell Priory, Yorkshire, 143, 150, 165–6, 172, 182, 206, **207, 217**, 236
Nottingham Castle, 13

Oakley Park, Shropshire, 203, 222
Oatlands Palace, Surrey, 122
Ockwells Manor House, Berkshire, 17
Old Place, Lingfield, Sussex, 264
Ombersley Hall, Hereford and Worcester, 155
Orleans House, Twickenham, 146, 178
*Osterley Park, Middlesex, 192, 200, 203, **204**, 213, 214, **215**, 222, **224, 227**, 228
*Oxburgh Hall, Norfolk, 24
Oxford Union Society Debating Room, 260

Packington Hall, Warwickshire, 218
Palladian style, 172–8, 181, 213, 225
panelling see wainscots; walls
papier-mâché, 258
parquetry, 79–80
*Paycockes, Essex, 44
Pembroke House, Whitehall, 206
*Penrhyn Castle, Gwynedd, 251, 264
Penshurst Place, Kent, 7–8, 18, 22
*Petworth House, Sussex, 83, 88, 89, 100, 118, 137–8, 158, **159**, 200
Pilton, Somerset, 3
Pitzhanger Manor, Ealing, 211
Pinkie House, Musselburgh, 16
plasterwork see ceilings; walls
*Polesden Lacy, Surrey, 256

Portman Square (20), London, 230–32, **231**
*Powis Castle, Welshpool, 97, 134–5
Prior Park, Avon, 143
privies see also water-closets, 23, 67–8, 184, 234–5
'prodigy houses', 37, 73

Queen's House, Greenwich, 70, 82–3, 93, 107, 143, 151

Raby Castle, Durham, 21
Ragley Hall, Warwickshire, 143
Raynham Hall, Norfolk, 70, 74
Red House, Bexleyheath, Kent, 252
Register House, Edinburgh, 173
Reigate Priory, Surrey, 63
Richmond Green, Surrey, 178
Richmond Palace, Sheen, 25, 32
Rococo style, 164, 172, 180, 188, 189, 205, 230, 267, 271
'Romayne' work, 45–6, **46**
roofs, 7–10, **10, 14**, 15, 37
rooms and their uses, 198–203, 243–56
Rousham, Oxfordshire, 163
Royal Pavilion, Brighton, 185
*Rufford Old Hall, Lancashire, **14**, 15
Rushton Hall, Northamptonshire, 105

St James Church, Piccadilly, 109
St James's Palace, 26, 42, 47, 264
St James's Square, London (15), 208; (20), 203, 217, 222, 227, 228, 229
St Martin's Palace, Norwich, 19
St Mary's Church, Derby, 264
St Nicholas Cole Abbey, Queenhithe, 110
St Paul's Cathedral, 88, 90, 132, 140
*Saltram, Devon, 165, 215–17, **216**, 222, **223**
Salutation, The, Sandwich, 254
Sandford Orcas Manor, Dorset, 21
Sandleford Priory, Berkshire, 209
Scarisbrick Castle, Lancashire, 248
seventeenth-century building, 70–138
Sezincote, Gloucestershire, 220–21
Shardeloes, Buckinghamshire, 222, 227
Sharpham House, Devon, 194
Sherborne Castle, Dorset, 214
Sheriff Hutton Park, Yorkshire, 104
*Sheringham Hall, Norfolk, 200–201, 221
*Shugborough, Staffordshire, 166, 208, 213, 220, 228
*Sizergh Castle, Cumbria, 46, 58
smoking rooms, 247
*Snowshill, Gloucestershire, 67
solars, 4, 6, 36, 76
Somerset House, 194; (Old), 27, 30, 63, 80, 93
Southill, Bedfordshire, 224
*Speke Hall, Lancashire, 30, 37

Spencer House, London, **212,** 212–13
staircases, 16, 65–7, 126–38, 181–4, 230–35,
  269–71
*Standen, East Grinstead, Sussex, 252–3, **253**
Stanford Hall, Leicestershire, 153
Stanton Harcourt, Oxfordshire, 21
Stockeld Park, Yorkshire, 184
Stoke Edith, Hereford and Worcester, 160
Stokesay Castle, Shropshire, 17, 18, 23
*Stourhead, Wiltshire, 144, 200, **201, 244**
Stowe, Buckinghamshire, 211, 218
Strawberry Hill, Twickenham, 209
*Sudbury Hall, Derbyshire, 76, **77,** 108–9,
  118, **119,** 131, 132, **133,** 134
Sutton Place, Surrey, 56, 58, 269
Sutton Scarsdale, Derbyshire, **154**
symmetry in building, 27, 70, 118, 239
Syon House, Middlesex, 192, **193,** 194, **197,**
  198–9, **199,** 213, 223, **224,** 228

Temple Newsam House, Leeds, 70, 151, 172,
  178
Thame, Oxfordshire, 46
Thoresby Hall, Nottinghamshire, 251
Thoresby House, Northamptonshire, 140
Thornbury Castle, Gloucestershire, 16, 25
Thorpe Hall, Northamptonshire, 107, **116,**
  132
Thurnalls, Royston, Hertfordshire, 95
timber-framed buildings, **xii,** 3, 4–6, 30
Towneley Hall, Burnley, 167
*Townend House, Troutbeck, Cumbria, 92
*Treasurer's House, Matlock, Somerset, 6, 17
Trentham Hall, Staffordshire, 260
Trinity College, Oxford, 90
Tudor building, 24–68

*Uppark, Surrey, 181

*Vyne, The, Hampshire, 32, **33,** 39, **40,** 42,
  233, **241,** 250

*Waddesdon Manor, Buckinghamshire, 263,
  269
wainscots, 15, 44, 85–6, **86,** 90–92, 153–8
*Wallington Hall, Northumberland, 180,
  247–8
walls
  leather, 261, 269
  medieval, 13–15

nineteenth century, 256–63
painted, 8, 13–15, 47–51, 92–102, 158–66,
  211–19
panelled, 84–92, 263
papered, 153, 165, 261–2
Tudor, 47–51
Wanstead House, Essex, 143, 189
Wardour Castle, Wiltshire, 151
Warwick Castle, 87–8, 109
water-closets, 23, 68, 137, 184, 234, 272
Wells, Somerset, 3
Wentworth Woodhouse, Yorkshire, 143, 151
*West Wycombe Park, Buckinghamshire, 164
Westminster Abbey, 16, 19, 29, 45, 211
Westminster Hall, **4**
Westminster Palace, 11
Weston Hall, West Midlands, 268
Westonbirt, Gloucestershire, 258
Wharram Percy Manor House, Yorkshire, 11
White Tower, London, 13
Whitehall Palace, 32, 93, 102, 116, 141
*Wightwick Manor, Wolverhampton, **262,**
  262–4
Willey Hall, Shropshire, 222
Wilton House, Wiltshire, 94, 106, 115, 118,
  122, **123,** 143
  Single and Double Cube Rooms, **78,** 79, 94,
    112
*Wimpole Hall, Cambridgeshire, 160, 195,
  196, 236, 237
Winchester Castle, 11
windows
  eighteenth century, 219–22
  medieval, 6, 16–18, 20, 29, 37
  nineteenth century, 263–5
  Palladian, 172–5
  seventeenth century, 113–16
  Tudor, 56–8
  Venetian, 114–15, 172–3
Windsor Castle, 16, 88, 95, 132, 139, 195, 211
Witham Park, Somerset, 192
Woburn Abbey, Bedfordshire, 172, 174, 180,
  213–14
Woodhall Park, Hertfordshire, 214
Wollaton Hall, Nottinghamshire, 37, 63–4, 68,
  184, 195
Wolseley Hall, Staffordshire, 134
Worksop Manor, Nottinghamshire, 34
Wrotham Park, Middlesex, 173, 189

York Minster, 211, 271